Wyoming Coroners and the Law
2nd Edition
A Review of Statutes, Regulations, with Suggested Policies and Procedures

By Mark R. Stratmoen

*Dedicated to those who give time and energy
in Public Service*

Commentary and Original Text © 2017 Mark R. Stratmoen,
All Rights, Reserved
2nd Edition Update © 2019 Mark R. Stratmoen
Documentation of Law, State Statutes, Policies and Procedures are
Public Records of the State of Wyoming and Fremont County, and other
Legal Sources

Published by Lenore Wyoming Publications
522 East Park Avenue, Riverton, WY 82501

ISBN-10: 1978105940
ISBN-13: 978-1978105942

Cover Photo: Mammoth Hot Springs, Yellowstone National Park
by the Author

About the Author:

Mark R. Stratmoen is currently the Coroner for Fremont County, Wyoming, and has been a certified death investigator since 1998. Before taking office in 2015, he also served as department administrator from 2004 to 2014, and as Chief Deputy from 2007 to 2014. Service also included being a member of DMORT (Disaster Mortuary Operational Response Team) under the Federal National Disaster Medical Service, Department of Health and Human Services, with deployment to work Hurricane Katrina in the New Orleans area in 2005.

Aside from the over 650 hours of State certified medical-legal training acquired up to this point, working in this area of Wyoming has involved experience in high altitude mountain recoveries, desert and remote area recoveries; air crash, fire incident, and water recoveries and investigations; vehicle collisions and traffic fatalities; industrial incidents; archaeological and anthropological recoveries and investigations; medical facility investigations; and the usual expected array of natural, accidental, homicide, and suicide deaths. This includes being the lead investigator on over 600 cases, including the lead on over 220 non-natural deaths.

He is also the author of *"Murder, Mayhem, and Mystery: Coroner Inquests in Fremont County, Wyoming 1885-1900"*, © 2010 Mark R. Stratmoen, Pub. Lenore Wyoming Publications, ISBN-10: 146362932X; and *"Finding Undetermined: Hard cases for Coroners and Death Investigators"*, © 2017 Mark R. Stratmoen, Pub. Lenore Wyoming Publications, ISBN-10: 197431376X

Preface

This book is published as a reference, and while any personal commentary is under copy write, that and all other materials are offered as "open source usage". The State of Wyoming documents referenced are public record, and likewise, Fremont County Coroner policies and procedures belong to the County and State and are also public record. It is hoped that by presenting a consolidated compilation of the various laws, statutes, policies and legal opinions that are relevant to coroners in the State of Wyoming, that we all can do a more accurate, complete, and compassionate job for the people, under the mandate and oath we take as an elected official.

Policies and procedures of Fremont County are presented as an example, to show some of the possible formats and issues. Any of those may be borrowed, copied, or otherwise used without permission if you can find them useful for your own situation and needs.

While the basis for this and for any commentary or opinions offered in this text, are based on the laws of Wyoming as researched and presented, realize that opinions may change from jurisdiction to jurisdiction. I am not an attorney, and the author and the Office of the Coroner of Fremont County are not responsible for any changes, variations, differing opinions, or alterations in the laws as of or after the date of publication, or in the application thereof.

On other words, do your homework and stay up to date on the law. Your job will be less complicated for the effort.

Preface to the 2019 Edition

This edition includes some major updates to matters of law and statute, including a significant addition to the coroner statutes and a recent Wyoming Supreme Court decision on inquest jurisdiction. Several existing statutes that are relevant to coroners have also been added to the "Other Related Statutes" section, as they have recently come to light in application. Statutes and law are always an evolving process, and it is important for coroners to keep an eye out for anything in the process that relates to their duties. When it comes to the law, relevant complications can sometimes pop up in the oddest places for even odder reasons.

Table of Contents

Introduction... 9

Part I: History
Coroner History.. 11
Wyoming History
      Section A: Old Statutes.. 13

      Section B: Other Notable Changes over Time.................. 18

Part II: Current Wyoming Statutes and Law
Establishment and Interpretation.. 20
    Section A: Coroner Statutes
W.S. 7-4-101. Election; oath; bond...................................... 23
W.S. 7-4-102. Deputy coroners.. 23
W.S. 7-4-103. Certification requirements; penalty; expenses....... 24
W.S. 7-4-104. Definitions.. 25
W.S. 7-4-105. Confidentiality of reports, photos and recordings; exceptions; penalties.. 27
W.S. 7-4-106. Archaeological human burial sites..................... 31
W.S. 7-4-201. Reports of death; investigation; summoning of jurors; fees and costs; inspection of medical records............................. 34
W.S. 7-4-202. Impaneling of bystanders as jurors; oath............. 37
W.S. 7-4-203. Issuance of subpoenas; witness fees; enforcement of attendance.. 37
W.S. 7-4-204. Oath of witness; recording of testimony; compensation of reporter... 38
W.S. 7-4-205. Return of inquisition by jury............................ 39
W.S. 7-4-206. Coroner's return to court................................. 39
W.S. 7-4-207. Disposition of body and effects of deceased.......... 39
W.S. 7-4-208. Authority of sheriff to perform duties of coroner... 41
W.S. 7-4-209. Postmortem examination; liability limitation........ 41
W.S. 7-4-210. Fees and mileage, salary................................. 42
W.S. 7-4-211. Board of coroner standards............................. 43

    Section B: Other Related Statutes
W.S. 1-11-303 Amount of fees *(jurors)*................................. 46
W.S. 1-12-102 "Dead man's statute" *(testimony)*.................... 46
W.S. 1-14-104 & 105 Fees of physicians in testimony and post-mortem examination... 47
W.S. 1-21-901 to 1-21-909 Attendance of witnesses, contempt.... 47
W.S. 2-7-101 Presumption of death....................................... 49

W.S. 2-17-101 Authority to authorize burial or cremation.......... 49
W.S. 6-4-501 & 502 Desecration of Graves and Bodies. 51
W.S. 6-5-106 through 118 Conflict of interest; penalties; disclosure of interest and withdrawal from participation. 53
W.S. 7-19-106 (k)(ii) Background checks, criminal history *(criminal justice agency).* 57
W.S 9-1-634 Training 58
W.S. 9-1-701 through 9-1-707 Peace officer standards and training commission. 58
W.S. 9-2-410 Records as property of state; delivery by outgoing officials and employees to successors; management and disposition 58
W.S. 14-2-708 Court ordered genetic testing of the deceased....... 59
W.S. 14-3-207 Reporting deaths,cases of suspected child abuse... 59
W.S. 16-1-104 Wyoming Joint Powers Act; Authorization for Inter-County Agreements 59
W.S. 16-4-201 through 205. Public Records 60
W.S. 16-4-203(d)(i) Public Records; *(dockets)*................... 62
W.S. 18-3-103 Offices and records to be kept within county; exceptions; records open to public inspection; removal for purposes of copying; penalty. 62
W.S. 18-3-504 County Commission; Powers and Duties Generally; Indigent Burials 64
W.S. 18-3-902 through 18-3-906 Causes for removal from office enumerated, procedure 65
W.S. 19-4-101 Veterans, Burial of Indigents 68
W.S. 22-2-105 Elections; *(Coroner listed as "elected official")*... 69
W.S. 33-16-502(a)(i) *(Human remains defined)*................... 70
W.S. 33-16-527 Duty of funeral director to ascertain cause of death prior to disposition. 71
W.S. 35-1-105 Public Health; Prohibited acts; penalty, violations.71
W.S. 35-1-241 Safe disposal in emergency circumstances.......... 72
W.S. 35-1-401(a) Public Health; Definitions 73
W.S. 35-4-107 Public Health; Report required of physician; record of each case to be kept; duty of individuals to report diseases. 75
W.S. 35-4-115(a)(i) Public Health Emergency; Definitions 77
W.S. 35-4-601 through 35-4-607. Unclaimed bodies; Who may have bodies in possession. 77
W.S. 35-5-201 to 225 Revised Uniform Anatomical Gift Act 80
W.S. 35-6-101(a)(vii) Abortions – Viability 82
W.S. 35-19-101 Determination of death. 84
W.S. 42-2-103 Department of Family Services; Burial Assist...... 84

Section C: Coroner Testimony 86

Section D: State Agency Rules
1. Records Retention 89
2. Public Records Policies 90
3. Wyoming Department of Health 92
4. Wyoming State Fire Marshal 93
5. State Law Enforcement, DCI, & Crime Lab .. 93
6. Board of Coroner Standards 93

Part III: Important Federal Regulations
Section A: First Responder Status 97

Section B: NAGPRA 98

Section C: OSHA & Biohazard Regulations 98

Section D; Incident Management 99

Section E: HIPAA 100

Part IV: County Government
a. Interactions and Obligations 101
b. County Policies and Procedures 103
c. Operations 103
d. Employment Manual and Policies 103

Part V: Inter-Agency Policies and MOUs
a. US Department of the Interior, BLM......................... 104
b. Tribal Relations 105
c. Mass Fatality 105
d. Donor Organizations 106
e. Inter-County 106

Part VI: Coroner Agency Policies
a. Disclaimers and provisions 108
b. General Duties 110
c. Internal Policies and Procedures 112

Part VII: Inquest Policies and Procedures 115

Part VIII: County Attorney and other Legal Opinions
a. Review of all MOUs and Agreements 128

      b. Policy Reviews 129
      c. Confidentiality 129
      d. Personnel File Access 131
      e. Film Productions and Name Permissions 131
      f. Records Release to a Private Investigator 132
      g. Release of Pre-2011 Records 132
      h. Release of the Body in a Criminal Case 133
      i. The Requirement to hold an Inquest 134
      j. Admission of Coroner Toxicology Evidence Obtained without Consent 135
      k. Coroner's Inquest as an Executive Matter conducted outside of the courts 135

Citations 138

Appendix A: Records Retention Policy for Fremont County 142

Appendix B: Records Request Policy for Fremont County 148

Appendix C: Biohazard/Infectious Disease Policies/Procedures .. 155

Appendix D: NAGPRA Policies 182

Appendix E: Anatomical Gifts, Procurement Agencies 185

Appendix F: Disaster Plan 187

Appendix G: Indigent and Unclaimed Policies, Fremont Co 193

Afterword: 199

Subject Index 200

Introduction

This is a presentation and discussion on the statutes, policies, and procedures applicable to coroners in the State of Wyoming. There is considerable variation in the needs and applications of duties for the various counties, due to the wide range of circumstances found across the state. Wyoming has 23 counties containing everything from urban settings to strictly small rural communities, as well as a wide range of environments found in the West, from range and farmland to remote mountains, forests, and deserts. Some counties are larger than several U.S. states, and jurisdictions are a patchwork and checkerboard of Federal, Tribal, State, County, Municipal, and Private lands.

While the policies of any one county may not always apply to another, the basics of law, statute, and procedural obligations are consistent. Application can be of many flavors, but the requirements of law are the same. One thing to keep in mind with this discussion, however, is the nature of legal opinion. Opinions on meaning and applications of law are just that, opinions, whether they come me, from your own county attorney, or the State Attorney General's Office. Unless meaning and application has been codified by case law in the Courts, or interpretation through judicial ruling, opinions can change. Such opinions do give you legal backing until overruled by the courts or a change in the public officer or administration, but things can change none the less.

The Wyoming Legislature can, and has in the past, also changed the laws and regulations relative to the duties of the coroner. It is important for any coroner to keep abreast and be proactive on any proposals that may affect the nature of the job. There have been many past improvements, but even more numbers of dubious proposals that, fortunately, never made it through the legislative process. Even the good changes of law will benefit from the input of those who will be affected by that law, so I recommend not being a passive citizen when it comes to the Legislature.

This book will cover a brief background of the coroner's office in general, and past Wyoming law and changes, to first give a feel for the history behind the position. Then we will present and discuss the current statutes applicable to coroners. Next it is appropriate to present other levels of law, such as Federal, that the coroner cannot avoid.

Finally as a resource, we will present the various recommended policies, procedures, and interactions with county government in Wyoming. A portion of all this might be applicable only to how Fremont County does things, but another larger part may be adapted to the needs of any county of the State. In any case, it can be helpful to see how things are done elsewhere, even if the individual run of things will have your own flavor and needs. There is often no need to reinvent the wheel. A good administrator will often borrow from others and adapt policies to their own particular needs for the county in which they serve.

Trying to ferret out and coordinate all the various aspects of law and how it affects the position of the coroner, can be both arduous and confusing, if not often surprising, especially for those new to the position. Hopefully this text will fill some of that gap in resource and help avoid some of the common pitfalls. No text can be 100% coverage, and even if it were, expect the legislature or some other agency to throw a change or monkey wrench into the works at some point. Such is the nature of government.

Part I: History

Coroner History

There are many resources that cover the early history of the coroner's office and how it has evolved over the years. Most agree that the only office that is older that has survived continuous existence within the Anglo systems of government is the position of sheriff. Through its evolution, which has taken several centuries, a variety of functions have come and gone. Initially the term and position shows documentation from the around year 1194, where it meant the "keeper of the pleas of the crown" in Medieval England. Then, in areas under the jurisdiction of the King, the "crowner" oversaw records and legal disputes, and collected revenue in the administration of justice. These executive and judicial functions also included investigation and determination of fines in the case of unnatural deaths, such as homicide, or seizures of property and estates in the case of suicide, which was forbidden by the Church. Early on this included a simple form of inquest, where local jurors would consider the evidence and witnesses and rule on the manner of death. By the seventeenth century, manners of death had been refined to such things as 'suicide while being of unsound mind', accidental death, acts of God, or 'simply found dead'. Over time, the position became more secular, less administrative, but still functioned as an investigator of death on behalf of the Crown.

The position and system moved with the English colonists to America in the 1700s. Inquests began to consistently employ examination of the body along with other evidence, and participation of physicians (or surgeons as they were known then) to give a medical appraisal. After independence from England, the position was retained within the governments of localities and states, even though the representation for the crown was no longer applicable. Society generally recognized that in cases of unknown or unexpected deaths, some official position was needed to ferret out the answers. In 1877 Massachusetts was the first state to abolish coroners and replace them with medical examiners, which had to be physicians, yet the functions basically remained the same as death investigators. We will not go into the pros and cons of medical examiner versus coroner here, and there has never been a national directive for either – the choice was just left to the individual state determination. Thus today in the U.S. there are both systems, and some systems that are a blend of both.

Instead of serving the interests of an individual like a king, today's M.E. or coroner now are public servants on behalf of society as a whole, and while the skills, tools and methods have evolved, the basic function of death investigation has endured.

Formal Wyoming history and government went through the usual early changes in the West, first as uncharted lands claimed by various colonial interests of Britain, France, and Spain, then as a portion of the vast acquisitions of the United States. While the "law" during those times had its own generalized forms, the specific history and position of the coroner was not usually implemented until an area was organized as a particular territory. Then as part of the procedures of territorial status, the involved citizens were required to start a documented and written set of laws for organization, and naturally turned to the forms and positions they were familiar with, and borrowed from past experience. Thus the position of coroner came to Wyoming as part of the first territorial statutes.

Next, let us take a look at exactly what the law and statutes had to say in the early Wyoming Territory.

Wyoming History

Section A: Old Statutes

Since it is the nature of government, law, and regulation to gravitate towards increasing complexity and detail, it is interesting (and sometimes amusing) to look at a simpler time for perspective. Following is the entire set of coroner statutes for the Territory of Wyoming from 1887:

REVISED STATUTES OF WYOMING

In Force January 1, 1887, By Authority of the Legislative Assembly
Prepared and Edited by John W. Blake, Willis Van Devanter, and Isaac P. Caldwell, Commissioners
Cheyenne, Wyoming: The Daily Sun Steam Printing House, 1887
[Page 482-483]

Coroner's inquests – Jury.
Sec. 1879. The coroner shall hold an inquest upon the dead bodies of such persons only, as are supposed to have died from unlawful means, or the cause of whose death is unknown. When he has notice of the dead body of any person supposed to have died from unlawful means, or the cause of whose death is unknown, found, or being in the country, it shall be his duty to summon forthwith six citizens of the county, to appear before him at a time and place named. [C.L. 1876, ch. 28, p. 214 § 4.]

Completing juries from bystanders – Oath.
Sec. 1880. If any juror fails to appear, the coroner shall summon the proper number from the bystanders immediately, and proceed to impanel them, and administer the following oath in substance: "You do solemnly swear (or affirm) that you will diligently inquire and true presentment make, when, how, and by what means, the person whose body lies here dead, came to his death, according to your knowledge and the evidence given you, so help you God." [C.L. 1876, ch. 28, p. 214 § 5.]

Attendance of witnesses may be enforced.

Sec. 1881. The coroner may issue subpoenas within his county for witnesses, returnable forthwith, or at such time as he may direct therein, and witnesses shall be allowed the same fees as in cases before a justice of the peace, and the coroner shall have the same authority to enforce the attendance of witnesses and to punish them and jurors for contempt in disobeying his process, as justices of the peace have in cases before them. [C.L. 1876, ch. 28, p. 214 § 6.] For witness fees, see § 1199

Oath of witness.
Sec. 1882. An oath shall be administered to each witness as follows: "You do solemnly swear (or affirm) that the testimony you shall give to this inquest concerning the death of the person lying here dead, shall be the truth, the whole truth, and nothing but the truth, so help you God." The testimony of the witness sworn, shall be reduced to writing under the coroner's order, and subscribed by each witness. [C.L. 1876, ch. 28, p. 214 § 7.]

Inquisition of jury.
Sec. 1883. The jurors having inspected the body, heard the testimony, and made all needful inquiries, shall return to the coroner their inquisition in writing under their hands, stating therein, as near as possible, the name of the person, and when, how, and by what means, if known, he came to his death. [C.L. 1876, ch. 28, p. 214 § 8.]

Arrest of persons charged with crime.
Sec. 1884. If the inquisition find a crime has been committed on the deceased, and the name of the person who the jury believes has committed it, thereupon, if the person charged be present, the coroner may order his arrest by an officer or any person, and shall then make a warrant requiring the officer or other person to take him before a justice of the peace. But if the person charged be not present, and the coroner believes he can be taken, and may escape unless immediately taken, he may issue a warrant to the sheriff or any constable of the county requiring him to arrest the person and take him before a justice of the peace; and the warrant of a coroner in such cases, shall be of equal authority with that of a justice of the peace, and when the person charged is brought before the justice, like proceedings shall be had as in similar cases commenced before a justice of the peace, sitting as court of inquiry. [C.L. 1876, ch. 28, p. 214 § 9.]

Coroner's return to court.
Sec 1885. The coroner shall then return to the district court, the inquisition, the written evidence, and a list of witnesses who testify material matter. [C.L. 1876, ch. 28, p. 214 § 10.]

Disposition of body and effects of deceased.
Sec. 1886. The coroner shall cause the body of a deceased person, which he is called to view, to be delivered to his friends, if there be any, if not, he shall cause him to be decently buried, the expenses of the same to be paid from any property found with the body, or if there be none, then from the county treasury, by certifying an account of the expenses to the board of county commissioners, which shall be acted upon by said board as in cases of other accounts presented to them. The coroner shall also, within forty-eight hours after completing the inquest, turn over to the probate judge of the county, all papers, property and effects of every kind, found upon, or belonging to the body of the deceased person. [C.L. 1876, ch. 28, p. 214 § 11.]

Justice to act in absence of coroner.
Sec. 1887. When there is no coroner, or in case of his absence, or inability to act, any justice of the peace of the same county is authorized to perform the duties of the coroner, in relation to dead bodies. [C.L. 1876, ch. 28, p. 214 § 12.]

Post mortem examination.
Sec. 1888. When an inquisition is being held. if the coroner or jury shall deem it requisite, he may summon one or more physicians or surgeons, to make a scientific examination. [C.L. 1876, ch. 28, p. 214 § 13. S.L. 1882, ch. 78, §§ 1 and 2.] For physician's fees, see §§ 1200 and 1201.

There are several interesting things to note here. The specific types of circumstances for what was to be a coroner case is not as well defined: *"supposed to have died from unlawful means, or the cause of whose death is unknown, found, or being in the country"* certainly gives a basic framework, but a lot of wiggle room for interpretation. Most suspected non-natural deaths would fall under suspected "unlawful means", as one would have to investigate even to eliminate "unlawful" in the case of accident. This could also explain why a good number of cases that would be the coroner's today, were not investigated or considered in the past. An example would be those accidental deaths that were considered 'routine' hazards of life or occupation. All would be a coroner case today, but from studying old newsprint, many were just assumed and not investigated. Also note that the main investigative tool is the inquest right off the bat (Section 1879), rather than just an option. The authority of the coroner in such circumstance is then the same as a lower level Justice of the Peace court, with those specified powers. Each county would have a single coroner, but multiple Justices in various locations and small communities, so it also made sense for JPs to be authorized to fulfill the role of the coroner. In the name of consolidation, the positions of Justice of the Peace (2004) and Constable (1971) were eliminated with statutory changes, with the judicial powers of a JP being distributed mostly to Circuit Courts, and the powers of the Constable going to the Sheriff. Rather than a JP, the Sheriff now can serve as the coroner under particular circumstances, which will be discussed later.

Consider the size of the early counties – when formed in 1884, Fremont County extended from the northern current border of Sweetwater, all the way to the Montana border (over 21,000 sq. mi.). With a single coroner located in the county seat of Lander, and the need for expedient examination and consideration of a body, it certainly made sense to authorize the local Justice of the Peace to perform the duties. Travel time alone was often days or weeks between locations by wagon or horseback, and often a risky proposition. Thus if you examine the older inquest texts from the Archives, you will often see a Justice of the Peace acting as coroner.

The responsibility for identification of the deceased is implied by the required return of the inquest jury: *"stating therein, as near as possible, the name of the person, ..."* (Sec. 1883). Section 1884 hold some arrest and warrant powers no longer valid in current statutes, although the subpoena power of Section 1881 remains intact today. A fun part of the old statutes is also in Section 1884: *"if the person charged be not present, and the coroner believes he can be taken, and may escape unless immediately taken, he may issue a warrant to the sheriff or any constable of the county requiring him to arrest the person..."*. This, if you think about it, was an expedient solution to the issue that a sudden reveal of a perpetrator during an inquest could cause the individual to jump on his horse and head for the hills – and at that time there was a lot of space and hills to head for.

The traditional responsibility of society to decently bury the unclaimed is noted in Section 1886, and the expenses for that act fell as today, to the county. What the county can claim in compensation, *"all papers, property and effects of every kind, found upon, or belonging to the body of the deceased person..."* is a bit broader than todays "on or with the body" as "belonging to" could have had wider implications. The authority to order an autopsy and examination is intact in Section 1888. All in all, many of the basics for today's statutes are seen. I have been told that at one time the coroner was the only official authorized to arrest the sheriff, but that is not seen here, unless he was determined a perpetrator, I suppose. It may have been noted in another section of statutes, or otherwise come and gone, and would make for interesting research.

Another change from this period to today is that the number of inquest jurors was reduced from six to three. Historically, coroners and inquest jurors were the main official application of death investigation. Detectives as specialists were non-existent in most areas, although the British and other European countries were starting to formalize the skill in the mid-1800s. Forensics was also just starting and in its infancy. Coroners and jurors had to rely on testimony if available, obvious evidence, a bit of medical analysis from the skill set at the time, and a whole lot of common sense application. Sometimes they did not do so well, but all in all, I think generally pretty good considering what they had to work with.

Section B: Other Notable Changes Over Time

Obviously, as we will see in presenting the current coroner statutes, a vast amount of changes occurred since the time of the laws of the Wyoming Territory. A lot of format and wording changes occurred to the statutes themselves, and it is the nature of the legislature to be constantly tweaking and altering statutes as conditions and circumstances of society change over time. Legislatures can be both reactionary, or engage in productive planning for the future, or change the statutes due to discovered deficiencies found in application. While the evolution to the current form will not be discussed in detail, there are several significant changes to the law that occurred in recent decades that greatly influenced how the coroner's office functions.

In the late 1980s a Board of Coroner Standards was established, with the intent on standardizing the functions and operations of the office in the 23 counties. This was altered, added to, and tweaked periodically by the legislature, with the last adjustment occurring in 2014. The benefits or deficiencies in this will be discussed later.

In 2004, as a 'housekeeping' change, the wording of the coroner statutes were adjusted to remove the reference that a Justice of the Peace could perform as a coroner in W.S. 7-4-203, since that position had been abolished by previous legislation. The significance of this is that, with only a couple of exceptions, the individual elected coroner became the only authorized official to act with the specified statutory duties. Those exceptions are found in W.S. 7-4-208, where the Sheriff is authorized in the coroner's absence or disability to perform those duties, or the State Health Officer under W.S. 35-1-241, or the coroner of another county (added in 2006) under a joint powers agreement. While over time counties have broken off into smaller units (5 to 23), some still leave vast territory for the individual coroner to cover, even with modern transportation. Fremont, for example, is almost 10,000 square miles. and response to a more remote location may take a couple of hours, and still on occasion includes horseback.

In 2005, as a part of initiating statutes that accounted for Hospice care in the State, the definitions under W.S. 7-4-104 were altered as to the meaning of an anticipated or attended death, and the time frame for "unattended" consideration. This will also be discussed in detail later.

Another recent change and addition occurred in 2011, when an entire section, W.S. 7-4-105, was added to create and regulate confidentiality of coroner records, and by who and under what circumstances, those records can be accessed. Prior to this change, all coroner records were considered public records, and subject to access by anyone. Circumstances and events nationally spurred the legislature to make this needed change, and now Wyoming has some of the strictest confidentiality law for coroners in the nation, and for good reason in my opinion. That will also be touched on later.

Major 2019 Additions and Updates

Legislative Changes: W.S. 7-4-106 added as an entirely new section to the Coroner statutes, dealing with archaeological burial sites.
Senate Enrolled Act 0072 also made changes related to the administration of public records in W.S. 16-4-201 through 205.

Wyoming Supreme Court: Decision S-18-0156, issued on 02/15/2019, established case law in regards to the lack of judicial jurisdiction over procedures involved in an Inquest. These new additions will be discussed in the appropriate sections.

A list of the major additions can be found at the end of the Subject Index.

Part II: Current Wyoming Statutes and Law

Establishment and Interpretation

Statutes are the bread and butter of what you do as coroner – the source for your authority, the framework for your duties, and the implementation of your responsibilities as coroner in the State of Wyoming. Not knowing the statutes that govern your job is as dumb as getting behind the wheel of a vehicle and not knowing the basics of the traffic laws. At some point, aside from not living up to your sworn duty and responsibility to the people that elected you to serve, you could actually get in serious legal difficulties. Anyone that gets spanked badly, whether civil or criminal in nature, through ignorance of the law, deserves what they get. No excuse, as the phrase says. It is important to know that even with the best knowledge and circumstances, even the most conscientious person can get caught with their pants down on occasion due to the obscure twists and turns of interpretation or application of the law, so it is important to narrow the opportunity as best you can through attentive knowledge and awareness.

As we cover the various portions of statute, I will offer commentary and examples to illustrate different aspects and applications. While my commentary is based on extensive research, personal experience, and a good deal of case law references, I offer that commentary conditionally.

First, compared to other contested statutory interpretation, coroner statutes have very little relative case law or judicial rulings, so there is not a whole lot to go on in that way. I will note what is available.

Second, a larger portion of analysis has been expressed in either County Attorney or Wyoming Attorney General opinions. Be aware that those opinions are just that – opinions. They are good as far as they go, but do not hold the certainty of judicial rulings and case law. Such opinions can change with a new or different public officer or official, change of party affiliation in the office, or be altered by later actual case law, if the same issue moves through the legal system in another jurisdiction. However, they usually will serve to back you up until changed or overruled.

Third, even judicial rulings can change over the course of time as legal interpretations change or progress. Luckily, and this is the main basis for my analysis, the Wyoming Supreme Court has expressed the main perspective in trying to interpret statutes:

> "A statute is clear and unambiguous if the words are such that reasonable minds are able to agree on its meaning in a consistent and predictable fashion." [1] *Mendoza v.State*, 2016 WY 31, ¶ 9, 368 P.3d 886, 891 (Wyo. 2016).
>
> "In any question of statutory interpretation, our primary objective is to give effect to the legislature's intent." [2] *L & L Enters. v. Arellano (In re Arellano)*, 2015 WY 21, ¶ 13, 344 P.3d 249, 252 (Wyo.2015). "Where legislative intent is discernible a court should give effect to the 'most likely, most reasonable, interpretation of the statute, given its design and purpose.'" [3] *Adekale*, ¶ 12, 344 P.3d at 765 (quoting *Rodriguez v. Casey*, 2002 WY 111, ¶ 20, 50 P.3d 323, 329 (Wyo.2002)).
>
> "In light of this objective, we have said: We therefore construe each statutory provision *in pari materia*, giving effect to every word, clause, and sentence according to their arrangement and connection. To ascertain the meaning of a given law, we also consider all statutes relating to the same subject or having the same general purpose and strive to interpret them harmoniously. We presume that the legislature has acted in a thoughtful and rational manner with full knowledge of existing law, and that it intended new statutory provisions to be read in harmony with existing law and as part of an overall and uniform system of jurisprudence. When the words used convey a specific and obvious meaning, we need not go farther and engage in statutory construction." [4] *Nicodemus v. Lampert*, 2014 WY 135, ¶ 13, 336 P.3d 671, 674 (Wyo.2014) (citing *Estate of Dahlke ex rel. Jubie v. Dahlke*, 2014 WY 29, ¶¶ 36–37, 319 P.3d 116, 125–26 (Wyo.2014)). *Robert L. Kroenlein Trust ex rel. Alden v. Kirchhefer*, 2015 WY 127, ¶ 22, 357 P.3d 1118, 1126 (Wyo. 2015) (citations omitted).
>
> **"If the language is sufficiently clear, we do not resort to rules of construction. We apply our general rule that we look to the ordinary and obvious meaning of a statute when the language is unambiguous."** [5] *Fontaine v. Bd. Of Cty. Comm'rs of Park Cty.*,

4 P.3d 890, 894 (Wyo. 2000) (citations omitted). **(Bold emphasis is mine)**

Whether we can "presume that the legislature has acted in a thoughtful and rational manner" may be a subject for hot debate, considering what often is proposed or goes on in our State Legislature, but that is a subject for discussion elsewhere, either over a hot cup of coffee, or a tall glass of scotch, depending on your need for perceptions of the legislative process.

As is true for most legal precedence cited and used by the various State Supreme Courts, these principles of interpreting the law along unambiguous, plain, and simple meaning of the words within the total context of a statute or law, are based on similar expressions and decisions by the U.S. Supreme Court over time. This may be hard to believe considering the way lawyers will argue and parse individual words or phrases, but the courts generally listen politely and then go with common sense, if available in the legislative construction.

Section A: Coroner Statutes

WYOMING STATUTES, TITLE 7, CHAPTER 4
COUNTY CORONERS
ARTICLE 1: IN GENERAL

7-4-101. Election; oath; bond.
A coroner shall be elected in each county for a term of four (4) years. He shall take the oath prescribed by the constitution of the state and give bond to the state of Wyoming, in the penal sum of one thousand dollars ($1,000.00), with sufficient sureties, to be approved by the board of county commissioners, conditioned that he will faithfully perform all duties required by law.

Commentary: This would be considered the 'authorizing' statute for the office, in other words, the source of its existence, or "creation of office". In other areas of statute, the coroner is often left off of the list of elected officials for various reasons, but this leaves no doubt that the office is an elected one. The sworn oath is the same, and a bond necessary like any other elected officer. If you do not file the appropriate bond as budgeted and approved by the County Commission, that in and of itself is a violation of statute and cause for removal. The fact the position is an elected one, is also reinforced in W.S. 22-2-105, noted later.

7-4-102. Deputy coroners.
The county coroner may appoint deputy coroners, who shall serve in the absence or inability of the coroner and who shall receive compensation as the board of county commissioners determines by resolution.

Commentary: The coroner may (but is not required to) hire and appoint deputies, but their compensation is subject to determination and approval by the County Commission, and whatever policies they set for the particular county. This is consistent with the fact that the Board is statutorily responsible for the financial welfare and disbursements for the county. In other words, the corner needs no permission to hire staff, but must work with the commission on how much they get paid. In other law for some elected officials, it is required that the Chief Deputy, if you have one, is required to get 80% of the elected official's salary in pay – logical since they basically have to serve all the functions if the elected official is absent. That however, is not set in statute for the coroner's staff, although probably a good idea if you expect that sort of responsibility from your chief deputy.

7-4-103. Certification requirements; penalty; expenses.
(a) After January 5, 1987, no person shall continue in office as county coroner or deputy coroner unless he has been certified under W.S. 9-1-634 as having completed:
    (i) Not later than one (1) year after assuming office, a basic coroner course;
    (ii) Continuing education requirements promulgated by the board of coroner standards pursuant to W.S. 7-4-211(c)(iii).
(b) Any person who knowingly fails to comply with subsection (a) of this section and continues in office is guilty of a misdemeanor punishable by a fine of twenty-five dollars ($25.00) for each day of noncompliance.
(c) Each coroner or deputy coroner attending approved classes to receive the certification required by subsection (a) of this section shall receive his present salary or per diem in the same manner and amount as state employees, whichever is greater, and shall be reimbursed for his actual travel and other necessary expenses reasonably incurred in obtaining the required training. The expenses shall be paid by the county in which the coroner or deputy coroner is serving.
(d) After July 1, 2001, no person shall serve as deputy coroner or as an employee of a county coroner who does not meet the employment standards adopted by the board of coroner standards pursuant to W.S. 7-4-211(c)(v).

Commentary: Certification is required through Police Officers Standards and Training (POST) and must be maintained to continue in office. Not only is it required, but you are liable for a misdemeanor penalty for non-compliance. This also requires the county to pay for the necessary training to stay in compliance. There is case law in this regards [1] (Veile v. Board of County Comm'rs, 860 P.2d 1174, 1993 Wyo.) in which the courts determined that the county could not be charged with the expenses of operating the county coroner's mortuary while the coroner attended the required certification courses. "Expenses reasonably incurred" does not anticipate the expenses of operating a private business, just the 'meals and lodging, etc.' costs of that training. The Board of County Commissioners is given discretionary authority to approve expenses, or not.

The subject of what to do with a coroner whose certification has lapsed has come up in a couple of instances over time. While the process to remove an *elected official can get complicated and time consuming (the particular statute is noted later), it has been firmly established that the person cannot act as coroner in the interim without regaining certification ('d' noted in the statute) even though he still holds the office. The rules of POST do allow one year after election or deputy appointment to obtain that certification, during which time the person can act in official capacity. The Coroner Basic course at the Academy for certification is only held once a year however, so if things are mistimed or you fail to attend, things could get complicated, so be aware. POST also requires 20 hours of continuing education every two years once certified, to retain that certification.*

7-4-104. Definitions.
    (a) As used in this chapter:
        (i)   "Coroner's case" means a case involving a death which was not anticipated and which may involve any of the following conditions:
        (A) Violent or criminal action;
        (B) Apparent suicide;
        (C) Accident;
        (D) Apparent drug or chemical overdose or toxicity;
        (E) The deceased was unattended by a physician or other licensed health care provider;
        (F) Apparent child abuse causes;
        (G) The deceased was a prisoner, trustee, inmate or patient of any county or state corrections facility or state hospital, whether or not the death is unanticipated;
        (H) If the cause is unknown, or cannot be certified by a physician,
        (J) A public health hazard is presented; or
        (K) The identity of the victim is unknown or the body is unclaimed.

(ii) "Coroner's office" means all personnel appointed and elected to the office of coroner, including the county coroner, deputies and assistants;

(iii) "County coroner" means the elected or appointed officer of the county whose task is to investigate the cause of death in a coroner's case.

(iv) "Anticipated death" means the death of an individual who has been diagnosed by a physician acting within the scope of his license as being afflicted with an illness or disease reasonably likely to result in death, and there is no cause to believe the death occurred for any reasons other than those associated with the illness or disease;

(v) "Unattended" means the deceased had not been under the care of a physician or other health care provider acting within the scope of his license within sixty (60) days immediately prior to the date of death.

Commentary: *Here we get to the meat of the matter – what exactly is a 'coroner's case'? As noted previously, in 2005 the legislature clarified the intent of "unattended" as part of a formalization of Hospice Care. "Other health care provider" was added to broaden the unattended definition to include other medical staff that might be in attendance at home or a facility for end-of-life care; the time frame was also shortened from 6 months to 60 days. This change was also promoted by corporate hospice providers who were upset at coroner staff in another county insisting on taking toxicology samples on Hospice patients at death. In conjunction with the definition for 'anticipated' death, a Hospice case is simply not the coroner's jurisdiction, period, unless it falls under (A) through (K). For example, if someone shoots a Hospice patient, it is a homicide under (A) and a coroner case, regardless of the Hospice status. As another example, if a family does not claim the body of a Hospice patient (K), the county has to deal with it as a coroner case and see to the burial. Please note, there is some uncertainty on which portions of this section retain primacy, as there has been no case law I am aware of that speaks to that determination in Wyoming. Another point to make here is that intentional or not, by making this change, the legislature effectively removed all oversight by anyone of a Hospice death. While the circumstance would probably be rare, the family of a Hospice patient could intentionally overdose the patient (i.e. assisted suicide, or homicide) and no one would ever know it. I personally have no objections to Hospice in general, but I do think that all medical providers should have some sort of oversight due to the potential for abuse of the system. It happens.*

Another thing this did clarify of note, is that by Fremont County Attorney written opinion, nursing homes are not coroner cases. While many residents of those facilities may have poor health or medical conditions, it would be a stretch to consider a facility death 'anticipated' in many cases; however, as a facility that has 24-hour attendance of "other health care providers" (nursing staff, therapists, and certification of an attending physician to even be a resident), they are attended deaths. 'Attended' does not necessarily mean physically present at the time of death specifically, as the definition in 'unattended' is a broad "under care" within the last 60 days. Again, if a resident goes down a flight of stairs and breaks his neck, that then falls under '(C) Accident', and is a coroner case. One must keep the logical and "plain meaning" of the law in mind.

Most of the other areas of jurisdiction are fairly obvious and fall under a non-natural death. Some are tied in with other areas of statutes, such as death from '(F) Apparent child abuse cases', or '(J) a public health hazard'. The latter one is where the Dept. of Health procedures and regulations regarding mass fatalities, pandemics, or other public safety and health events come into play. All deaths in those instances are coroner cases, anticipated or attended, or not. The two departments of coroner and Health work together on mitigating the event.

The final one to make a point about here is (G) – regardless of attended or anticipated death, all inmates, or those in custody, at a medical facility or otherwise, whether local or State jurisdiction, are coroner cases and must be investigated. This included prisons, jails, any State facility, or any location where the "custody" is intact, regardless of circumstance. This particular part of the statute is a good recognition that even the State need oversight in the circumstances of a death, and the traditional role of the coroner as an independent investigator is upheld. The policies of most correctional facilities require an autopsy regardless of initial apparent manner of death, which the coroner is to facilitate. I have no argument with those policies, as the public needs an assurance of proper oversight and verification of the circumstances.

While the definition of jurisdiction on what is a coroner case has obviously evolved and been clarified since Territorial times, just by the varied nature of death, you will encounter cases where there is a question of whether it is your jurisdiction or not. Since those decisions are often those that have to be made in immediate circumstances, and usually without time to consult the County Attorney for an opinion, the best advice I have is to treat it as a case and proceed appropriately. The coroner can always terminate jurisdiction later if it is found not to apply.

7-4-105. Confidentiality of reports, photos and recordings; exceptions; penalties.

(a) After viewing the body and completing his investigation, the coroner shall draw up and sign his verdict on the death under consideration. The coroner shall also make a written docket giving an accurate description of the deceased person, his name if it can be determined, cause and manner of death, including relevant toxicological factors, age of decedent, date and time of death and the description of money and other property found with the body. The verdict and written docket are public records and may be viewed or obtained by request to the coroner, pursuant to W.S. 16-4-202.

(b) Except as provided in subsections (c), (d), (e), (g) and (o) of this section a toxicology report, a photograph, video recording or audio recording made at the scene of the death or made in the course of a postmortem examination or autopsy made or caused by a coroner shall be confidential and are not public records.

(c) A surviving spouse, surviving parent, an adult child, personal representative, legal representative, or a legal guardian may:

> (i) View and copy a toxicology report, a photograph or video recording made at the scene of the death or made in the course of a postmortem examination or autopsy made by or caused by a coroner; and
>
> (ii) Listen to and copy an audio recording made at the scene of the death or made in the course of a postmortem examination or autopsy made by or caused by a coroner.

(d) Upon making a written request, a law enforcement entity of the state of Wyoming or United States government, a district attorney, the United States attorney for the district of Wyoming, a county, state or federal public health agency, a board licensing health care professionals under title 33 of the Wyoming statutes, the division responsible for administering the Wyoming Workers' Compensation Act, the state occupational epidemiologist, the department and the division responsible for administering the Wyoming Occupational Health and Safety Act, the office of the inspector of mines, insurance companies with legitimate interest in the death, all parties in civil litigation proceedings with legitimate interest in the death or a treating physician, while in performance of his official duty may:

> (i) View and copy a toxicology report, photograph or video recording made at the scene of the death or made in the course of a postmortem examination or autopsy made by or caused by a coroner; and
>
> (ii) Listen to and copy an audio recording made at the scene of the death or made in the course of a postmortem examination or autopsy made by or caused by a coroner.

(e) Unless otherwise required in the performance of official duties, the identity of the deceased shall remain confidential in any record obtained under subsection (d) of this section.

(f) The coroner having custody of a toxicology report, a photograph, a video recording or an audio recording made at any scene of the death or made in the course of a postmortem examination or autopsy may allow the use for case consultation with an appropriate expert. The coroner may also allow the use of a toxicology report, a photograph, a video recording or an audio recording made at the scene of the death or made in the course of a postmortem examination or autopsy by legitimate scientific research organizations or for training purposes provided the identity of the decedent is not published or otherwise made public.

(g) A court upon showing of good cause, may issue an order authorizing a person to:

    (i) View or copy a toxicology report, photograph or video recording made at the scene of the death or made in the course of a postmortem examination or autopsy made or caused by a coroner; and

    (ii) Listen to and copy an audio recording made at the scene of the death or made in the course of a postmortem examination or autopsy made or caused by a coroner.

(h) In determining good cause under subsection (g) of this section, the court shall consider:

    (i) Whether the disclosure is necessary for the public evaluation of governmental performance;

    (ii) The seriousness of the intrusion into the family's privacy;

    (iii) Whether the disclosure of the toxicology report, photograph, video recording or audio recording is by the least intrusive means available; and

    (iv) The availability of similar information in other public records regardless of form.

(j) A surviving spouse shall be given reasonable notice and a copy of any petition filed with the court under subsection (g) of this section and reasonable opportunity to be present and be heard on the matter. If there is no surviving spouse, the notice of the petition being filed and the opportunity to be heard shall be given to the deceased's parents and if the deceased has no living parent, the notice of the petition being filed and the opportunity to be heard shall be given to the adult children of the deceased or legal guardian, personal representative or legal representative of the children of the deceased.

(k) A coroner or coroner's designee that knowingly violates this section shall be guilty of a misdemeanor punishable by imprisonment for not more than six (6) months, a fine of not more than one thousand dollars ($1,000.00), or both.

(m) A person who knowingly or purposefully uses the information in a manner other than the specified purpose for which it was released or violates a court order issued under subsection (g) of this section is guilty of a misdemeanor punishable by imprisonment for not more than six (6) months, a fine of not more than one thousand dollars ($1,000.00), or both.

(n) In all cases, the viewing, copying, listening to, or other handling of a toxicology report, photograph, video recording, or audio recording made at a scene of the death or made in the course of a postmortem examination or autopsy made or caused by a coroner shall be under the direct supervision of the coroner, or the coroner's designee, who is the custodian of the record.

(o) In the event that the coroner, or the coroner's designee, determines that a person's death was caused by an infectious disease, biological toxin or any other cause which may constitute a public health emergency as defined in W.S. 35-4-115(a)(i), the coroner shall release to the state health officer or his designee all information and records required under W.S. 35-4-107. If the state health official or his designee determines upon an examination of the results of the autopsy and the toxicology report that a public health emergency may in fact exist, he shall release the appropriate information to the general public as provided by department of health rules and regulations.

***Commentary:** W.S. 7-4-105 was added and passed by the legislature in 2011to address the issue of confidentiality. This came to the fore in some very public national instances, such as the media publication of autopsy photos in other States, and Wyoming coroners were very active in getting this addition passed. Prior to this time, <u>all</u> aspects of the investigation were considered public record – photos, autopsy reports, everything in the file. Part (a) now determines exactly what is a public record, no more, no less, and requires the coroner to issue a public docket on the completion of every case. Anything else is protected from exposure as confidential non-public information. Specific instances and allowances for release of the confidential materials are defined in detail, and will be discussed later in the section on suggested department policies. There is one good bit of case law regarding the detail of the required public information* [2] *(Williams v. Sundstrom, 2016 WY 122, 385 P.3d 789, 2016 Wyo.). The court ruled that if the verdict and case docket clearly included the reason for the death of the individual, the coroner did not have "an absolute, clear, and indisputable duty" to provide additional detailed information or diagrams requested by a party when listing the cause of death.*

This section can get sticky in implementation, and took a while to work out in the public's mind exactly what is, or is not allowed. For example, for some reason, siblings are not listed in the allowed family members for receiving the materials, and sometimes they may be the only family left for the deceased. They can access if they are the "legal or personal representative" for the deceased, but that is defined elsewhere in statutes by legal requirements. Thus, it is our policy, and advisable, to require copies of such paperwork rather than depending on what a person says verbally. The public has some misconceptions on these legalities, such as in many cases, a "Power of Attorney" ends at death, and they are not aware that what they legally could previously do, does not apply once a person is deceased. It all depends on the wording of a document, and this section also obligates the coroner, under penalty of law, to safeguard the materials. There is also a penalty if the receiver of the information misuses it in a manner other than for which it was intended.

General summary data, such as that requested by various agencies, groups, or prevention organizations, is not prohibited from release, as long as the individual identification is redacted or removed. Anyone can petition a court for release of information, and the protections for that are spelled out in detail as to what concerns and justifications need to be addressed by the judge. This reference is different from the civil or criminal legal process, where attorneys on both sides need information for a case and are bound by other statutes and rules of legal procedure to obtain it.

7-4-106. Archaeological human burial sites.
    (a) The county coroner shall have jurisdiction over all archaeological human burials discovered in the county on state or private lands.
    (b) When human remains are discovered:
        (i) The person who discovers the remains shall cease the activity that caused the discovery of the remains and immediately notify law enforcement. If the remains are discovered on private land and the person who discovers the remains is not an agent of the landowner, the individual shall also notify the landowner;
        (ii) When law enforcement is notified that human remains have been discovered within the limits of the county, law enforcement shall notify the coroner who shall determine the approximate age of the burial site. If the human remains constitute an archaeological human burial:
            (A) On private land, the coroner shall notify the state archaeologist and the landowner;
            (B) On state land, the coroner shall notify the state archaeologist and the office of state lands and investments. The office of state lands and investments shall notify any leaseholder;

(C) The state archaeologist's investigation to determine the forensic value and archaeological context shall be:

(I) Commenced within two (2) business days of the discovery to protect the integrity of the remains;

(II) Limited to the discovered human burial site.

(c) When human remains are exhumed:

(i) An archaeological human burial shall only be exhumed under the direction and supervision of the state archaeologist in coordination with the county coroner, and provided:

(A) The coroner shall notify the landowner of exhumation; and

(B) If the state archaeologist determines that the remains are Native American, the state archaeologist shall notify the Eastern Shoshone and Northern Arapaho Tribes before exhumation.

(ii) Absent extraordinary circumstances, exhumation shall be completed not more than six (6) business days from the date the coroner notifies the state archaeologist of the archeological human burial discovery to protect the safety and integrity of the remains.

(d) When human remains are reinterred:

(i) When the state archaeologist determines that an archaeological human burial is Native American, after archaeological human remains are exhumed and before reinterment or repatriation, the state archaeologist and county coroner shall:

(A) Notify and consult with culturally affiliated Native American tribes in accordance with the protocol developed pursuant to subsection (f) of this section; and

(B) Expend reasonable effort to identify present day descendants.

(ii) When the state archaeologist determines that an archaeological human burial is not Native American, the state archaeologist shall expend reasonable effort to identify present day descendants and consult with them before reinterment;

(iii) If no descendants of the person whose remains were exhumed are identifiable, remains may be reinterred on state lands;

(iv) Subject to the notification of law enforcement, the coroner and the state archaeologist and the procedures in this section, nothing in this section precludes a landowner from working with descendants or Native American tribes to reinter human remains on private lands with the landowner's consent.

(e) Human remains shall be treated with respect, dignity and with consideration of religious, spiritual and ethnic evidence present at the burial site.

(f) The state archaeologist in cooperation with the state historic preservation office and county coroners shall work with culturally affiliated tribes including the Eastern Shoshone and Northern Arapaho tribes to develop a protocol for consultation, repatriation and reinterment or other disposition of Native American human remains.

(g) For purposes of this section, "archaeological human burial" includes human remains and funerary objects that, as part of the death rite or ceremony of a culture, are reasonably believed to have been placed with individual human remains at the time of death or later but does not include remains found in known or marked graves, found in established cemeteries or that demonstrate present medicolegal significance.

(h) A person who knowingly violates this section is guilty of a misdemeanor punishable by imprisonment for not more than six (6) months, a fine of not more than five thousand dollars ($5,000.00), or both.

Commentary: *This section represents a major addition to the coroner statutes by the Legislature in 2019. I had the opportunity to discuss and offer input with the sponsors prior to introduction, and followed this effort through the legislative session. The main impetus was to codify a consistent procedure throughout the State, and involve all the various agencies and departments appropriate to the area of archaeological remains. Note that (a) spells out the jurisdiction of the coroner in this matter on state or private lands within his county – Federal lands are covered under similar laws discussed elsewhere.*

The first section covers the procedure when remains are found – logically, the coroner and law enforcement must determine if they are indeed older and archaeological in nature, or of medical-legal significance. Obviously, if a recent burial that might involve criminality, regular procedures come into play and the balance of this section is not applicable. However, if of historic or archaeological time frame (generally considered 70 years of age since burial or older), other parties must be notified and involved. This is spelled out in detail, and time frames for investigation established. Quite plainly, the proper expertise is summoned to deal with the site.

If the remains are to be removed, it is to be done along proper archaeological methods, to protect the integrity and historic value of the site, as well as insure proper and methodical documentation. If the remains show evidence of being a Native American site, then Tribal considerations come into play and further notifications made. **It is important to note that if the state agency or the coroner take possession of the remains after removal, the Federal NAGPRA regulations must be followed, as that is specifically required by Federal law for the state and its political subdivisions, which includes the county coroner.** *Believe me, you do not want to run afoul of the Feds in this case, as that can involve long-term legal issues and heavy fines for non-compliance. NAGPRA is discussed in a later section.*

Section (f) notes that a protocol and procedure will be developed to further detail consultation, repatriation, and reinterment if the remains are Native American, and this portion gives the whole section the ability to comply and be consistent with Federal law. If historic, but not Native, other procedures are spelled out for disposition.

This section was well-designed and allows for further protocols to address the details. Many interests came together in creating this section, from historical, tribal, energy industry concerns, law enforcement, and coroner jurisdictions, all to try and set and expedite, as well as standardize these procedures across Wyoming. Some coroners may only run into this every few years, others more frequently. It should be also noted that the last penalty section not only covers the public or land owners that do not comply, it also includes each responsible agency, like the coroner. Failure to comply could result in grounds for removal from office if convicted.

ARTICLE 2: INQUESTS

7-4-201. Reports of death; investigation; summoning of jurors; fees and costs; inspection of medical records.

(a) When any person is found dead and the death appears to have occurred under circumstances indicating the death is a coroner's case, the person who discovers the death shall report it immediately to law enforcement authorities who shall in turn notify the coroner. A person who knowingly violates this section is guilty of a misdemeanor punishable by imprisonment for not more than six (6) months, a fine of not more than seven hundred fifty dollars ($750.00), or both.

(b) When the coroner is notified that the dead body of any person has been found within the limits of the county or that the death resulted from injury sustained within the county and he suspects that the death is a coroner's case, he shall conduct an investigation which may include:

(i) An examination of the body and an investigation into the medical history of the case;
(ii) The appointment of a qualified physician to assist in determining the cause of death;
(iii) An autopsy if the physician appointed to assist the coroner under this subsection determines an autopsy is necessary;
(iv) An inquest; or
(v) Any other reasonable procedure which may be necessary to determine the cause of death.

(c) If the coroner determines to hold an inquest he shall summon three (3) citizens of the county to appear before him to act as jurors at the time and place named. The jurors shall receive the same fee paid jurors in district court as provided in W.S. 1-11-303 and per diem and travel expenses in the same manner as state employees. The coroner may furnish transportation for the jury and witnesses to and from the place of inquest and for the removal of the dead body.

(d) If a coroner determines the injuries which caused the person's death were received in a county other than that in which the body was found, he shall transfer authority for the investigation and inquest to the coroner for that county.

(e) The expense and costs of conducting the investigation or holding the inquest shall be paid by the county in which the injuries were received. The accounts of the claimants shall be attested by the coroner or acting coroner, and shall be presented in duplicate to the board of county commissioners of the proper county. If the board of county commissioners finds that the inquest was necessary and in accordance with law, and the accounts are correct and just, the accounts shall be paid in warrants properly drawn upon the order of the county commissioners.

(f) Notwithstanding any other provision of law to the contrary, the coroner may inspect medical and psychological data relating to the person-whose death is being investigated if the coroner determines the information is relevant and necessary to the investigation.

Commentary: While the title of Article 2 is "Inquests", there is a wealth of information and law that is applicable to more than just that procedure. To start with (a) in this section established the legal obligation of any citizen to report a death, under penalty of law. An interesting note is that the citizen shall report it to law enforcement, who shall "in turn" report the death to the coroner. In a past homicide case here in Fremont County, law enforcement did not report the case to the coroner for about 10 hours, and we were not admitted to the scene for about 15 hours. Aside from the circumstances that action, or inaction, could have as an effect on the loss of evidence and change in condition of the body to hinder our investigation, this was improper under the meaning of the phrase "in turn". As determined by the WY Supreme Court, reasonable interpretations look to "the ordinary and obvious meaning of the word". "In turn" means simply, "one after the other, as an equal and related effect". Under no logical interpretation would that be taken to mean informing the coroner over 10 hours after a homicide is discovered. How such things are resolved or mitigated depends on your relationship with the law enforcement agency of jurisdiction, but needless to say, we were not happy about it, especially as in a homicide, we would probably end up testifying in court as to circumstances and time of death, manner and cause, and appropriateness and validity of an investigation. Since such a delay could greatly impact the main piece of evidence, the body, it would not have looked good for the law enforcement investigators or the case. Luckily, the perpetrator pled out, so that aspect did not occur.

(b) provides the framework for authority to investigate. Note that it clearly states the jurisdiction as within the county boundaries, or that the originating injury occurred within the county. Thus any injury that occurs that results in death, is this particular county coroner's case, even if they end up being transferred to another medical facility in another county and dying there. As a side note, By Department of Health rules for Vital Records, if a patient dies during air or ground transport, the 'location' of death is where the vehicle stops or lands. Jurisdiction though still remains with the county of incident origin. The subparts of (b) give authority to examine the body and medical history of the case, seek a physician to assist and order an autopsy, and order an inquest. Part (v) allows "any other reasonable procedure which may be necessary" and that gives the open-ended ability to adjust investigatory needs and procedures to the specific case needs, and incorporate new or better procedures and technology as they come along. This also is consistent with the traditional coroner's place as an independent investigator into the manner and cause of death, outside of the procedures or methods of law enforcement.

(c) starts the procedure for an inquest, which will be discussed in detail later, and as a process is referred to periodically throughout this section.

(d) reinforces (b) in that the jurisdiction is transferred to the county of the originating incident.

(e) specifically states that the originating county where the incident occurred is responsible for the costs of the investigation, as submitted to the Board of County Commissioners by the coroner. This is tempered by

the court decision in "Veile" noted earlier, where the Board does have discretion in determining that the expenses are valid.

(f) gives undisputed authority to the coroner to inspect medical and psychological records of the deceased without question or denial of any party. The phrase "not withstanding" means "in spite of", in other words, any other law or regulation that limits access to such records does not apply to the coroner in the matter. Even the Federal [3.]HIPAA laws specifically allow access of coroners and medical examiners to all medical records regardless of any objection. This makes perfect sense if we are to do our job in determination of manner and cause of death as an independent investigator.

7-4-202. Impaneling of bystanders as jurors; oath.

If any juror fails to appear, the coroner shall immediately summon the proper number from the bystanders and proceed to impanel them. He shall administer the following oath: "You do solemnly swear (or affirm) that you will diligently inquire and truly present if known or determinable, the time and date of death, and by what means and manner the death of (NAME OF DECEASED) was caused, according to your knowledge and the evidence given you, so help you God."

Commentary: *This section is amusingly pretty much intact from the territorial language. If a juror for an inquest fails to show, you can pick anyone nearby and they have no choice but to serve, like it or not.*

7-4-203. Issuance of subpoenas; witness fees; enforcement of attendance.

The coroner may issue subpoenas and compel the attendance of witnesses to testify at the inquest. Witnesses shall be allowed the same fees as in cases before a circuit court, and the coroner shall have the same authority to enforce the attendance of witnesses and to punish for contempt as provided by W.S. 1-21-901 through 1-21-909.

Commentary: *In the instance of an inquest (and only that instance) the coroner has the authority to issue subpoenas, the same as the circuit courts. Failure to obey the subpoenas has the same punishment for contempt of court in that venue. There has been some quibbling legally by defense attorneys over how that applies to various documentations, but the courts have generally upheld the ability to subpoena documents as well as witnesses, in the same manner as a circuit court.*

The ability to subpoena documents, however, is not a settled issue in Wyoming. While other states and previous attorney's general opinions have allowed it, in 2019 the current Wyoming attorney general's office had some doubts about that. In an Inquest earlier this year, I subpoenaed State Division of Criminal Investigation (DCI) records as evidence, and that agency objected. The current AG administration upheld their objection, mostly due to not wanting their confidential reports exposed in a public proceeding, however, their interpretation of the statute was that subpoenas only applied to witnesses. DCI appeared as a witness, but without their reports. Regardless of previous interpretations, the current one must hold sway and be adhered to, unless differently determined by a court, so I had to agree (unless I wanted to challenge the AG opinion in court, which would not have been constructive at the time). This also only addressed a subpoena for just documents. An alternate possibility is to issue a "subpoena duces tecum", which is for an individual to appear and bring documents as a single subpoena – I may have to try that one next time and see what happens.

In the complexities of legislative interpretation and design, the issue would be clear if they had placed a comma after 'subpoenas' and before 'and compel…' in the first line, grammatically establishing two subjects, eliminating the possible interpretation of subpoenas only applying to witnesses. Such minute language marks have often been the subject of legal arguments. In any case, the current opinion, as noted before, is just an opinion, and can change later. It is hard to say what the original intent of the legislature was at the time, unless decided by a court in case law. There is adequate grounds to challenge the current opinion, as the statute references the powers of a circuit court in this instance, and circuit courts can subpoena documents.

7-4-204. Oath of witness; recording of testimony; compensation of reporter.

An oath shall be administered to each witness as follows: "You do solemnly swear (or affirm) that the testimony which you shall give to this inquest concerning the death of the person about whom this inquest is being held, shall be the truth, the whole truth and nothing but the truth, so help you God." The coroner shall insure that all testimony in an inquest shall be recorded. The compensation of the court reporter or of the person transcribing the audio tape shall be as prescribed by the board of county commissioners. Unless specifically requested by the coroner or prosecuting attorney, audio tapes need not be transcribed.

Commentary: This part is pretty self-explanatory. Court reporters are a usually a private business and as such can be hired to record the procedures of an inquest, which is a process that will result in less error than an audio recording for later transcription. With audio recordings you can end up with unintelligible portions, and can run into historical archive problems. We have inquest testimony in old files that was recorded via an eight-inch blue floppy 'record' "Dictaphone" system... Where in the world do you find that technology now, and at what expense, even if you could? Do you even know what a 'Dictaphone' is? I do, but don't often admit it, as that somewhat reveals my age. Sort of like making a phone call on a "brick", or by "dropping a dime" – young people, look it up, I'm not going to make it easy for you.

In any case, a good court reporter will ask for a repeat if testimony is not audible, or for spelling on terms and names, thus a more accurate text when reproduced into a transcript. Paper transcripts from over 120 years ago are still readable, whereas technology from 20 years ago may not be available to access data.

7-4-205. Return of inquisition by jury.
After hearing testimony and making necessary inquiries, the jurors shall return to the coroner their signed inquisition stating the name of the person and when, how and by what means, if known, he came to his death.

Commentary: The details and traditional format for this will be discussed in the section on inquests.

7-4-206. Coroner's return to court.
The coroner shall return to the district court the inquisition, the written evidence and a list of witnesses providing material testimony.

Commentary: The details and traditional format for this will be discussed in the section on inquests.

7-4-207. Disposition of body and effects of deceased.
    (a) When the coroner investigates the death of a person whose body is not claimed by a friend or relative within five (5) days of the date of discovery and whose death does not require further investigation, he shall cause the body to be decently buried. The

expense of the burial shall be paid from any property found with the body. If no property is found, the expense of the burial shall be paid by the county in which the investigation occurs.
(b) The coroner shall within a reasonable time after completing the investigation, turn over to the appointed personal representative of the estate of the deceased or, if none, to the clerk of the district court of the county, all money or other property found upon the body of the deceased. Personal items valued at less than fifty dollars ($50.00) and items necessary for the convenience of the deceased's next of kin may be released to the deceased's next of kin.

Commentary: *This section states the obligation of the county as a public service to see to the "decent burial" of unclaimed remains once an investigation is completed, a social contract of government that goes back hundreds of years in tradition and law. It is notable that while disposition of property is determined by other statutes, and in most cases through a chain of relation, anyone can claim a body for burial. The five-day limit is only mitigated by the need of an open investigation, not by the preference of relatives, so there is motivation to make the arrangements in a reasonably quick time. We have in some cases had to force the decision when various family members cannot decide, or argue about what to do with Uncle Joe. Figure it out, or we by law will have to do it by our policies, not your preferences (more about that later). This probably goes back to the days before consistent availability of proper storage or embalming, to prevent things from "stacking up" with the usual process of decomposition. Still, even today, there are practical limits to what any coroner office can do or store, so still a good statute to have.*

In regards to property, there are two "word" references here: "with" and "upon" the body. While more defined then territorial law, there is still a lot of argument over the meaning of "upon" or "with" the body, and there has been no guidance by case law in the courts. This will be discussed later in detail in the section on indigent and unclaimed policies for the county, and a majority of those policies are based on County Attorney review and opinion. There is a packrat's nest of issues regarding disposal of property, and that will come back to bite you if done haphazardly and without a formal procedure in place.

One previous Fremont Coroner took possession of a herd of sheep when there was no one else to do so available. Another former coroner would have staff inventory and store entire households pending distribution. Aside from the ridiculous time and expense such things cost the county, my *opinion was that this was inappropriate under the law, and the County Attorney's office agreed, stating that this could be seen as an illegal seizure of personal property, regardless of disposition, with great possible liability on the county. We now go by the interpretation of a very narrow "on or with" in the plain and simple meaning of the words. The body is the custody of the coroner, and the scene is the jurisdiction of law enforcement, so it is up to them to decide what to do with that $50,000 in cash sitting on the kitchen table (that actually happened in a Fremont case).*

7-4-208. Authority of sheriff to perform duties of coroner.
If there is no coroner, deputy coroner or in case of their absence, or inability to act, the county sheriff of the same county, the state health officer pursuant to W.S. 35-1-241, or the coroner of another county if there is a joint powers agreement pursuant to W.S. 16-1-102 through 16-1-108 between the counties authorizing the coroner to so act, is authorized to perform the duties of coroner in relation to dead bodies.

Commentary: This also is fairly straight forward in meaning, and I have used this statute periodically to give the Sheriff a hard time in that I will disappear and leave him to deal with a particularly odd or 'ripe' case. Other aspects of this regarding health officers or joint powers will come up when we review other statutes.

7-4-209. Postmortem examination; liability limitation.
    (a) When an inquisition is being held, if the coroner or the jury shall deem it requisite, he may summon one (1) or more physicians or surgeons, to make an autopsy or postmortem examination.
    (b) If it is necessary to obtain or preserve evidence of the cause of death, the district attorney may order that a qualified physician perform an autopsy or postmortem examination of the body of any person who appears to have died by unlawful means, by violence, or when the cause of death is unknown.
    (c) No person is subject to civil liability solely because he requested or was involved in the performing of an autopsy that was ordered by a coroner or district attorney.

Commentary: By law, only two people have the authority to order an autopsy (other than an inquest jury) – the coroner or county/district attorney. Normally if a case is serious enough to warrant an inquest, an autopsy will already have been ordered and completed, but the inquest jury could in fact order additional examinations if it felt it necessary. This goes back to the days when an inquest jury was summoned in the immediate circumstance of a death. These days, in order to have a complete presentation of the evidence, most inquests would not be held until the investigation and procedures have already had time to provide adequate materials for the presentation. And no physician or coroner can be held liable for the process of an autopsy so ordered.

I personally have never had an instance where the county attorney insisted on an autopsy when I did not feel one was necessary. In any major case, we discuss the need at the time and in most cases concur without argument as the logical thing to do, or not. Note that while the need for autopsy is often also discussed with law enforcement, they cannot order one on their own, but would have to convince the county attorney to do so on their behalf if the coroner declines.

This statute is in conjunction with the authority described for investigations in W.S. 7-4-201. While it is appropriate to discuss with a family the need, or lack of need, for an autopsy, they can neither demand nor forbid one. That decision is the coroner's, based on the needs of the investigation, like it or not.

7-4-210. Fees and mileage, salary.
    (a) The coroner or deputy coroner of each county within this state shall receive fees and mileage, if any, as set by the board of county commissioners.
    (b) The board of county commissioners shall set the salary of the coroner and deputy coroner. A coroner or deputy coroner shall not be prohibited from receiving other fees for their services unrelated to their official duties as coroner or deputy coroner.

Commentary: *Part (a) further details the obligations of the county to pay for certain expenses as set within the policies of that county. Part (b) was added in 2005, and up to that point, there was no legal requirement to pay the coroner as an elected official, other than the expenses noted here or for an investigation as in W.S. 7-4-201(e). As noted previously, coroners were often left out of other statutory guidelines for county officials. W.S. 18-3-106 does not include coroners with other officials as being considered a full-time position. W.S 18-3-107 does not include coroners in regards to requiring a salary be paid (other elected county official even have the maximum amount that can be paid as periodically adjusted by the* *legislature). County Commissions can pay less, but not more, than a specified amount for each office. This 2005 addition to the law requires that coroners be paid a salary, but both the legislature and County Commissioner's Association balked at setting a specified amount. That may sound unfair, but realize that the smaller counties, with limited budgets and irregular or low numbers of case load for their coroner, do need some leeway in appropriate compensation. Since coroners in those counties are effectively part time or less, this statute also allows for the need to make a living wage by other means. It should be noted, however, that the common meaning of "salary" is a fixed compensation paid periodically to total a yearly amount. This is versus a "wage" that is a fixed amount paid by an employer to an employee. Coroners are elected officials in their own right and not employed by the Commission, so their compensation must fit being a salary, and not a wage. That salary may be a dollar per year, but since 2005 the Commission is at least required to set one. Historically, coroners were often paid by the case, but that technically would not work these days, as that is a wage, not a yearly salary.*

Again, it must be specifically noted that approving budgets and determining compensation are expressly statutory functions within the duties of the Board of County Commissioners. In another part of the "Veile" decisions in 1993, the WY Supreme Court stated that allegations of inadequate budget allocations or compensation could not be the basis of a claim of tortuous conduct (a civil act that causes harm or infringes the rights of an individual) against the Commission. The Wyoming Constitution, Article 3, Section32, also forbids the Commission from increasing the salary of any elected official during their term of office. They can only set new salaries for after the next election cycle.

7-4-211. Board of coroner standards.
    (a) There is created a board of coroner standards. The board shall consist of one (1) chairman and six (6) members appointed by and who shall serve at-the pleasure of the governor as follows:
        (i) One (1) shall be a physician with a specialty in pathology who is licensed to practice in this state;
        (ii) Three (3) shall be duly elected coroners in this state;
        (iii) One (1) shall be a funeral director in this state;
        (iv) One (1) shall be a duly elected district attorney in this state;
        (v) One (1) shall be a peace officer certified under W.S. 9-1-701 through 9-1-707.

(b) The members of the board shall be appointed to terms of four (4) years which are concurrent with the terms of the office of coroner. Board members not otherwise compensated for attending board meetings shall receive travel expenses and per them in the same manner and amount as state employees, and any other reasonable expenses upon board approval. Board members not otherwise compensated shall have their expenses paid from the general fund by appropriation to the office of the attorney general.

(c) The board shall:

    (i) Meet at least biannually and at the call of the chairman or of a majority of the membership;

    (ii) Promulgate standards dealing with the investigation of coroner's cases;

    (iii) Promulgate educational and training requirements for coroner basic and continuing education requirements and review those requirements annually;

    (iv) Cooperate with the peace officer standards and training commission in developing basic and continuing education courses for coroners;

    (v) Promulgate employment standards for deputy coroners and coroner employees. The standards may include the requirement that deputy coroners and coroner employees provide to the employing coroner fingerprints and other information necessary for a state and national criminal history record background check and release of information as provided in W.S. 7-19-106(k)(ii) and federal P.L. 92-544 and consent to the release of any criminal history information to the employing coroner.

    (vi) Promulgate rules and regulations to provide for the review of complaints if a coroner or deputy coroner has failed to comply with any provision of W.S. 7-4-103 or this subsection or has failed to meet any educational or training requirement provided under this section. The board shall make recommendations to the peace officer standards and training commission regarding revocation of certifications based on these investigations;

    (vii) Provide for a system to offer educational programs to assist coroners and deputy coroners in meeting educational and training requirements provided under this section.

(d) The peace officer standards and training commission shall cooperate with the board of coroner standards in establishing course requirements and continuing education requirements required by law.

(e) The board shall contact the district attorney for the county or the attorney general to initiate an action and may serve as complaining party in an action under W.S. 7-4-103 (b) or 18-3-902 to remove any coroner who is not in compliance with W.S. 7-4-103.

(f) In addition to any action under subsection (e) of this section, the board shall notify the county commissioners for the county of any coroner or deputy coroner who has had his certification revoked.

***Commentary:** In recognition of the need for requirements and standards for the duties of a coroner and how they are performed, over the last two decades the Board of Coroner Standards was created and formed, and the portions of this statute variously tweaked over time. Part (c)(ii) took years to complete, but is in place, and subject to discussion in another section of this text. Coroners should note that rules, as authorized by statute, once completed through the process and in place, have the effect and authority of statute – so the established rules for investigations cannot be ignored. Standards for employment and certification are determined by statute, the Board, and Police Officers Standards and Training (POST). In 2014, parts (c)(vi), (c)(vii), and (f) were added by the legislature in an attempt to put some teeth in compliance with the standards, but as of 2019 the Board has not established any regulations in regards to a complaint process that I know of. Removal of an elected official can only be determined for cause and process as it exists in other statutes. This did add the Board's legal standing as a party in a complaint for removal.*

Removal of an elected official should be a specified and not necessarily an easy process, in my opinion, as removal should only be for just cause, and publically spelled out. After all, the public granted the office, and the will of the public in an election needs to be protected from special interest or individual vindictiveness. This is not to say that the public always chooses wisely, or is an informed electorate. That is our system, however, and it should not be overthrown on a whim. The main issue these additions have struggled to address is compliance with the standards, and maintaining certification, in an effort to encourage some uniformity in job performance. After all, that is the meaning and intent of 'standards'.

Section B: Other Related Statutes

Don't think for a minute that once you get a handle on the Coroner Statutes themselves, that you have grasped all the implications of the laws of Wyoming in regards to coroners. Coroners are mentioned and interrelate in many other ways and locations in the law, either specifically by being named, or by inference. Sorry to disappoint. Any set of laws and regulations have a cat's cradle web of interactions, which can be both fascinating and frustrating, so it pays to account for the main areas you need to be aware of or reference, depending on need and application. These are presented in numerical order and have varying degrees of significance to the duties of the coroner.

W.S. 1-11-303 Amount of fees *(jurors)*
    1-11-303. Amount of fees.
    Jurors shall receive thirty dollars ($30.00) for each full or part day of actual attendance. A juror in attendance for more than five (5) consecutive days, exclusive of Saturdays, Sundays and holidays, may, in the discretion of the court, be allowed an additional twenty dollars ($20.00) per day for each day actually in attendance.

Commentary: This is the statute referenced by W.S. 7-4-201 regarding fees for inquest jurors. Amounts may be periodically updated at the whim of the legislature, so in this and any other similar statute, make sure you have the most recent version for the proper amount of compensation. These bills are vouchered with other costs of an inquest to the county commission for payment.

W.S. 1-12-102 "Dead man's statute" *(testimony)*
    1-12-102. When party incapable of testifying.
    In an action or suit by or against a person who from any cause is incapable of testifying, or by or against a trustee, executor, administrator, heir or other representative of the person incapable of testifying, no judgment or decree founded on uncorroborated testimony shall be rendered in favor of a party whose interests are adverse to the person incapable of testifying or his trustee, executor, administrator, heir or other representative. In any such action or suit, if the adverse party testifies, all entries, memorandum and declarations by the party incapable of testifying made while he was capable, relevant to the matter in issue, may be received in evidence.

Commentary: *This is not relevant to coroners just because of the name. This is applicable for a coroner inquest, where statements or documents made by the deceased may indeed be offered to the jury as evidence, just as in a regular judicial proceeding.*

W.S. 1-14-104 & 105 Fees of physicians in testimony and post-mortem examination.

1-14-104. Physician testifying as expert or performing postmortem or autopsy; fees.
Any physician or surgeon shall receive a reasonable fee as determined by the coroner when testifying as an expert before a coroner or other officer for each half day or portion thereof, and when conducting a postmortem examination or autopsy.

1-14-105. Physician testifying as expert or performing postmortem or autopsy; postmortem fee certificate; exceptions.
The coroner or other officer who has ordered a postmortem examination shall issue to the physician or surgeon a certificate for the fees provided, which shall be paid by the board of county commissioners by issuing a county warrant on the treasurer of the county in which the services were rendered in the amount of the certificate. W.S. 1-14-104 and 1-14-105 do not apply in the case of any physician regularly employed by the county.

Commentary: *These citations from the Code of Civil Procedure duplicate and reinforce W.S. 7-4-209 and note that the fees for autopsy or physician testimony are part of the legitimate expenses billed to the Commission.*

W.S. 1-21-901 through 1-21-909 Attendance of witnesses, contempt.

1-21-901. Grounds.
(a) A circuit court judge may punish for contempt in the following cases and no others:
(i) Persons guilty of disorderly, contemptuous and insolent behavior toward a judge engaged in any judicial proceeding, which tends to interrupt such proceedings or impair the respect due the judge's authority;
(ii) Persons guilty of resistance or disobedience to any lawful order or process made or issued by the judge.

1-21-902. Repealed By Laws 2005, ch. 90, § 2.

1-21-903. Hearing required; warrant of attachment.
No person shall be punished for contempt before a circuit court judge until after an opportunity to be heard and for that purpose the judge may issue his warrant of attachment to bring the offender before him.

1-21-904. Summary proceedings if offender present.
If the offender is present he may be summarily arraigned by the circuit court judge and proceeded against as if a warrant had been previously issued and the offender arrested thereon.

1-21-905. Warrant of commitment.
The warrant of commitment for contempt must set forth the particular circumstances of the offense or it is void.

1-21-906. Commitment of witness; generally.
Any witness attending before a circuit court who refuses to be sworn in some form prescribed by law or to answer any pertinent or proper question, may by order be committed to the jail of the county.

1-21-907. Commitment of witness; order.
The order shall specify the cause for which the order was issued. If it is for refusing to answer any question, the question shall be specified. The witness shall be closely confined pursuant to the order until he is sworn or answers.

1-21-908. Commitment of witness; adjournment.
The circuit court shall adjourn the case at the request of either party for a reasonable time or until the witness testifies in the case.

1-21-909. Failure of witness to attend.
If any person subpoenaed as a witness fails to attend, he is guilty of contempt and shall be fined all the costs for his apprehension unless he shows reasonable cause for his failure to attend, in which case the party requiring the appearance shall pay the costs.

Commentary: These are the contempt statutes cited in W.S. 7-4-203 applicable to coroner inquests. While seemingly fairly straight forward, the issues of subpoenas and the resulting charge of contempt for failure to comply, have rarely been an issue, but can get complicated. As our County Attorney noted originally when the subject came up of contempt, he had not encountered that before as very few individuals ever do not show up for a subpoena. After they did extensive research, I do have a County Attorney opinion on the matter, in quite lengthy detail. Here in Fremont, the whole issue is complicated by the presence of a Reservation, which in some legal circles, can be considered "foreign nationals" due to tribal sovereignty. In circumstances where I need to subpoena tribal members on the Reservation, I submit them to the Tribal Court, where a Tribal Judge can sign them and direct the tribal police to serve them. Then any occasions of failure to appear are also handled by those authorities within that system.

Another issue to note is the legal principle of "specificity" in subpoenas. In terms of documentation, rarely will it pass to simply subpoena "everything you have" – the subpoenas need to specify exactly what is required or at the minimum, specific ranges of documents and time frames. There is an enormous amount of court rulings and citations regarding subpoenas which we won't go into here, but basically courts do not allow subpoenas that are "fishing expeditions", or are unreasonable. The same would most likely apply to inquest subpoenas. Also note that the issues and procedures for contempt are very specific.

W.S. 2-7-101 Presumption of Death; how estate is handled.

When any person leaves his usual place of abode and is not seen or heard from by his relatives or other persons reasonably expected to hear from him for a period of seven (7) years, the person is presumed to be dead. If the person owned any real or personal property in Wyoming, administration of the estate of the person may be had in the manner provided by law.

Commentary: *This statute is in conformity with most other states when it comes to presumed death. Next-of-kin may petition the District Court for an Order of Presumptive Death. The Court will weigh the facts presented, and may issue such an order. The order will designate an effective date of death. This procedure is frequently used in cases where a body is never recovered, and legal counsel on behalf of the family must provide all documents that support Court's declaration. Upon the ruling of the Court that an individual is declared dead, an order is issued, and a certified copy of that order must be presented to the Coroner in order for a Death Certificate to be issued. If no date of death is determined by the Court, then the date of issue of the order serves that purpose.*

W.S. 2-17-101 Authority to authorize burial or cremation
2-17-101. Authority to authorize burial or cremation; immunity for funeral directors and undertakers.

(a) If a decedent leaves written instructions regarding his entombment, burial or cremation, or a document that designates and authorizes another person to direct disposition of the decedent's body the funeral director or undertaker to whom the body is entrusted shall proceed with the disposition of the body in accordance with those instructions or the instructions given by the person designated to direct disposition of the decedent's body. A document that designates another person to direct disposition of the decedent's body drafted pursuant to service in the military and in a form mandated by federal law at the time it was signed shall be recognized as valid for purposes of this section. In the event a decedent does not leave written instructions regarding his entombment, burial or cremation, or fails to leave a document designating another person to direct disposition of the decedent's body, the funeral director or undertaker to whom the body is entrusted shall obtain a signed consent before the entombment, burial or cremation proceeds.

(b) Any of the following persons, in order of priority as stated, may consent to the entombment, burial or cremation of the decedent, provided no written instructions or a document designating another person to direct disposition of the decedent's body were left by the decedent:

(i) The decedent's spouse at the time of death;
(ii) An adult child of the decedent;
(iii) Either parent of the decedent;
(iv) An adult sibling of the decedent;
(v) A grandparent of the decedent;
(vi) A stepchild of the decedent;
(vii) A guardian of the decedent in accordance with W.S. 3-2-201(a)(x).

(c) If a funeral director or undertaker receives written consent from a person specified in subsection (b) of this section, he may act in accordance with the consent, unless a person with a higher or equal priority provides the funeral director or undertaker a contrary written consent within three (3) days. If the funeral director or undertaker has been provided contrary written consents from members of the same class with the highest priority as to the entombment, burial or cremation of the decedent, the director or undertaker shall act in accordance with the directive of the greatest number of consents received from members of the class. If that number is equal, the director or undertaker shall act in accordance with the earlier consent unless the person providing the later consent is granted an order from the district court for the county in which the funeral home or mortuary is located. The district court shall order disposition in accordance with the later consent only if it is shown by a preponderance of the evidence the disposition is in accordance with the decedent's wishes.

(d) If the decedent is not survived by any member of the classes listed or no member of those classes is competent to sign a consent, any person who comes forward and legitimately identifies himself as another level of relation or friend of the decedent is authorized to sign the consent. If no consent is received within seven (7) days of the decedent's death, the coroner for the county in which the funeral home or mortuary is located is authorized to sign the consent.

(e) A funeral director or undertaker acting in accordance with this section, or attempting in good faith to act in accordance with this section, shall be immune from civil liability.

(f) Nothing in this section abrogates or amends the intestate succession laws of W.S. 2-4-101 through 2-4-214.

Commentary: *Authority to cremate is strictly regulated and detailed in this State, both to protect the deceased, the body as evidence, the funeral director, and the wishes of family. Note that there is no authority for anyone to see to any sort of disposition in a coroner case until the coroner has released the body from his possession. In an odd quirk, this statute states that after 7 days the coroner can sign an authorization, where as W.S. 7-4-207 states the coroner shall see to decent burial after 5 days... <u>if the investigation is completed</u>. That last part gives a bit of wiggle room so there is no conflict within the law. In practical terms, our investigation is not completed until we get toxicology results at the minimum, which takes about a week. Also note that there are no restrictions that disposition cannot happen sooner, if the coroner releases the body. This is also one of several areas in statute where the 'pecking order' of next of kin is established. There are some variations in that order within statute, depending on the subject matter, especially for organ donation or property disposition.*

W.S. 6-4-501 & 502 Desecration of Graves and Bodies.
6-4-501. Opening graves and removing bodies; penalty; exception.

(a) A person who opens a grave or tomb and removes a body or remains of a deceased person for any purpose without the knowledge and consent of near relations of the deceased commits a misdemeanor punishable by a fine of not more than seven hundred fifty dollars ($750.00).

(b) This section does not prohibit exhumation if ordered by a court of competent jurisdiction or if performed in accordance with W.S. 7-4-106(c).

6-4-502. Mutilation of dead human bodies; concealing a felony; penalties; exceptions.

(a) Except as provided in this section, a person who dissects or mutilates a dead human body is guilty of a felony punishable by imprisonment for not more than five (5) years, a fine of not more than ten thousand dollars ($10,000.00), or both.

(b) This section does not apply to:

    (i) The state health officer acting pursuant to W.S. 35-1-241, or a physician or surgeon acting on the order of a court of competent jurisdiction, a coroner or other qualified officer;

    (ii) Dissection to determine the cause of death when authorized by the nearest living kin of deceased, a court of competent jurisdiction or other qualified officer;

    (iii) Unclaimed dead human bodies delivered by state or county authorities to regularly chartered institutions for scientific research or persons certified by a state or local law enforcement agency to train search and rescue animals;

    (iv) The necessary mutilation incident to embalming a dead human body when authorized by nearest living kin, a court of competent jurisdiction or other qualified officer; or

    (v) Conduct authorized by the Revised Uniform Anatomical Gift Act, W.S. 35-5-201 through 35-5-225.

(c) A person who mutilates a dead human body or disposes of a dead human body in a hidden, undisclosed or transient location in order to conceal a felony offense is guilty of a felony punishable by imprisonment for not more than ten (10) years, a fine of not more than ten thousand dollars ($10,000.00), or both.

Commentary: While this has protections for officials or professionals doing their job, keep in mind this does not just refer to your standard local cemetery. Nor does it just apply to whole bodies. The requirement to report in W.S. 7-4-201 also applies to parts and pieces, or skeletal remains. This statute also applies to archeological digs or illegal robbing of older or ancient burials. If a body (or a part) is found, the coroner must be notified, and what happens next depends on the jurisdiction and location, as determined by other laws and regulations. A small bit of language was added in 2019 to W.S. 6-4-501(b) to coincide with the new W.S. 7-4-106.

W.S. 6-5-106 through 118 Conflict of interest; penalties; disclosure of interest and withdrawal from participation.
(a) Except as provided by subsection (b) of this section, a public servant commits an offense if he requests or receives any pecuniary benefit, other than lawful compensation, on any contract, or for the letting of any contract, or making any appointment where the government employing or subject to the discretion or decisions of the public servant is concerned.
(b) If any public servant discloses the nature and extent of his pecuniary interest to all parties concerned therewith and does not participate during the considerations and vote thereon and does not attempt to influence any of the parties and does not act for the governing body with respect to the contracts or appointments, then the acts are not unlawful under subsection (a) of this section. Subsection (a) of this section does not apply to the operation, administration, inspection or performance of banking and deposit contracts or relationships after the selection of a depository.
(c) Violation of subsection (a) of this section is a misdemeanor punishable by a fine of not more than five thousand dollars ($5,000.00).

6-5-107. Official misconduct; penalties.
(a) A public servant commits a misdemeanor punishable by a fine of not more than five thousand dollars ($5,000.00), if, with intent to obtain a pecuniary benefit or maliciously to cause harm to another, he knowingly:
    (i) Commits an act relating to his official duties that the public servant does not have the authority to undertake;
    (ii) Refrains from performing a duty imposed upon him by law; or
    (iii) Violates any statute relating to his official duties.
(b) A public officer commits a misdemeanor punishable by a fine of not more than seven hundred fifty dollars ($750.00) if he intentionally fails to perform a duty in the manner and within the time prescribed by law.

6-5-108. Issuing false certificate; penalties.
(a) A public servant commits a felony punishable by imprisonment for not more than ten (10) years, a fine of not more than ten thousand dollars ($10,000.00), or both, if he makes and issues an official certificate or other official written instrument which he is authorized to make and issue containing a statement which he knows to be false with intent to obtain a benefit or maliciously to cause harm to another.

(b) A public servant commits a misdemeanor punishable by imprisonment for not more than one (1) year, a fine of not more than one thousand dollars ($1,000.00), or both, if he makes and issues an official certificate or other official written instrument which he is authorized to make and issue containing a statement which he knows to be false.

6-5-109. Repealed by Laws 1984, ch. 44, § 3.

6-5-110. Wrongful appropriation of public property; penalties.

(a) A public servant who lawfully or unlawfully comes into possession of any property of any government and who, with intent temporarily to deprive the owner of its use and benefit, converts any of the public property to his own use or any use other than the public use authorized by law is guilty of wrongful appropriation of public property.

(b) Wrongful appropriation is a misdemeanor punishable by imprisonment for not more than one (1) year, a fine of not more than one thousand dollars ($1,000.00), or both.

(c) This section shall not apply to limited use of government property or resources for personal purposes if the use does not interfere with the performance of a governmental function and either the cost or value related to the use is de minimis or the public servant reimburses the government for the cost of the use.

6-5-111. Failure or refusal to account for, deliver or pay over property; penalties.

A public servant who fails or refuses to account for, deliver and pay over property received by virtue of the office, when legally required by the proper person or authority is guilty of a felony punishable by imprisonment for not more than five (5) years, a fine of not more than five thousand dollars ($5,000.00), or both.

6-5-112. Mistreating persons in institutions or mental hospital; penalties; no bar to other criminal action.

(a) A person commits a felony punishable by imprisonment for not more than three (3) years, a fine of not more than three thousand dollars ($3,000.00), or both, if he:

    (i) Is an employee of, or is responsible for the care of a person in, a reformatory, penal or charitable institution or a mental hospital and treats him with unnecessary severity, harshness or cruelty; or

    (ii) Is an officer required by law to perform an act with regard to persons in a reformatory, penal or charitable institution or a mental hospital and he intentionally refuses or neglects to perform the act.

(b) This section does not bar prosecution, under any other criminal statute, of a person responsible for the care of a person in a reformatory, penal or charitable institution or a mental hospital, even if he also violates this section.

6-5-113. Removal from office after judgment of conviction.

A judgment of conviction rendered under W.S. 6-5-102 through 6-5-112 and 6-5-117 against any public servant, except state elected officials, supreme court justices, district court judges and circuit court judges, shall result in removal from office or discharge from employment.

6-5-114. Notarial officers; issuance of certificate without proper acknowledgment; penalties.

A notarial officer commits a misdemeanor punishable by imprisonment for not more than six (6) months, a fine of not more than seven hundred fifty dollars ($750.00), or both, if he signs and affixes his seal to a certificate of acknowledgment when the party executing the instrument has not first acknowledged the execution of the instrument in the presence of, as defined in W.S. 34-26-101(b)(xxi), the notarial officer, if by law the instrument is required to be recorded or filed and cannot be filed without a certificate of acknowledgment signed and sealed by a notarial officer.

6-5-115. Neglect or refusal of ministerial officer to perform duty in criminal case; unnecessary delay in serving warrant; penalties.

(a) A person commits a misdemeanor punishable by imprisonment for not more than six (6) months, a fine of not more than five hundred dollars ($500.00), or both, if he is:

> (i) A clerk, sheriff, coroner or other ministerial officer who refuses or neglects to perform any duty he is required by law to perform in any criminal case or proceeding; or
>
> (ii) An officer who unnecessarily delays serving a warrant legally issued in any criminal case when it is his duty to execute and in his power to serve the warrant.

6-5-116. Public officer acting before qualifying; penalty.

An elected or appointed public officer or his deputy commits a misdemeanor punishable by a fine of not more than one thousand dollars ($1,000.00) if he performs any duty of his office without taking and subscribing the oath prescribed by law or before giving and filing the bond required by law. This section shall not apply to training and similar minor preparation for taking office.

6-5-117. Public officer demanding kickback from deputy; penalties.

A public officer who requires a deputy appointed by him to divide or pay back to the officer a part of the deputy's salary or requires any type of compensation of any form in return for the deputy's continued employment is guilty of a felony punishable by imprisonment for not more than three (3) years, a fine of not more than five thousand dollars ($5,000.00), or both.

6-5-118. Conflict of interest; public investments; disclosure required; penalty; definitions.
(a) No public servant who invests public funds for a unit of government, or who has authority to decide how public funds are invested, shall transact any personal business with, receive any pecuniary benefit from or have any financial interest in any entity, other than a governmental entity, unless he has disclosed the benefit or interest in writing to the body of which he is a member or entity for which he is working. Disclosures shall be made annually in a public meeting and shall be made part of the record of proceedings. The public servant shall make the written disclosure prior to investing any public funds in any entity, other than a governmental entity, which:
> (i) Provides any services related to investment of funds by that same unit of government; or
> (ii) Has a financial interest in any security or other investment made by that unit of government.

(b) A violation of subsection (a) of this section is a misdemeanor punishable by imprisonment for not more than six (6) months, a fine of not more than seven hundred fifty dollars ($750.00), or both.
(c) The definitions in W.S. 6-5-101 shall apply to this section except "pecuniary benefit" shall also include benefits in the form of services such as, but not limited to, transportation and lodging. As used in this section, "personal business" means any activity that is not a governmental function as defined in W.S. 6-5-101(a)(ii).

Commentary: This set of statutes covers public officers and elected officials in regards to activities that could be considered grounds for removal from office, and thus should at least be reviewed by any elected official. In general, aside from the expected conflict of interest idea, there are interesting points to be noted that in essence, proper performance of your duties including the accurate filing of documentation is in reality, required by law. The oath administered on assuming public office is not just a mere formality.

W.S. 7-19-106 (k)(ii) Background checks, criminal history *(criminal justice agency)*.

(k) Notwithstanding subsection (a) of this section, the division may disseminate criminal history record information concerning a record subject, or may confirm that no criminal history record information exists relating to a named individual:

    (i) In conjunction with state or national criminal history record information check under W.S. 7-19-201; or

    (ii) If application is made for a voluntary record information check, provided:

        (A) The applicant submits proof satisfactory to the division that the individual whose record is being checked consents to the release of the information to the applicant;

        (B) The application is made through a criminal justice agency in this state authorized to access criminal history record information maintained by the division which application shall then be forwarded to the division by the criminal justice agency; and

        (C) The applicant pays the fees required by W.S. 7-19-108.

Commentary: *This statute documents the authority of the Division of Criminal Investigation to perform and provide the background checks required by POST for certification as a coroner or deputy, as noted under W.S. 7-4-211 in the coroner statutes. As an interesting side note, the statute requires fees to be paid. Several years ago DCI decided to require the fees upfront, rather than billing after the fact, to save paper and administration costs. I noted to the Division that such policy makes it difficult for the county to pay, as such things must have a completed invoice for services rendered <u>before</u> the county can prepare a voucher and cut a check, as required by other statutes... so they created a classic 'Catch-22' situation in billing. I cannot have the county cut a check in advance, if I do not have an invoice that they won't issue. Counties never pay in advance. The answer to that question was a bureaucratic shrug of the shoulders – not their problem.*

We resolved that by making the fingerprint back ground fee part of a non-refundable charge for the application process, accepting only cashier's check or money order for the fee, so it could be sent with the cards to DCI. Government bureaucracy can be absurd sometimes.

W.S 9-1-634 Training
9-1-634. Academy to provide coroner training; certification of completion.
(a) The director of the Wyoming law enforcement academy shall provide at the academy or other location within the state a basic coroner's course of at least forty (40) hours. The course shall comply with standards promulgated by the peace officers standards and training commission and the board of coroner standards.
(b) The executive director of the peace officers standards and training commission shall issue an appropriate certificate of completion to any coroner or deputy coroner who completes a coroner training course offered by the academy or which the board of coroner standards has certified as meeting board standards.

Commentary: This codifies that the Academy will provide for the training and certification for coroners and their deputies under the standards and curriculum as defined by the Coroner Board

W.S. 9-1-701 through 9-1-707 Peace officer standards and training commission.

Commentary: Statutory authorization for POST, which we will not list or review in detail, other than to say that they get to make the rules for the documentation you have to turn in to be certified, and keep that certification. The rules on what is acceptable training are very specific.

W.S. 9-2-410 Records as property of state; delivery by outgoing officials and employees to successors; management and disposition thereof.
All public records are the property of the state. They shall be delivered by outgoing officials and employees to their successors and shall be preserved, stored, transferred, destroyed or disposed of, and otherwise managed, only in accordance with W.S. 9-2-405 through 9-2-413.

Commentary: <u>This is important to remember.</u> As coroner, you have discretion on some of the formatting for your records, or what you choose to document in some areas, <u>but the records themselves, of any type, are not yours to do with as you please.</u> The statutes referenced refer to the Wyoming State Archives, which makes the rules on what exactly you can or cannot do with particular records. Specific policies are best to have in this *area, but the Archives get to approve or disapprove your policies. Improper handling of records could result in civil or criminal action, or be justification of removal from office. Examples of records policies and procedures will be discussed later in this book.*

W.S. 14-2-708 Court ordered genetic testing of the deceased.
14-2-708. Deceased individual.
For good cause shown, the court may order genetic testing of a deceased individual.

Commentary: *A very simple and easy statute – and while a coroner may only use DNA rarely in identification, obtaining a toxicology and DNA sample are part of the investigation standards set by the Board. The most common circumstance we encounter in Fremont is where an individual or agency requests our samples for paternity testing, which we may or may not still have due to the time frame and viability of the sample. In any case it is best to require a copy of a court order to release such samples, and document in detail such releases. It is up to the requesting party, not the coroner, to pursue such court orders.*

W.S. 14-3-207 Reporting deaths in cases of suspected child abuse.
14-3-207. Abuse or neglect as suspected cause of death; coroner's investigation.
Any person who knows or has reasonable cause to suspect that a child has died as a result of child abuse or neglect shall report to the appropriate coroner. The coroner shall investigate the report and submit his findings in writing to the law enforcement agency, the appropriate district attorney and the local child protective agency.

Commentary: *This further details the requirement under W.S. 7-4-104 (a)(i)(F) that suspected child abuse is a coroner case and jurisdiction, regardless of any other circumstances. The coroner has the resources and authority to order an autopsy and complete an investigation into such causes of death, which may be necessary for other agencies to pursue criminal prosecutions. This also is why medical providers, or any other person for that matter, are required to report such suspected cases.*

W.S. 16-1-104 Wyoming Joint Powers Act; Authorization for Inter-County Agreements

16-1-104. Joint powers, functions and facilities

(a) Any power, privilege or authority exercised or capable of being exercised by an agency may be exercised and enjoyed jointly with any other agency having a similar power, privilege or authority. No cost shall be incurred, debt accrued, nor money expended by any contracting party, which will be in excess of limits prescribed by law. If the joint business council of the Eastern Shoshone and Northern Arapaho Indian tribes, the business council of the Eastern Shoshone Indian tribe or the business council of the Northern Arapaho Indian tribe participates in a joint powers board under this act with political subdivisions and special districts of Wyoming, the powers of the joint business council, the powers of the business council of the Eastern Shoshone Indian tribe, the powers of the business council of the Northern Arapaho Indian tribe, Wyoming political subdivisions and Wyoming special districts are neither increased or decreased by that participation. Rather the participation of the joint business council, the business council of the Eastern Shoshone Indian tribe or the business council of the Northern Arapaho Indian tribe is intended to facilitate implementation of programs and projects designed to more effectively benefit Wyoming's citizens.

(b) A county may enter into and operate under a joint powers agreement with one (1) or more counties, cities, school districts or community college districts for the performance of any function that the county, city, school district or community college district is authorized to perform, except the planning, expansion, creation, financing or operation of municipally owned electrical facilities.

Commentary: *This is the statute referenced in W.S. 7-4-208 that allows another coroner to act in another county of jurisdiction if that coroner is unable to do so. These agreements must be in writing prior to any such action and are usually completed through the County Attorney's civil attorney if needed, and are in a specific format.*

W.S. 16-4-201 through 16-4-205 Public Records Act

Commentary: *Rather than display the entirety of W.S. 16-4-201 through 16-4-205, the Wyoming Public Records Acts, the coroner and interested individual is referred to the State web site for this voluminous detail, or to the written publications such as those printed by LexisNexis. The reason for this is that these statutes have been revised on almost a yearly basis by the legislature, and a coroner must keep up on such changes. Public advocacy groups have been pushing state government for years to revise various aspects of these statutes, for reasons of transparency in government, charges for duplication issues, or other tweaks and adjustments.*

The 2019 State Legislature made a major change in the definitions of "Official Custodian" of records, and what an all-encompassing "government entity" is. In addition, and most significantly, there are new time frames for legal compliance with request for records, and each agency must have a "designated public records person". This designee must be identified to the state department of administration and information, and available on a public listing. A whole new procedure for complaints on lack of compliance has been also added, and whole new areas regarding grounds for denial of access.

Other changes are sure to follow in the next few years, as this is one of the most contested and convoluted areas in the relationship between government and the public. We can however make a few suggestions generally on what each coroner office should have in place. Luckily, as far as case files, we have our own W.S. 7-4-105 that specifically rules the day, and other than the case verdict and docket, they are not public records, so most of this does not apply. Remember however, the administrative records of your department not only belong to the State, but may also be considered public records.

First suggestion: have policies and procedures. Statutes give you the authority to make rules in regards to documents and requests, and if you do, and they are on file, they have the effect of law, as long as they conform the statutory requirements. In Fremont, for the confidential records, we require such things as ID and specific forms, which not only gives a record of who to and what records are dispensed, but documents our compliance.

Second suggestion: work with your county clerk and attorney to see what your particular county is doing in this regard. In Fremont, all public records requests go through the county civil attorney, who is in charge of compliance within the statutory time frames. So for anything other than requests for the confidential records under W.S. 7-4-105, that is our "designated public records person". Compliance made simple, from this office's perspective.

Third suggestion: W.S. 16-4-204(c) requires that the fees charged be enacted by due process, and in our case, this was done by resolution by the County Commission. So figure out what you need and have it on file as an official resolution, or document if your county has a fee schedule as a whole.

One thing to keep in mind is that the law does require a response within a set time limit to anyone who requests public records, even if that is to tell them 'no', they are not public records. As far as what is public for a coroner, the docket is usually easy to produce and send once completed. The other circumstance would be the information from a public inquest. My preference on those is that in my opinion, it does not become a 'record' until I file it as required by statute with the Clerk of District Court. If anyone wants a copy of that record, they can request it from that Office by their procedures. Otherwise my files are confidential.

W.S. 16-4-203 Public Records; Right of inspection; grounds for denial; access of news media; order permitting or restricting disclosure; exceptions.
>   (d) The custodian shall deny the right of inspection of the following records, unless otherwise provided by law:
>>   (i) Medical, psychological and sociological data on individual persons, exclusive of coroners' verdicts and written dockets as provided in W.S.7-4-105(a);

Commentary: *This specific portion of the public records act deserves a special mention. This portion was changed in 2011 when the coroner records were made legally confidential, except for the written verdict and docket, as noted in W.S. 7-4-105. Previous wording prior to 2011 stated "exclusive of coroner's autopsy reports" which at that time meant that anyone could get ahold of an autopsy report simply by asking for it. Considering all the issues, and the fact that coroners have access by state and Federal law to medical records, the legislature in 2011 acted wisely in restricting access to our reports and autopsies to those with a verified need for the information... otherwise, just imagine an autopsy report exposed to the now prolific social media without protection.*

W.S. 18-3-103 Offices and records to be kept within county; exceptions; records open to public inspection; removal for purposes of copying; penalty.
>   (a) Each county officer except the county attorney, the county coroner and the county sheriff if the county jail is not located in

the county seat, shall keep his office at the county seat of the county in an office provided by the county. If the county does not provide an office then the office shall be maintained at a place approved by the board of county commissioners:

 (i) The county clerk, county sheriff and county treasurer shall be furnished offices in the courthouse or building used as such;

 (ii) The county and prosecuting attorney and the county attorney shall be furnished suitable office space at the expense of the county which shall if practicable be located at or near the courthouse;

 (iii) The office of the county assessor may be with the office of another county officer as determined by the board of county commissioners;

 (iv) The office of the county coroner may be located at any suitable location determined by the county coroner with the approval of the board of county commissioners.

(b) All county officers shall keep their offices open during the usual business hours of each day excluding Saturdays, Sundays, legal holidays and other days as established by the county commissioners through resolution.

(c) All books and papers required to be in county offices are open to the examination of any person without fee. The officer in charge of any documents may temporarily remove them for lawful reproduction purposes and during the period of removal shall not be subject to any penalty. Any officer or person not complying with the provisions of this subsection shall forfeit five dollars ($5.00) for each day he fails to comply.

***Commentary:** Historically, many coroners had no office, or worked out of their home or business. This statute generally relieves the county commission from having to provide the coroner an office in the county court house, but that they will support one somewhere with the coroner's approval. Coroners as elected officials sometimes seem like the "ugly red-headed step children" of county officers and often are ignored or not mentioned, and often have to struggle for every scrap of facility, budget, or recognition of need. This poor situation is not the current one in Fremont, as we have a good relationship with the commission, and that attitude should always be encouraged. Coroners do have a trump card if needed, in that statute W.S. 7-4-201 does require the county to pay the costs of the investigation, among other costs, whether they like it or not. The best resolution however is to respectfully work together for that end, rather* *than waiving a confrontational flag, as the Commission does have some discretion by statute in determining what is a reasonable expense.*

The provision for in-office inspection for the most part does not affect coroner files, since they are confidential, but may apply to administrative files that contain no confidential information. Note: personnel files are restricted by Federal regulations and the individual county policies. I don't get too concerned about the "usual business hours" portion of this statute, as we are available 24-7, and office hours are usually subject to immediate change depending on the needs of the job... there really is no "usual" for this profession. If someone were to complain, that can be mitigated by making an appointment, which is the "usual" mode if you want to make sure someone is in the office. If nothing is going on, we maintain office hours, but most of the public realizes that can change in an instant.

One complication for small counties where the coroner has no office in a county building (which was even the case in Fremont prior to 1998): where ever your "office" is, such as a private home or business, that location could be considered 'public' as far as access.

W.S. 18-3-504 County Commission; Powers and Duties Generally; Indigent Burials

(c) Each board of county commissioners shall provide for the burial of the human remains of any deceased person not receiving personal opportunities with employment responsibilities (POWER) assistance, supplemental security income or Medicaid under the Wyoming Public Assistance and Social Services Act at the time of death and without sufficient means in his own estate or other resources to provide burial or cremation.

Commentary: *While worded oddly, this statute works in conjunction with W.S. 7-4-207 that enumerates the county responsibility to see to the disposition of indigent remains, except for those that are receiving public assistance through the Department of Family Services programs of POWER, SSI, or Medicaid. The county actually cannot help in that circumstance, and responsibility falls to DFS, whether they like it or not. This is also restated in W.S. 42-2-103(c): "No board of county commissioners shall be responsible for any burial or cremation expenses in excess of the amount paid under this subsection". The DFS statutes on assistance are antiquated and insufficient as far as amount of assistance* *allowed, in my (and most funeral home's) opinion, but we have to obey the law as it is until someone changes it.*

W.S. 18-3-902 through 18-3-906 Causes for removal from office enumerated, procedure

18-3-902. Governor to direct district attorney or attorney general to commence action; petition served with summons; pleading; trial; judgment; change of judge.

(a) Whenever it appears to the governor on the verified complaint of qualified electors or the board of county commissioners of the county that any county officer is guilty of misconduct or malfeasance in office he may direct the attorney general to commence and prosecute an action in the district court of the county in which the officer is an official asking for the removal of the officer. The action shall be commenced by the filing of a verified petition in the name of the state of Wyoming signed by the attorney general setting forth the facts constituting the misconduct or malfeasance in office.

(b) Upon filing of the petition a summons and a copy of the petition shall be served on the defendant as in civil cases. The answer day shall be the same as provided for civil suits. The petition and answer are the only pleadings allowed and the allegations of the answer so far as they conflict with the petition shall be considered denied without a reply.

(c) The action shall be tried in a summary manner by the district court with or without a jury not less than five (5) days nor more than thirty (30) days after answer day. At the trial all questions touching the sufficiency or certainty of the allegations of the petition or answer shall be heard and determined and amendments which are not inconsistent with the original pleadings shall be authorized to be made at once and shall not delay the trial. If the court finds the defendant is guilty of misconduct or malfeasance in office as charged in the petition, a judgment shall be entered removing the defendant from office and taxing against him the costs of the action.

(d) The judge of a district court in which an action for the removal of an officer is pending, if unable to try the action within the period provided by this section, shall call in another district judge.

(e) No change of judge is allowed unless proper application therefor is filed with the answer but if the judge of that district is unable to try the action and has designated another district judge to try the same, the application must be filed within three (3) days after the filing of the order designating the judge to whom the action is referred.

(f) As used in this section, "misconduct or malfeasance" includes, but is not limited to, instances when:

>(i) The officer absents himself from his office for an aggregate of sixty (60) days in any three (3) month period unless such absence is caused by illness or other disability;
>
>(ii) The officer is absent from his office for more than ninety (90) days because of illness or other disability and the illness or disability will probably not terminate during the unexpired portion of the officer's term of office.

(g) Whenever a vacancy occurs in any county office under the provisions of this section, it shall be filled as provided by law.

(h) This section is supplemental to all other statutes concerning removal of county officers.

18-3-903. Suspension of officers by the governor pending outcome of proceedings; notice; order to be filed; filling of vacancies; restoration of office upon verdict of not guilty; reimbursement of compensation and expense of trial.

(a) Whenever a proceeding as specified by W.S. 18-3-902 has been commenced in the district court, the governor may cause notice to be served upon the accused officer setting forth the misconduct or malfeasance in office as charged in the petition and requiring the officer to appear before him at a designated time and place not less than five (5) days after service of the notice. The governor shall hear the charges against and the defense of the officer, which may be presented by affidavits or otherwise. If the governor determines that the officer is guilty of misconduct or malfeasance in office he may by an order signed by him and filed in the office of the secretary of state, suspend the officer from the further exercise of his duties until the termination of the trial of such officer as provided by W.S. 18-3-902. Duplicate copies of the order of suspension shall be filed in the offices of the county clerk and the clerk of the district court of the county in which the accused is an officer.

(b) Whenever any county officer is suspended as provided by this section the person or board having authority to fill vacancies in the office shall appoint some qualified elector to temporarily fill the office and perform the duties thereof so long as the suspension continues. If the officer suspended is a county commissioner the governor shall appoint some qualified elector to temporarily fill the office and perform the duties thereof so long as the suspension continues. Whenever any officer is removed by a final judgment entered in such proceeding the vacancy shall be filled as provided by law.

(c) Any county officer who has been suspended under the provisions of this section and who is found by the district court to be not guilty of the misconduct or malfeasance in office charged against him shall be restored to his office and shall receive the compensation provided for the office during the period of his suspension. He shall be reimbursed by the state of Wyoming for all actual and necessary expenditures made by him in connection with all trials and hearings provided for in this section.

18-3-904. Hearing by the supreme court.
Either party may commence a proceeding in error in the supreme court by filing a petition in error as in civil actions within thirty (30) days after the entry and judgment provided by W.S. 18-3-902. The supreme court may upon motion of the attorney general fix a time within which the necessary records of the proceedings and the briefs of the parties shall be filed and advance the cause for hearing. No proceeding in error shall suspend or supersede a judgment of the district court removing such officer, but such officer shall be suspended and barred from performing the duties of his office from the time of the entry of such judgment so long as the same remains unreversed.

18-3-905. Criminal statutes neither repealed nor barred.
Nothing in W.S. 18-3-902 through 18-3-904 shall be construed as repealing any law making it a crime or misdemeanor for county officers to violate statutes of this state and providing a punishment for the violation. Proceedings under W.S. 18-3-902 through 18-3-904 shall not bar proceedings under any criminal statute.

18-3-906. Prima facie malfeasance in office by sheriffs, district attorneys and county assessors.
Every sheriff and district attorney shall prima facie be guilty of malfeasance in office and subject to removal where open and continuous violations of any law occur in the county for which such officers are employed. Every county assessor is prima facie guilty of malfeasance in office and subject to removal where the county assessor has failed to carry out and follow the legal directives and legal orders of the state board of equalization relative to assessment of property.

***Commentary:** This series details the steps for removal of an elected official from office, which hopefully is never needed, however, politics being what it is, it is important to know your rights of due process. One point to note, is W.S. 18-3-902(f) which defines that 'malfeasance' can* include a period of absence or being unable to perform the duties of the office. When you take the oath of office, you are swearing to be available and be there.

W.S. 19-4-101 Veterans, Burial of Indigents
19-14-101. Burial of indigents.

(a) The board of county commissioners of each county shall provide for the preparation of the body and transmittal to and burial in the veteran's cemetery of any other than a dishonorably discharged veteran of the armed forces of the United States who served on behalf of the United States in any war or conflict as defined in section 101, title 38, United States Code and who dies leaving insufficient funds to defray the necessary funeral expenses. The amount expended for transporting the body shall not exceed five hundred dollars ($500.00).

(b) Before assuming charge and expense for preparation and transmittal of the body and burial, each board of county commissioners shall first determine according to procedures they establish that the deceased veteran of the armed forces of the United States whose body they are called upon to bury served in the armed forces of the United States during World War II or any preceding war in which the United States was a party or during the Korean or Vietnam conflicts, was other than dishonorably discharged and died in the county leaving insufficient means to defray the necessary funeral expenses.

(c) The county commissioners of each county, shall:

    (i) Keep a complete record of all the facts relating to any veteran of the armed forces of the United States who is buried in accordance with this section; and

    (ii) Draw a warrant on the treasurer of their county for the payment of the expenses out of the general funds of the county.

Commentary: *While this will be discussed and detailed in policies and procedures later, the main point to understand here is that indigent and unclaimed veterans are treated as special cases for assistance by society, as well they should be.*

There has been periodically some discussion on whether the county should pay for veterans that technically did not serve directly in a "war or conflict" as specified in the statute. That detail is generally not specified on the DD-214 form that verifies veteran status of discharge. We generally treat all veterans the same in need if honorably discharged, regardless. No one has disputed that, that I am aware of, and I would argue we should honor their service, whether they spent the entire term stateside or not.

W.S. 22-2-105 Elections; *(Coroner listed as "elected official")*
22-2-105. Terms of office and offices voted on at general elections.
(a) The terms of office and offices voted on at general elections are as follows:
> (i) Two Year Term.-At every general election there shall be elected the number of representatives in congress to which this state is entitled and members of the Wyoming house of representatives;
> (ii) Four Year Term. - At the general election in 1974 and in every fourth (4th) year thereafter, there shall be elected the following officers: one (1) governor, one (1) secretary of state, one (1) state treasurer, one (1) state auditor, one (1) superintendent of public instruction, county clerks, county treasurers, county assessors, county coroners, county and prosecuting attorneys, district attorneys, sheriffs, clerks of the district court. At every general election there shall be elected the necessary member or members of the Wyoming senate and county commissioners. The question of retention of a circuit court judge or a magistrate of the circuit court shall be submitted:
>> (A) For a circuit court judge, to the electorate of all counties within the circuit;
>> (B) For a magistrate required by law to stand for retention, to the electorate of the county wherein the magistrate serves.

Commentary: *In Title 18: Counties; W.S. 18-3 County Officers; Coroners are not listed as an elected official, and in this statute, they are. One of the quirks of law is that as long as it is defined in one location, the balance of mention of inclusion does not have to be consistent. Just because coroners are not stated as an elected official under Title 18: Counties, does not mean you aren't one. I have actually heard that argument from some people trying to make a point, which was wrong.*

W.S. 33-16-502 Definitions *(Funeral Services Practitioners Act)*
    W.S. 33-16-502(a)(xix) "Human Remains" means the body of a deceased person or part of a body or limb that has been removed from a deceased person, including the body, part of the body or limb in any stage of decomposition. The following are not "human remains":
        (A) The cremated remains of any human;
        (B) Powder resulting from chemical disposition of a human body;
        (C) Any body part removed and held for testing, research or other medical or law enforcement purposes; or
        (D) Hair or nail clippings.

Commentary: *This statute was noted in amongst the large set of statutes set up for funeral directors, embalmers and crematories. Several things of importance here should be noted. Over the years, the coroner's office has had several occasions where relatives find cremains in an estate, and wonder what to do with them. Formerly under other administrations, these containers were collected by the coroner's office and later buried as unclaimed remains at county cost. Technically, however, this was a legal error by previous coroners. Since cremains are not, by this statute, "human remains", the coroner has no obligation nor jurisdiction to collect, retain, or see to their disposition, especially at county cost.*

Many states and jurisdictions have very strict laws on what you can do with cremains, and restrictions on where they can be scattered – but Wyoming is not one of them. Since they are not legally "human remains", you can pretty much do with them what you want, although most sensibilities in society would regard that they should be treated with a certain modicum of respect. Many retain them in a nice container on a shelf (thus to be found later by your descendants after you're gone, resulting in the above noted call to the coroner). Others scatter them in a favorite place or location, and there is no law against that here. I know of one horseman friend that wanted his scattered in his favorite rodeo arena. Often they are buried in a cemetery, or placed in a specialized mausoleum. Whatever the disposition, since they are not "human remains", there is no prohibition on possessing them in Wyoming.

This statute also exempts toxicology samples, other medical uses, and anything retained by law enforcement as evidence, thus alleviating some of the questions on legally disposing of leftovers after testing or the judicial process is finished. Hair or nail clippings seem obvious, and one wonders what issue originally prompted they be listed here?

I have also heard tales of particular "dispositions" by spurned spouses or other disgruntled family members, most unverified, and all too far beyond the boundaries of good taste to repeat here, except to characterize some of them as "poetic justice".

W.S. 33-16-527 Duty of funeral director to ascertain cause of death prior to disposition.

33-16-527. Duty to ascertain cause of death; funeral service practitioner to prepare body for transportation or removal if death due to communicable, contagious or infectious disease. It shall be the duty of every funeral director and funeral service practitioner, when called to take charge of a dead body, to first ascertain the cause of death from the coroner or medical professional. If death has occurred from any communicable, contagious or infectious disease, the funeral director or funeral service practitioner shall not remove or transport the body until after the body has been prepared for transportation or removal by a licensed funeral service practitioner of this state.

Commentary: *Title 33 defines the statutory obligations of various professionals including funeral directors. Many funeral directors are also registrars for certification of deaths with State Vital Records. This statute emphasizes the rule that only coroners and medical professionals can certify a cause of death, and it is the funeral director's duty to obtain that information.*

W.S. 35-1-105 Public Health; Prohibited acts; penalty for violations.

(a) No person, corporation or other organization nor representative thereof shall:

(i) Willfully violate, disobey or disregard the provisions of the public health laws of Wyoming or the terms of any lawful notice, order, rule or regulation issued pursuant thereto;

(vi) Knowingly transport or accept for transportation, interment or other disposition a dead human body without an accompanying permit issued in accordance with the public health laws of Wyoming or the rules of the department; or *(balance redacted)*

Commentary: *Title 35, which include quite a few of the next listed statutes, covers public health and safety generally, and the Wyoming Department of Health specifically. Obviously, in any regulation of health and safety, there would be assorted areas regarding death, bodies, and related realities that will imply obligations for the coroner, or be associated with other aspects of the deceased. Under part (a) which has been edited here to show just (i) and (vi), <u>everybody</u> has to obey the law. One of those regulations is that the transport of human remains requires a permit from the Dept. of Health. There are notable exceptions under the law as stated in other statutes or rules, such as those covering organ donation organizations for example. Also, as long as the coroner's office has remains under its custody, transport needs no permit, and this includes transport out of state for an autopsy.*

W.S. 35-1-241 Safe disposal of corpses in emergency circumstances.
   (a) The state health officer in consultation with the appropriate county coroner, during the period that a public health emergency exists, may:
        (i) Adopt and enforce measures to provide for the safe disposal of corpses as may be reasonable and necessary for emergency response. These measures may include the embalming, burial, cremation, interment, disinterment, transportation and disposal of corpses;
        (ii) Take possession or control of any corpse;
        (iii) Order the disposal of any corpse of a person who has died of an infectious disease through burial or cremation within twenty-four (24) hours after death;
        (iv) Compel any person authorized to embalm, bury, cremate, inter, disinter, transport or dispose of corpses to accept any corpse or provide the use of his business or facility if the actions are reasonable and necessary for emergency response. The use of a business or facility may include transferring the management and supervision of the business or facility to the state health officer and granting the right for the state health officer to take immediate possession for a limited or unlimited period of time, but shall not exceed beyond the termination of the public health emergency.
   (b) Every corpse prior to disposal pursuant to subsection (a) of this section shall be clearly labeled with all available information to identify the decedent and the circumstances of death. Any

corpse of a deceased person with an infectious disease shall have an external, clearly visible tag indicating that the corpse is infected and, if known, the infectious disease.

(c) Every person in charge of disposing of any corpse pursuant to subsection (a) of this section shall maintain a written record of each corpse and all available information to identify the decedent and the circumstances of death and disposal. If a corpse cannot be identified, prior to disposal a qualified person shall, to the extent possible, take fingerprints and one (1) or more photographs of the corpse, and collect a DNA specimen. All information collected under this subsection shall be promptly forwarded to the state health official.

(d) As used in this section "public health emergency" means as defined by W.S. 35-4-115(a)(i).

Commentary: Pandemics, mass fatality incidents, or other emergencies where there are large numbers of fatalities or deaths, obviously may need extraordinary tools to deal with the circumstances and realities of the situation. The Health Department, in working with the coroner, is given great authority to order and see to the disposition of remains in an orderly manner. The framework is defined in this statute in an attempt to insure that the response is conducted in that orderly manner, but leaves no doubt that in a declared emergency of this nature, broad powers are needed and can be enforced by both departments to mitigate the situation. Periodic exercises in pandemic events or mass fatality are conducted by the State Health Department in response to possible events, and all coroners should have policies and procedures in place for potential situations of this nature.

W.S. 35-1-401(a) Public Health; Definitions –

(v) "Live birth" means the complete expulsion or extraction from its mother of a fetus, which after such expulsion or extraction, breathes or shows any other evidence of life such as beating of the heart, pulsation of the umbilical cord, or definite movement of voluntary muscles, whether or not the umbilical cord has been cut or the placenta is attached;

(vi) "Stillbirth" means a birth after twenty (20) completed weeks gestation in which the child shows no evidence of life after complete birth;

(vii) "Dead body" means a lifeless human body, or such severed parts of the human body, or the bones thereof, from the state of which it reasonably may be concluded that death occurred;

(viii) "Final disposition" means the burial, interment, cremation, or other disposition of a dead body or stillbirth;

(ix) "Person in charge of interment" means any person who places or causes to be placed a deceased, stillbirth, or dead body, or after cremation the ashes thereof, in the earth, a grave, tomb, vault, urn or other receptacle, either in a cemetery or at any other place, or otherwise disposes of a body;

Commentary: *These sections of the large number of definitions in the Public Health statutes have a direct impact on the duties of the coroner. While the definition of "life" in a fetus is a subject fraught with emotional, religious, and legal baggage in society, coroners swear to uphold the law as it is, not as you wish it would be. It is imperative to perform your duties objectively under the law separate from the influence of personal beliefs, as best you can.*

Note that "dead body" here is defined as a whole, or parts and pieces, which is why other statutes referencing dead remains also mean any parts and pieces. A definition in one statute applies within the whole of statute, unless specifically excepted elsewhere. In those cases, a conflict of definitions are usually clarified by case law or a later statutory fix by the legislature.

Stillbirths are by definition, not coroner cases, as without being born alive as defined under the law, there is no death. Vital Records does not even issue a standard death certificate, but only a shortened version signed by the physician to record the event. Prior to the 20 weeks gestation, legally in Wyoming the fetus is not even considered viable and needs no certification of any sort with the state. It is merely the medical event of a miscarriage and handled within the individual medical health record.

While the law is clear, aside from the abortion controversies in society, coroners may find themselves involved in certain circumstances as they have the resources, such as autopsy, to bring into play for those cases in the 'grey' areas, or those which are unknown. The medical or legal communities will often turn to the coroner for assistance to determine if it was a "live" birth or not – and if it is, it may be a coroner case anyway. And unfortunately, remains are sometimes found after the fact of birth or miscarriage, and an investigation must be completed to even know if it is a case or not. An experienced forensic pathologist can often determine after the fact the reason for the termination of a fetus, or if the lungs ever inflated, which would mean, however briefly, that the birth was live, and thus a coroner case.

The complicating factors a coroner may encounter in these situations are numerous. One example from Fremont County was a good number of births or miscarriages that occurred about a decade ago during the surge of methamphetamine use. Prosecutors and law enforcement wanted to know in cases if the birth was "live" and thus a possible homicide overdose, or a stillbirth and not prosecutable. The complicating factor at that time was that no studies had been done to establish what might be a fatal level of meth in a fetus or infant, so even the pathologists could not say with certainty at the various levels found on toxicology in cases, whether the death was the result of overdose, or a natural factor complication. Most cases could not be pursued in any manner legally, regardless of your personal opinion in the event. Currently there is no law regarding drug abuse in a mother and the effect on a pregnancy. There is a statute that provides for penalty for any perpetrator of assault on a pregnant mother that results in miscarriage or termination of the pregnancy, if it can be proven the perpetrator knew the female was pregnant at the time of the assault – but that is another matter, and not regarding the behavior of the mother herself.

There is a further issue with the term 'viable' as defined in W.S. 35-6-101(a)(vii) which will be noted at that time.

W.S. 35-4-107 Public Health; Report required of physician; record of each case to be kept; duty of individuals to report diseases.

    (a) Pursuant to department of health rules and regulations, the state health officer or his designee shall publish a list of communicable diseases or conditions to be reported by licensed physicians and laboratories in the state. It shall be the duty of every practicing or licensed physician or other health care provider as provided by department rules and regulations in the state of Wyoming to report immediately to the state health officer or his designee in the manner established by department rule and regulation through published reporting procedures provided to each licensed physician or laboratory. The state health officer or his designee shall collect and provide information which may include the name of the person suffering from disease only to the county health officer or health representatives where disease control efforts are required. For purposes of this section, "health representatives" means those health care workers assigned by federal, state or local health authorities to assist with disease control and investigation efforts under the direct supervision of the state health officer or his designee and local county health officer. Any person knowing of a case of a serious contagious or infectious disease, not under the care of a physician, may report the same to the state health officer or his designee or the health officer of the county in which the disease exists.

(b) Pursuant to department of health rules and regulations, there may be a review of medical records by the state health officer, his designee or their designated health care representatives who shall be under the direct supervision of the state health officer or his designee to confirm diagnosis, investigate causes or identify other cases of disease conditions in a region, community or workplace in the state to determine if proper measures have been taken to protect public health and safety. Notwithstanding other provisions of state law, the review of records may occur without patient consent, but shall be kept confidential and shall be restricted to information necessary for the control, investigation and prevention of disease conditions dangerous to the public health. Any person who receives medical information under this subsection shall not disclose that information for any other purpose other than for purposes of the investigation and disease control efforts. Any violation of this subsection is a misdemeanor punishable by imprisonment for not more than six (6) months, a fine of not more than one thousand dollars ($1,000.00), or both.

Commentary: *This regulation concerns the establishment of a list of reportable diseases, and the requirement to report them. This list is usually updated yearly by the Department of Health, and has various methods of notification required depending on the disease. While coroners are not named specifically, we would fall under the "any person" designation, aside from the fact there are other statutes that mandate cooperation between the coroner and Health Department in this area. This is also one of the statutes that gives the Department of Health the logical right to review case files and records. Even though in most cases, the attending physician has already reported the disease if needed, cases may come up where there was no medical care prior to death, or the care occurred in another State, thus the coroner is obligated to report such incidents should they occur, or at the minimum verify that they have been reported, especially in the case of the more severe communicable diseases.*

W.S. 35-4-115(a)(i) Public Health Emergency; Definitions
(a) As used in this article:
(i) "Public health emergency" means an occurrence or imminent threat of an illness or health condition caused by an epidemic or pandemic disease, a novel and highly fatal infectious agent or a biological toxin that poses a substantial risk of a significant number of human fatalities or incidents of permanent or long-term disability. The governor shall declare when a public health emergency exists or has ended;

Commentary: *This is a pretty clear definition, and is considered with other statutory areas where Hazmat, terrorist acts, disaster, or other incidents have the potential for mass fatality and involve the coroner.*

W.S. 35-4-601 through 35-4-607. Unclaimed bodies; Who may have bodies in possession.
35-4-601. Delivery of unclaimed bodies for anatomical study. Any member of the following boards or officers to-wit: The board of health of any city, town or county in the state; the mayor or common council of any city, and the officers or board having direction or control of any almshouse, prison hospital, house of correction or jail, in the state, shall, when so requested, surrender the dead bodies of such persons as may be required to be buried at the public expense, to any regularly licensed physician or dentist or medical college in the state or to a person certified by a state or local law enforcement agency to train search and rescue animals, in accordance with such rules as may be prescribed by the state department of health; such bodies to be used by said physician, dentist, medical college or person, for the advancement of anatomical science or the training of search and rescue animals; preference being given to the faculty of any legally organized state medical college or school of anatomy, for their use in the instruction of medical students; provided that in no case shall the faculties or other officers of such medical college or school of anatomy require or receive from any medical student or students, for such body so furnished therein, any sum of money in excess of the actual cost of procuring the same.

35-4-602. Exceptions as to certain bodies.
(a) No such body shall in any case be surrendered if:
(i) The deceased in his or her last illness requested to be not dissected; or

(ii) If within forty-eight (48) hours after his or her death, any person of kindred or a friend of the deceased shall request the body for burial; or
(iii) If such deceased was a stranger or a traveler who died suddenly before making himself or herself known; or
(iv) If such deceased person was honorably discharged from any arm of the military or naval service of the United States.

35-4-603. Restriction upon use of bodies; bond required of applicant; prohibited acts.
It shall not be lawful for any person so receiving dead bodies to use the same, except for the prosecution of anatomical science or the training of search and rescue animals, or elsewhere than in this state; and the state department of health in its rules and regulations in regard to the distribution of the same, may require each applicant to furnish a good and sufficient bond that the provisions of this act will be observed. Whosoever shall use said body for any other purpose, or shall remove the same beyond the limits of the state, or whosoever shall traffic, trade or deal with said bodies for a commercial purpose shall be deemed guilty of a misdemeanor and shall be fined, on conviction, not less than one hundred dollars ($100.00) and be imprisoned in the county jail for a period of not less than thirty (30) days or more than one (1) year; the fine accruing from said conviction to be paid to the school fund of the county, wherein such offense was committed.

35-4-604. Penalty for refusing to deliver body.
Any officer refusing to deliver the remains or dead body of the deceased person, when demanded in accordance with the provisions of this act and the rules and regulations set forth by the state department of health, shall pay a penalty of not less than fifty dollars ($50.00), nor more than one hundred dollars ($100.00); such penalties to be sued for by the department of health as the case may be.

35-4-605. Burial or cremation after use.
It shall be the duty of all parties, who may secure dead bodies under provisions of this act, to bury the same decently in some public cemetery within a reasonable time after dissection or use, or cremate the same or make such other disposition as may be prescribed by the state department of health. For any violation of this provision, the party or parties so neglecting shall on conviction, forfeit or pay a penalty of not less than fifty dollars ($50.00), nor more than one hundred dollars ($100.00), or be imprisoned in the county jail not less than six (6) months nor more

than twelve (12) months or both, at the discretion of the court; such penalties to be sued for by the school officers or anyone interested therein, for the benefit of the school fund of the county in which the offense shall have been committed.

35-4-606. Rules and regulations.

The state department of health shall, within thirty (30) days after passage of this act, promulgate rules and regulations as called for by W.S. 35-4-601.

35-4-607. Who may have bodies in possession.

Any regularly licensed physician or dentist of the state, any medical student who is a regular matriculate of a recognized medical college, under authority of such physician, any person certified by a state or local law enforcement agency to train search and rescue animals or any person authorized by the Revised Uniform Anatomical Gift Act may have in his possession human dead bodies, or parts thereof, lawfully obtained, for the purpose of anatomical inquiry or dissection or for training of search and rescue animals.

Commentary: Part 601 is somewhat moot in Wyoming, as we have no medical schools or facilities that would regularly use this section – note that this concerns unclaimed remains buried at county expense, and they cannot be sold, although costs can be recovered. Part 602 specifically denies donation for study if the deceased left specific instructions against it, has been otherwise claimed, is unidentified, or is a veteran. Part 603 notes that trafficking in human remains is a criminal offense; and Part 604 notes that failure to follow the rules is also a crime. If the specified persons or institutions obtain remains as allowed it is their obligation under Part 605 to see to proper disposition once done. Part 606 is the standard statute to allow for rule making capability, in this case by the Department of Health. An interesting portion of the statute is Part 607: who is allowed to possess human bodies, parts, and pieces? Coroners have their own authorization by statute. Donor organizations are allowed here for obvious reasons relative to their own statutes; physicians, dentists, and medical students for analysis and training may also seem obvious, although we did have a case where the TSA questioned one of those having bones in their luggage prior to boarding a plane. People who train and maintain search & rescue or cadaver dogs was added a few years ago at the push of those organizations, as they need actual samples to properly train their dogs.

Per other statutes, none of this applies to cremains that are given back to family members after cremation. It is up to a family whether they want to scatter, bury, or keep the urn on a shelf at home. At least no one at this point has challenged that as a legal matter (and I'm not sure why anyone would want to). This does apply, however to that human skull Uncle Joe found one year out hunting that he displays on his fireplace mantel. That is illegal under State law, as are any other human bone collections by private citizens. And if the remains are Native American, another world of trouble Federally can open up. We run into this mostly where a private citizen is discovered to have remains on a shelf or in storage, usually by relatives going through their property after they have died. Then we get the call, and we have procedures in place for how to handle such events.

W.S. 35-5-201 through 225 Revised Uniform Anatomical Gift Act
35-5-221. Cooperation between coroner and procurement organization.

(a) A coroner shall cooperate with procurement organizations to maximize the opportunity to recover anatomical gifts for the purpose of transplantation, therapy, research or education.

(b) If a coroner receives notice from a procurement organization that an anatomical gift might be available or was made with respect to a decedent whose body is under the jurisdiction of the coroner and a post-mortem examination is going to be performed, unless the coroner denies recovery in accordance with W.S. 35-5-222, the coroner or designee shall conduct a post-mortem examination of the body or the part in a manner and within a period compatible with its preservation for the purposes of the gift.

(c) A part may not be removed from the body of a decedent under the jurisdiction of a coroner for transplantation, therapy, research or education unless the part is the subject of an anatomical gift. The body of a decedent under the jurisdiction of the coroner may not be delivered to a person for research or education unless the body is the subject of an anatomical gift. This subsection does not preclude a coroner from performing the medicolegal investigation upon the body or parts of a decedent under the jurisdiction of the coroner.

35-5-222. Facilitation of anatomical gift from decedent whose body is under jurisdiction of coroner.

(a) Upon request of a procurement organization, a coroner shall release to the procurement organization the name, contact information and available medical and social history of a decedent whose body is under the jurisdiction of the coroner. If the decedent's body or part is medically suitable for transplantation, therapy, research or education, the coroner shall release postmortem examination results to the procurement organization. The procurement organization may make a subsequent disclosure of the post-mortem examination results or other information received from the coroner only if relevant to transplantation or therapy.

(b) The coroner may conduct a medicolegal examination by reviewing all medical records, laboratory test results, x-rays, other diagnostic results and other information that any person possesses about a donor or prospective donor whose body is under the jurisdiction of the coroner which the coroner determines may be relevant to the investigation.

(c) A person who has any information requested by a coroner pursuant to subsection (b) of this section shall provide that information as expeditiously as possible to allow the coroner to conduct the medicolegal investigation within a period compatible with the preservation of parts for the purpose of transplantation, therapy, research or education.

(d) If an anatomical gift has been or might be made of a part of a decedent whose body is under the jurisdiction of the coroner and a post-mortem examination is not required, or the coroner determines that a post-mortem examination is required but that the recovery of the part that is the subject of an anatomical gift will not interfere with the examination, the coroner and procurement organization shall cooperate in the timely removal of the part from the decedent for the purpose of transplantation, therapy, research or education.

(e) If an anatomical gift of a part from the decedent under the jurisdiction of the coroner has been or might be made, but the coroner initially believes that the recovery of the part could interfere with the post-mortem investigation into the decedent's cause or manner of death, the coroner shall consult with the procurement organization or physician or technician designated by the procurement organization about the proposed recovery. After consultation, the coroner may deny the recovery.

(f) The coroner and procurement organization shall enter into an agreement establishing protocols and procedures governing relations between them when the coroner believes that the recovery of a part for anatomical gift from a decedent whose body is under the jurisdiction of the coroner could interfere with the post-mortem investigation into the decedent's cause or manner of death or the documentation or preservation of evidence. Decisions regarding the recovery of a part from the decedent shall be made in accordance with the agreement.

(g) If the coroner or designee denies recovery under subsection (f) of this section, the coroner or designee shall:
> (i) Explain in a record the specific reasons for not allowing recovery of the part;
> (ii) Include the specific reasons in the records of the coroner; and
> (iii) Provide a record with the specific reasons to the procurement organization.

(h) If the coroner or designee allows recovery of a part under subsection (d), (e) or (f) of this section, the procurement organization, upon request, shall cause the physician or technician who removes the part to provide the coroner with a record describing the condition of the part, a biopsy, a photograph and any other information and observations that would assist in the post-mortem examination.

(j) If a coroner or designee is required to be present at a removal procedure under subsection (f) of this section, upon request the procurement organization requesting the recovery of the part shall reimburse the coroner or designee for the additional costs incurred in complying with subsection (f) of this section.

***Commentary:** The above are the portions of the Anatomical Gift Act that apply to coroners. Coroners are required to have procedures and agreements with the appropriate recovery organization for their jurisdiction. This will be discussed in more detail under the Policies and Procedures sections. Note that while coroners are required by law to be a party to such agreements, nowhere in the law does it state that the donor organizations get to stipulate all the details or rules of that agreement, especially if it requires a violation of other statutes by the coroner. One area would be in the area of veterans, where in W.S. 35-4-602(a)(iv) the unclaimed body of a veteran is forbidden from being used for research – which is what happens in some cases with "left overs" deemed by the donor organization as unsuitable for use after recovery. That is a cautionary restriction to be aware of. Also, while the statute notes that an autopsy should be completed in a "period compatible" with recovery, that does not take into account the realities of Wyoming in that the time frame to set up and transport for autopsy may put the body outside of such time frames just by the distances involved. More on this later.*

W.S. 35-6-101(a)(vii) Abortions - Viability

> (vii) "Viability" means that stage of human development when the embryo or fetus is able to live by natural or

life-supportive systems outside the womb of the mother according to appropriate medical judgment;

Commentary: *As mentioned earlier, in conjunction with W.S. 35-1-401(a) definitions, the term 'viability' has meaning in the context of a live birth, and here in the context of abortion law. Viability is literally "the ability to live", which means a live birth. Federal law as established by Supreme Court decisions has established the current standard for this term as related to gestation, and is reflected in state statute previously noted.*

Regardless of your personal opinion on the subject of abortion, this statute does illustrate the complications and problems that can arise when the legislature tries to alter a current law, especially one that is so integrated into multiple areas of other statutes. In the 2017 legislative session, a change was proposed to amend the definition of viability to include the ability to feel pain. Again keep in mind I am staying out of the moral or ethical aspects of the subject, but just addressing the literal word of law. While medical methods are always improving, there is a current established medical average, and legal determination by case law of gestational viability. If you change the law to include the ability to feel pain, how is that scientifically or legally determined? And by what verifiable standard? The definition of life and viability is key to the definition of a minor under W.S 8-1-102; the definition of a child homicide under W.S. 6-2-101; the definition of a child under W.S 14-3-202(iii) and mandatory reporting to the coroner under W.S. 14-3-207; the definitions for Vital Records certifications under W.S. 35-1-401(v) and stillbirth under W.S. 35-1-401(vi); the definition of a dead body under 35-1-401(vii); and other ties within statutory law. How are coroners and Vital Records to address certifications and whether it is a case or not, if jurisdiction is not clearly determined, and who is to pay for that determination in each case, either medically or judicially? Without addressing all those issues, such a change would have made a legal and costly mess for the office of the coroner and others to wade through, one that would have probably taken years to sort out, separate from anyone's opinion on abortion law itself. Fortunately, the legislature recognized the problem with such a change, and removed the language and issue.

This is also a good example why coroners need to pay attention and be involved in tracking proposed legislative changes to statutes that might affect the office. Otherwise, if your jurisdictional world is turned upside-down without your input to the legislature, it is your own fault. Legislative activism can also decrease your case load. This office in 2017 actively supported increasing the legal availability of opiate antagonists to first responders in the state, as the more overdoses that survive, the less work for coroners, and less tragedy for families. We deal with enough tragedy as it is.

W.S. 35-19-101 Determination of death.
35-19-101. Determination of death.

An individual who has sustained either irreversible cessation of circulatory and respiratory functions, or irreversible cessation of all functions of the entire brain including the brain stem, is dead. A determination of death shall be made in accordance with accepted medical standards.

Commentary: *This definition is in accord with national and medical current standards. One thing to keep in mind on this is the relationship to organ donation. Legally, the coroner has no jurisdiction until the individual is dead by definition. Some donor organizations will try and get coroner permission for donation prior to the person being declared dead. While I can appreciate their interest in expediting the process, the coroner has no authority to give permission on anything prior to death, which is where jurisdiction is established. Indicating and investigating a probability or not prior to the upcoming event is one thing, but recording the time of actual release or permission is another. That time had better be after the physician records a time of death. Due to the variability of their documentation wording, I insist the organizations confirm and communicate with me after the patient is declared, regardless of pre-event planning. Otherwise you could open yourself to a whole civil or criminal legal can or worms if someone objects.*

W.S. 42-2-103 Department of Family Services; Burial Assistance

(c) Notwithstanding any other provision of this article, the department shall pay the burial or cremation expenses of any recipient of aid under the personal opportunities with employment responsibilities (POWER) program, supplemental security income or Medicaid at the time of his death and without sufficient means in his own estate or other resources to provide burial or cremation. The amount paid under this subsection shall not exceed one thousand dollars ($1,000.00) after consideration of funds available to the recipient from all other sources. In determining eligibility under this subsection, the department shall not consider as available funds, an amount up to or equal to one thousand five hundred dollars ($1,500.00) of the corpus of a Medicaid qualifying trust meeting the requirements of W.S. 42-4-113. No board of county commissioners shall be responsible for any burial or cremation expenses in excess of the amount paid under this subsection. Burial or cremation expenses under this subsection shall not include those expenses relating to cemetery costs.

Commentary: *This statute goes in conjunction with W.S. 18-3-504 as far as responsibility for the county to assist in the burial of persons on particular public welfare programs. Clearly here the responsibility is in the hands of DFS and not the coroner or county. Unfortunately, this amount is terribly inadequate in today's funeral markets, so the people that need it the most, are left without proper assistance. Since the wording contains the phrase "shall not exceed", that means the amount can be lower, and in that regards, DFS in 2017 cut this portion of their budget to allow only $500 for each case. This caused a bit of consternation and complaint, but it is a state issue that county coroners cannot resolve on their own. We have to follow the law.*

While this section has covered the coroner statutes, and many of those other statutes that directly refer to the office of the coroner or how duties are performed, the reader should realize that there are many other statutes that affect how the coroner will do his job within the interplay of government. There are rules on how the county is to conduct business, rules for how each of the other elected officials do their jobs, rules for the various state departments, criminal and civil law, and others. While many may not mention or directly involve the coroner, the rules for the county, clerk, and treasurer, for example, control how you will have to administer the office, and others partially determine what you can or cannot do as an elected official. In other interactions, such as with the Department of Family Services, Vital Records, or the State Archives, as other examples, they have their own statutes to determine how they are to do their jobs and the corner needs to accommodate and work within the structure of government to accomplish a task. Serving as an elected official is a continuous learning process, and the legislature, or a court ruling, may change the rules in any given year. It is your obligation as an elected official to stay on top of things and changes, in order to remain in compliance with the law.

Also remember, that while court judgements and opinions are firmer ground than those from the County Attorney or even the Wyoming Attorney General, even these can, and do, change over time with the evolution of the courts and those who are chosen to sit on the bench.

Section C: Coroner Testimony

Another critical aspect of the duties of the coroner are how the office integrates into judicial cases as a witness. The authority of the coroner is based in statutes, as are the standards of an investigation. How this is applied in testimony, also involves established case law, and both the Wyoming and Federal Rules of Evidence.

General Expert Testimony on Coroner Cases

1. Coroner authority for investigation in Wyoming Statutes: see W.S. 7-4-201. Reports of death; investigation; summoning of jurors; fees and costs; inspection of medical records. In addition, a basis can be found in rules as directed by W.S. 7-4-211(c)(ii), where the Wyoming Board of Coroner Standards has promulgated specific rules regarding the investigation of coroner cases under "Section D. Board of Coroner Standards" (detailed later in this text).

2. Coroner Testimony as an Expert Witness:
    a. Basis for testimony has been secured through case law[1] and both Wyoming Rules of Evidence (WRE), Article VII; and Federal Rules of Evidence (FRE), Article VII.
    b. Per WRE Rule 702, the coroner if qualified by knowledge, skill, experience, training, or education, may testify in the form of an opinion or otherwise. FRE Rule 702 further specifies that the witness's knowledge should (a) help the trier of fact understand the evidence or determine a fact in issue; (b) testimony is based on sufficient facts or data; (c) testimony is the product of reliable principles and methods; and (d) these principles and methods have been reliably applied to the facts of the case.
    c. The notes on FRE Rule 702 also state that the expert may give a dissertation or exposition of the scientific or other principles relevant to the case; and that by being broadly phrased, the rule allows for all "specialized" knowledge, or "skilled" witnesses[2].
    d. Trial judges are considered the gatekeeper on the admissibility of a skilled witness[3].
    e. Additional case law regarding FRE Rule 702 further defines issues relevant to coroner testimony that may be significant. In particular, the coroner/witness must be able to adequately account for obvious alternative explanations, and reasonably rule them out[4]. In this way, the coroner needs not only to justify his decision on manner of death, but be able to justify why alternative manners are eliminated, and ground that decision in the facts of the investigation.

3. Bases of Opinion in Coroner Testimony:

    a. WRE Rule 703 notes that the facts of data as a basis for opinion or inference may be those made known at or before a hearing; and that if those facts and data are of a type reasonably relied upon in the particular field for forming an opinion or inference upon the subject, the facts or data themselves need not be admitted into evidence *[see citation 1]*.

    b. Notes included by the Advisory Committee for FRE Rule 703 use the analogy of a physician in that in practice, the professional uses information from numerous sources of considerable variety, including statements, reports and opinions from other professionals, technicians, records, and diagnostics such as x-rays. To assess each component individually for admissibility would require the expenditure of substantial time to produce authenticating witnesses. Therefore the expert's validation, expertly performed and subject to cross-examination, ought to suffice for judicial purposes[5]. The key point is that these facts or data be those "reasonably relied upon by experts in the particular field".

    c. Thus, for the coroner, any of the investigative tools or procedures specified by Statute or the Coroner Standards, or those generally used by "experts in the field", could be included as a component of testimony. All testimony should be probative, that is proven by the evidence, which can be either by first hand observation or that which one was made aware of.

4. Knowledge of the Underlying Facts:

    a. WRE Rule 705 notes that the expert may testify in terms of opinion or inference and give the reasons, without prior disclosure of the underlying facts or data, unless the court requires otherwise. It is important to note, however, that the expert may have to disclose or explain the underlying data/facts on cross-examination.

    b. What this means for the coroner witness, is that if questioned, they would need to understand and explain to a lay jury in reasonable terms, the justification for the procedures and meaning of the data or facts that form a basis for a conclusion on manner and cause of death. This does not mean that the witness would have to know the detailed technology, procedures, techniques, or specifics of say, how a toxicology test is performed and analyzed; but rather be able to relate the general value and meaning of individual data, facts, or reports. Detailed testimony in an individual field should be the job of the expert in that particular field – coroners appraise, combine, and analyze component fields of investigation for a summary judgement on manner and cause.

5. <u>Autopsies and Other Specialties in the Course of an Investigation</u>:

      a. An autopsy is one of many procedures possibly used in an investigation caused by a coroner, under the authority noted above, and is a portion of the investigation used in conjunction with other aspects to arrive at a manner and cause of death. While an integral part of some investigations, it is important to keep in mind that the forensic pathologist findings and opinion is only a part of the investigation, and the ultimate decision on manner and cause is the coroner's, based on the entire findings of the investigation, not just the autopsy. The pathologist is often working with the investigative information as known only at the time of the autopsy, not necessarily the total facts eventually known at the end of the investigation. In that context, the coroner may change the manner from what is stated in the autopsy report, as the investigation is completed with additional facts. In addition, even the National Association of Medical Examiners[6] notes that the manner of death is circumstance dependent, not autopsy dependent.

      b. As a witness, the coroner may testify as to the conclusions of an autopsy as an integral portion of the determination of manner and cause, much like any other component such as toxicology, summary medical records, reports, property and evidence, and photographs, or other facts and data. The key is being able to explain that these are all reliable principles and methods involved in and relied upon as standard facts or data gathered in the field for determination of manner and cause of death.

Section D: State Agency Rules

As noted before, many agencies, boards, or commissions in the state have created rules to govern the functioning of government or a specific department. There is a specific legal procedure for the creation of rules that involve review by the Attorney General, public comment periods, and other requirements. If the legislature has authorized a body to create rules through statute, once those rules are adopted through due process, the rules have the effect and authority of statute. A complete resource for the rules for any authorized body in the State of Wyoming can be found in various locations in the state government web site. There are several main areas where the coroner will interact with or be subject to agency rules, and this is by no means an exclusive list.

1. Records Retention: The only specific coroner statute that deals with records, other than the sections of W.S. 7-4-105, is W.S. 7-4-206, in which the documents of an inquest must be filed with the Clerk of District Court. This does not, however, mean that is the only records rule you must follow. Statutes define that all your records are property of the State of Wyoming, in any form, and give the Wyoming State Archives the authority to make rules on how those records are to be retained, disposed, or otherwise handled (and this includes all digital forms of record). Penalties are also provided for mishandling of records, so my best advice is to have policies in place for your office that conform to the rules of the Archives. A copy of the policy developed for Fremont County can be found in the Appendix as an example.

Historically, in many cases coroner records were quite frankly, a mess. Through many terms of office, and especially in those cases where a coroner had no official facility, records were lost, misplaced, or otherwise gone. I know of one southern Wyoming county where the previous coroner took all the case files due to a disagreement with the newly elected coroner – an act that by statute is patently illegal, since statute specifically states all records must be turned over to the incoming office holder. In the case of Fremont, prior coroners either did not keep accurate files, or kept every piece of paper that existed, so that when I took office I inherited a disorganized set of storage rooms filled to the brim with paper. This is not an efficient way to do business.

As Chief Deputy, prior to taking office as coroner, one of my projects was to go through files and make sure everything was in a database for basic access, and we ended up with over 7,500 case files at that time, going back to 1885. And even at that, a lot of older files are missing everything other than basic information. In 2014 I started work with the State Archivists to develop a retention policy for Fremont. At that time, there was not even a State specific policy for coroners, although there was a general retention policy that applied – many other departments or officials had their own lists devised by the Archives. Since that time the State has developed rules for everyone generally, with the ability to tailor a set for your specific agency. And all records policies must be approved by the Archives prior to implementation. Once this was completed, having a policy enabled me to get the paperwork under control – many cubic feet of old documents and duplications could be disposed and cleared out. (Note: the method of destruction is also mandated by the Archives.) With organization and clearing, and State Approval, we are able now to keep the paper build up to reasonable proportions, and secure what we need to keep. Remember, with the 2011 addition of confidentiality statutes, coroners must secure the confidentiality of the records, so the less you have to keep, the less space you will need to keep them in.

Contact the State Archives for questions and assistance if you have no policies in this regard, or have questions. The archivists are a pleasure to work with in my experience, extremely helpful, and with policies in place, can make the administrative job of a coroner much easier. Good policies in this regard not only help in clearing and controlling documentation, but protect the coroner and staff from the consequences of mishandling records. While there is a structure to go by, compliance with the rules and law can be built according to your needs.

2. Public Records Policies: Public records and access is an often contentious and problematic issue these days, especially with the media. While some of the specific statutes have already been noted, it is worthwhile for a coroner to review and be familiar with the entire set of statutes that deal with the public records aspects of the law. The main sections are W.S. 9-2-401 through 9-2-415, and W.S. 16-4-201 through 16-4-204, although, like a lot of cases, aspects of public records law are scattered throughout the statutes. If you have a copy of the Wyoming Statutes Annotated, just look in the index under "Records" and you will see what I mean. Paper and records are the beating heart and circulatory system of government, and records have a large amount of statutory language to talk about themselves.

In the public records arena, the 2011 legislative changes in many ways simplified some things, because except for a few exceptions, coroner case records are not public. The complications come in however in that even though that is the law, that does not mean that people, organizations, or agencies will not seek them, and you will need to determine, under the law, what the various parties can or cannot have, under what circumstances, and by what procedures. And again, any slip-ups in this area, under the statutes, leave you criminally liable for the consequences. The law does permit you to establish procedures for disseminating and compliance with requests for records, and having those procedures in place is your best protection for everyone's benefit. Agencies you work with that have the right of access to coroner records, such as law enforcement or certain social services, need your information to do their job. It is the coroner's responsibility to document, as custodian of the records, verification of the requesting party's right to the information, identification of the requestor, and that dissemination is provided to the legitimate party. More paperwork, absolutely, but it documents compliance and protects you and your staff. Knowledge of the law and documentation in this area also provides justification for denial of information to those not eligible to receive it, and can deflect many of the conflicts other parts of government have to deal with. As an example, the media here know that a public records request under the Public Records Act, for photos or a coroner autopsy text, will not go anywhere. They get the Public Records Docket as specified by law, and nothing more. Since some people, and especially the media, will whine about the restrictions, we are specific on most forms to reference the appropriate statutes in this regards, so they can look it up, if they like.

As another caution regarding public information and the coroner's office, remember the confidentiality statutes refer to information, not just documents. You can get in the same trouble by releasing confidential information verbally, the same as if you hand out a document. Dealing with the media, or the skills needed in even talking about a case, could be a whole instructional text in and of itself. Openness about discussing case information should only be in regards to explaining the policies, procedures, and laws that restrict what you can say, not the details of the case.

Like the laws themselves, policies in this area should be customized and tweaked periodically to your needs, as new circumstances will bring up situations not previously encountered. Current Fremont County policies in this area are available in the Appendix as an example for reference.

3. WY Dept. of Health: As seen in the statutes, there is a lot of cross-over and common ground in the duties of the coroner and responsibilities of the Health Department. Public Health Emergencies have their own rules and authority, and the coroner needs to have policies and procedures for mass fatalities, disasters, or other such events. Jurisdiction and authority can change drastically, and the need to work well and interact between agencies becomes a paramount concern. In something like a pandemic event, the duties and authority of State Health Officers escalate, and coroners will be involved. The county health officer is usually a local physician appointed by the Department of Health, and generally an uninvolved position that may be out of their league in a large event, unless unusually well trained and aware, so it helps the coroner to not only know his own job, but what the health officer needs to do in such situations.

'Reportable Diseases' is another area where it helps the coroner to be aware and verify when these instances pop up in cases. The Department of Health web site has access to this yearly updated listing, with the required method of contact for each disease. Most often I have found that the personal physician or hospital has already done the required reporting, but cases will occur where it has not been done. The contacts with the State can usually verify fairly quickly if the procedures have been completed in any particular deceased instance. These things are statutorily required, and not a choice.

Vital Statistics Services (commonly called Vital Records) is under the Department of Health. This agency is one you will have regular interactions with in the area of filing death certificates. They have instructions and programs for coroners available regarding their rules, and the on-line system of certification. They also are the collectors of statistics and demographics for the State, which are passed along to the Center for Disease Control (CDC) and correlated under the national vital statistics departments. Most of this area has at this point been standardized nationally, but different regions will have their own quirks and variations.

The Department of Family Services has been under the Department of Health, off and on, over the years, depending on the whims of the legislature and agency. The interactions between this agency and the coroner is most notable in the areas of child deaths, but also involves adults on Medicaid, other adult protective services, or legal issues with family dynamics. Cooperation with this department on the part of the coroner is mandatory by their statutes and rules, as is their cooperation with the coroner. How this proceeds and is accomplished often depends on the personalities of staffing or situations that arise, and while both are working to particular justifiable ends, the means of getting there sometimes conflicts, even within the law (especially in the area of confidentiality). We take it as it goes and work through it.

Some facilities in the state are under the Department of Health, such as the State Hospital in Evanston (psychiatric), the Wyoming Life Resource Center in Lander (brain injury and disabilities) and several retirement facilities like the State Veteran's Home in Buffalo. Deaths at these facilities are automatically coroner cases under W.S. 7-4-104(a)(i)(G).

4. Wyoming State Fire Marshal: In any circumstance of a fire related death, the Fire Marshal's office will be a part of the investigation. Statutes and rules are specific in their authority in this area, but that does not negate the coroner's authority over the body. It is imperative for agencies to work together in these circumstances, as fire deaths can be some of the most complicated investigations. The coroner will often be dependent on the results of the Fire Marshal investigator's investigation report to determine manner of death. The investigative powers of the Fire Marshal are defined in W.S. 35-9-107 through 35-9-110.

5. State Law Enforcement and Division of Criminal Investigation / State Crime Laboratory: These agencies are under the State Attorney General's Office. Coroners will mostly be involved with these state agencies when they are brought in by request or associated with local law enforcement investigations. In some circumstances the state lab will send an evidence team to a scene, and in most cases, the coroner investigation is held until, or in conjunction with, these investigators. The statutory jurisdiction and rules for these departments are pretty much not the concern of the coroner, other than how that interaction occurs. Other areas of State law enforcement may involve State Parks personnel or Wyoming Game and Fish, if a death occurs in their jurisdiction. Game and Fish is also an invaluable resource for any death that involves wildlife, and we have even used their expertise to eliminate wildlife as a cause. A recent case involved determination that the wounds were feral canine, rather than bear, cougar, or wildlife. Another involved the death of a hiker by bear. They were able to not only define the circumstances of the event but also prove the "perpetrators" – that experience and assistance is an asset to any coroner.

6. Board of Coroner Standards: This state appointed board is authorized by the noted section of the coroner statutes. The most significant portion of the rules for the board are as follows, established in 2009:

CHAPTER 6
STANDARDS DEALING WITH THE INVESTIGATION OF CORONER'S CASES

Section 1. Definitions. W.S. 7-4-104 is appended to these standards as Appendix A and adopted and incorporated herein.

Section 2. Conduct. Coroners shall act in accordance with all relevant state and federal law. In addition, in dealing with the deceased, the family of the deceased, and the general public, the Coroners shall conduct themselves in a manner consistent with the highest standards of professionalism, compassion, and respect.

Section 3. General.

(a) The Coroner shall work jointly with all law enforcement agencies having jurisdiction in a death scene investigation.

(b) The Coroner has jurisdiction over and shall take custody of the body.

(c) The Coroner shall assume responsibility for the property of the deceased.

(d) Evidence is the responsibility of law enforcement and/or the Coroner.

(e) The Coroner shall protect the chain of custody for any evidence in their custody.

(f) The Coroner shall provide for transportation, security, and preservation of the deceased until released to the next of kin or their designee.

(g) The Coroner shall pronounce death, and record the date, time, and location.

(h) The Coroner shall provide for the notification of next of kin.

(i) The Coroner shall provide the office staff and investigators:

    (i) Safe and adequate equipment to perform any duties of the office; and

    (ii) Adequate and appropriate safety and personal protective equipment suitable for the circumstances of the investigation.

Section 4. Investigations.

(a) The Coroner shall identify the deceased and determine the Manner and Cause of death as accurately as possible.

(b) In determining the Manner and Cause of death, the investigation shall include:

    (i) Scene Investigation;

    (ii) Toxicology sample on the deceased;

    (iii) Inventory of property, evidence, and medications;

(iv) Photographs;
(v) External Exam; and
(vi) DNA sample.

(c) The Coroner shall issue a written report for all death investigations. The written reports may include but are not limited to, data from measuring devices, diagrams, evidence and body labeling, interviews, psychological and social histories, medical histories and consultation with physicians, autopsy, fingerprints, radiology, odontology, or DNA profiles or any other method necessary to determine the cause and manner of death.

(d) Investigations requiring a forensic autopsy of the deceased shall be conducted by a Forensic Pathologist who has been certified in that specialty by a nationally recognized certification board.

(e) All investigations will be completed in a reasonable time. The term 'reasonable time' is defined as that time period necessary to complete and collect data and information from toxicology, autopsy, or other investigation procedures, to determine with medical certainty a manner and cause of death.

Section 5. Records. The Coroner shall maintain all public records in accordance with W.S. 9-2-405 through 9-2-413.

Commentary: I participated with the Board in creating these set of standards for investigations, which had considerable input and discussion, along with a long time frame to go through the rule making process. The basis for this basic set of standards is a combination of recommendations from the National Institute of Justice, and the needs of the varied size and nature of coroner offices in the state. Just as in the fact that forensic pathologists follow standard procedures and techniques in their exams, having a standard for coroner investigations in the state give direct credibility to what we do. This is important in court cases, as well as ensuring that every death receives the same standard of investigation, regardless of circumstance. Some interesting conversations and discussions occurred during the formation of these standards. For example, all investigations should include photographs. Some wanted to define in the rule the megapixel standard for cameras, others the nature and subject matter that should be photographed. Since technology changes so rapidly, and some small offices can't afford high-end cameras, it was decided that the principle is to take photos, not the type of camera. And how to do so in a scene should be left up to education, not rule. The same for many of the other standards – make this a framework, not a textbook on method. The last part under Section 4 (e) has an interesting background. At the time, personnel at Vital Records had an on-going dispute with some coroners over the issue that the state wanted death certificates filed in three days, as that is what was stated as a reasonable time by their rules. Obviously to anyone who has worked in this business, manner and cause of death is not so neatly packaged like that. In research, it was found that the term "reasonable time" had never been defined in either any statute, or any rule in Wyoming. So, coroners and the Board established our own definition as stated, which once passed through the rule making process, has the effect of law and precedence, at least for coroners. End of argument. This is a great example of how knowing the process and foibles of the law, can work to your advantage.

Part III: Important Federal Regulations

The web of Federal regulations reaches into all aspects of society, and Coroners are not exempt. We will not attempt to cover all the intricacies of Federal involvement, but there are several main areas of regulation that the coroner needs to be immediately familiar with, and the impact they have on the duties of the office. For example, several Wyoming statutes involve deceased veterans, and how they are handled, which will be covered in the suggested policies later. Interactions with the Veteran's Administration will be frequent also in terms of obtaining medical records on the deceased. This is only one of the Federal Agencies you may encounter in your duties, and the most common other instances will be those agencies associated with lands, such as the Bureau of Land Management, Forest Service, National Park Service; or those associated with law enforcement such as the Drug Enforcement Administration, Bureau of Indian Affairs, or the FBI. Some may be more common here in Fremont County (like the FBI) due to our unique inclusion of a Reservation, but almost all areas of Wyoming will have Federal public lands or parks. Each area or department will have their own policies and procedures if a death occurs in their jurisdiction.

    Section A: First Responder Status: [1.]*The Homeland Security Act, Section 2, 6 U.S.C. 101, (6)* defines 'emergency response provider – "The term "emergency response provider" includes Federal, State, and local public safety, law enforcement, emergency medical (including hospital emergency facilities), and related personnel, agencies, and authorities." A general misconception is that the title of first responder only belongs to EMS or Fire personnel, when actually it is a Federal umbrella term for a multitude of staff and agencies. The Department of Homeland Security under *HSPD-8* further defines first responders as a trained or certified individual, who on arriving at an incident or emergency assumes immediate responsibility for the protection and preservation of life, property, evidence and environment. Since by law the coroner takes

97

custody of the body, which in many cases is a critical piece of evidence, there is little to question that we fall under that definition. 'First responder' is not limited to first on the scene. This is the reason that coroners are considered under interoperability standards and issues, mass fatality response, and even eligible under Federal regulations for certain Homeland Security Grants.

Section B: NAGPRA: Coroners in regards to the disposition of the skeletal remains of Native American individuals are subject to the applicable provisions of the [2] *Native American Graves Protection and Repatriation Act (NAGPRA; 25 U.S.C. 3001-3013 (2016)) and its implementing regulations (43 C.F.R. Part 10 (2017)). See Appendix A, Section L.: Native American Human Remains.* This refers only to skeletal remains that are of historic nature, not those that are more recent and of medical-legal significance. Obviously those would be handled like any other death. In the case of those skeletal remains discovered or otherwise turned up from graves, burials or on someone's shelf, the location, determination of race, and tribal affiliation are the prime determiners for procedure. Whether private, State, Federal, or Tribal lands, the procedures for Native American remains are specific and penalties possibly severe for not following the law in these cases. Coroners need to have a policy in place noting their compliance with Federal law, but it does not have to be complicated – it can be as simple as a notation in your policy manual that you will comply with NAGPRA per the citation noted above. A copy of the specific Fremont Policy for this area is located in the Appendix, as approved by the Solicitor General's Office for the Department of the Interior and the County Civil Attorney.

Section C: OSHA and Biohazard Regulations: Coroners and deputies obviously deal with and can be exposed to biohazards in the course of their duties, therefor they are subject to the rules and regulations of the Occupational Safety and Health Administration (OSHA), and are required by Federal law to have policies and procedures in place. Like the NAGPRA rules, a policy manual can simply have a reference to the appropriate citation: "All employees of the Coroner's Office will have a copy of the Biosafety Manual and be familiar with the policies and procedures regarding infectious disease protocols and response prior to any case work in the field. This includes response for exposure protocols and required immunizations as an employee under OSHA regulations. Copies of these procedures and policies are available as a separate publication at the coroner office." [3] [Ref. OSHA Standards 29 CFR Subpart I, Personal Protective Equipment, 1910.132 General Requirements; 29 CFR

1910.1030 Subpart Z: Toxic and Hazardous Substances, Bloodborne Pathogens].

Here, however, it gets a bit more complicated. While your policy manual can get by with the citation, the regulations require that you have an actual procedure manual in place, and that your employees are trained to use it. In addition, you can go through the regulations and pare down to only what is applicable to the duties of the job, <u>as long as your policies justify why certain parts do not apply.</u> For example, our policy notes that in most circumstances of case investigation, disposable gloves are the only biohazard equipment needed. Also, in the case of respirators, the usual encounters at the most would require an N-95 face mask. It is not required that you account for biohazard suits or full breathing gear like a fire department, as long as your policy defines the most common hazards encountered. Coroners also need to have policies and procedures for any exposures to blood-borne pathogens (commonly referred to as "Ryan White Act" compliance), such as needle sticks, etc. There are also required immunizations that must be obtained, like Hepatitis B, and since they are required, the county must pay for them, either directly or through a health plan. And finally, like most Federal regulations, you are required to maintain forms and documentation of employee awareness of hazards, training, immunizations obtained (or voluntary refusal), and any incidents and their mitigation. A copy of the Fremont County policies can be found in the Appendix for reference.

Section D: Incident Management: The system under the Federal Emergency Management Agency (FEMA) has coordinated resources and mandates under the National Incident Management System (NIMS) and the Incident Command System (ICS). Periodically requirements for certain training or proposed rules from the Federal level are passed along through the State Department of Homeland Security. Most fire commands, county emergency management agencies, law enforcement, and other responders are familiar with ICS and use it to great effectiveness. The Federal adoption and push came after the 9-11 terrorist incidents, however since that time there appears to be a constant revision, alteration, or change to how things work at the Federal level. The Federal agencies and Wyoming Dept. of Homeland Security periodically offer training in these areas, and have made periodic attempts at requiring the training for certain agencies, but the implementation has been inconsistent in my opinion, and funding generally non-existent for paying for the training as far as that goes. While you cannot beat ICS for dealing with major incidents, it would be unusual at any major incident not to have an agency trained and familiar with the process already. At this time, such training is probably not required, but should be taken advantage of if possible, just to be familiar with the system on a basic level, if not already. A lot of this is incorporated into the disaster and mass fatality policies for other county agencies, and gets experience and review during the various exercises and table tops performed periodically by those departments. A 'mass fatality' is any event that has more deaths than your capacity to deal with them, and a coroner should have a plan in place for those events

Section E: HIPAA: The final Federal regulation we will mention is [4.] The Health Insurance Portability and Accountability Act of 1996 (HIPAA). *[Code of Federal Regulations] [Title 45, Volume 1] [CITE: 45CFR164.512] Subpart E--Privacy of Individually Identifiable Health Information. Sec. 164.512*

This has been referenced before in the fact that as seen in the regulation, coroners and medical examiners are exempt from the disclosure restrictions on medical records. For once, at least, a Federal regulation simplifies things for coroners. This section is handy to have on your request forms in case someone balks at giving you medical records of any type, as the paranoia at violating this is great in the medical community. This is used in conjunction with W.S. 7-4-201(f) to emphasize the coroner's authority to obtain what they need in a case. The one caution to keep in mind, is that the same Federal law that gives you unlimited access, also forbids any secondary release. This includes any case records given to families or other agencies as permitted by the confidentiality statutes – unless by court order or within the judicial process. In most cases they have to obtain or subpoena their own copies of such records within other areas of the law. You may have anything you need in this area, but are required to protect them once you have them. Also, since over time, medical records can be a large volume of paper to deal with, have a policy for disposal included in the records retention policies approved for your office by the Archives.

HIPAA also applies in reference to your employees – while as an employer you have a right to require certain medical information as a part of sick leave or other policies, or document required medical care such as immunizations, that information is highly restricted within the office setting and may only be accessed by a coroner head of the department, or an administrator. Like other personnel files, this information must be locked away in limited access.

Part IV: County Government

This will be a brief discussion on the interactions of the office of the coroner with other county agencies and elected officials. Each county will have their own policies and procedures in these areas, and are of main concern in the administrative aspects of the job. Each elected official for the county is an independent and equal office, but each elected official will have their own set of statutes that govern what and how they do their jobs, just as the coroner does. And like the coroner, while aspects of the job are determined by your own needs, style, and flavor of management, each has a job to do and all officials should strive to interact in a coherent and respectful manner. You cannot require another elected official to violate their own statutes, any more than they can require you to violate yours. Some interactions will be defined by statute and the law, regardless of the opinions of an individual official.

a. Interactions and Obligations

1. Treasurer – This office is in charge of State mandated monetary policies, receipts, collections, and disbursements; projections and documentation of funding. These are complicated duties that other than determining what is available in county funding that would include a coroner's budget, has minimal interaction with the office. Most coroners will account for little income to report, although any income received should be documented by policies as approved by the Treasurer. *(Reference W.S. 18-3-801 through 18-3-814)*

2. Clerk – Along with all the other myriad duties of the county clerk, most are also in charge of documenting and filing elected official policies and performing other administrative duties for the county, including acting as a repository for county records, and running elections. Some perform or oversee personnel responsibilities, such as payroll. Budgets and their procedures usually run through the clerk, and these are just a few of the interactions that will involve the coroner. *(Reference W.S. 18-3-401 through 18-3-402)*

3. Clerk of District Court – As noted, inquests are required to be filed with this office, and in some circumstances, property that is unclaimed in the course of a case is required to be turned over to this office. The other main area of interaction would be in the case of trials where the coroner is involved as a witness. The Clerk of District Court, like the Coroner, is not included in Title 18 with the other county officers, but is elected as a county officer with their own authorizing statutes. *(Reference W.S. 5-7-101 through 5-7-107)*

4. Commission – Counties in Wyoming may have either a three or five person Board, as decided by the particular county. The main area of interaction will be in setting and approving your budget, as the Board is responsible for the general operations of the county, determining aspects of funding, general county policies, and in charge of various county departments other than the elected officials. Any area that has developed policies for the coroner that directly involve approval of payments, such as Indigent and Unclaimed Policies, must be worked out and approved with the input of the county commission. The interactions with the Board are too numerous to go into, and vary from county to county depending on the circumstances. *(Reference W.S. 18-3-501 through 18-3-524)*

5. Sheriff – The main interaction will be in investigations that are in this law enforcement agency's jurisdiction. Cooperation and how the two offices work together also varies depending on the policies set between the coroner and sheriff. *(Reference W.S. 18-3-601 through 18-3-611)*

6. Assessor – While the interactions with this elected official and the coroner are usually not common, due to the duties of the office, the Assessor often has scene and mapping resources and information that may be of use in a case. *(Reference W.S. 18-3-201 through 18-3-206)*

7. County or District Attorney – Interactions include trials and judicial workings, and sometimes some offices request presence at scenes or particular notifications, such as homicides. In addition, one of the duties of the county attorney is that they are the legal representative for all elected officials. Here in Fremont, we have a Deputy Attorney in charge of civil matters, who also reviews and approves all MOUs, agreements, and certain policies, handles employment matters, and researches opinions on questions of law. How some of this is handled, again, often depends on the county. *(Reference W.S. 18-3-301 through 18-3-305)*

b. County Policies and Procedures – while another elected official is not necessarily required to go by all or specific policies as set by the Commission, common sense demands that everyone work together in the best interest of the county. Cultivating an atmosphere of input and interaction, as well as cooperation and respect, will make the administration of the coroner's job go much smoother.

c. Operations – Certain operations of the county, which usually involve other departments that work under the commission, will directly have interactions with the coroner. These would include things like emergency management, or building and vehicle maintenance, to name a few.

d. Employment Manual and Policies – County employment, usually through the Clerk, will have its own policies and procedures. Some will have a 'Human Resource' officer or department. In any case, a coroner will need to have their own job descriptions and employment manual/policies that mesh with those of the county.

This by no means describes all the duties of the various officials and departments of county government, and like the coroner, while there are specific sections for each elected official, they too have and interconnecting set of obligations within the whole of statute.

One final comment on being a county officer and elected official is regarding elections: those procedures have their own set of statutes and guidelines or requirements in law, and it is important to follow those laws, or the result can be prohibition from office, or removal.

Part V: Inter-Agency Policies and MOUs

As a part of operations of the office of the coroner, the necessity will arise to have agreements on procedures with other assorted agencies, departments, or organizations. These sort of agreements can streamline and clarify just whose responsibility is what, settle jurisdictional conflicts, and pre-empt other issues that will pop up in situations not previously encountered, or unprepared for. Each agency will have its own obligations and requirements under the law, and most likely will require legal review within each agency prior to approval. While the process of creating these agreements can be quite involved and drawn out, once completed, in the long run they can greatly simplify your job in particular situations. Some of the examples we have in Fremont County are as follows:

a. The U.S. Dept. of Interior, Bureau of Land Management: This agreement is between the coroner's office and the Lander Field Office of the BLM, and covers the discovery, recovery, and disposition of human remains found on BLM land within the boundaries of Fremont County. It determines the parameters of the working relationship between agencies in their mutual jurisdictions. The Lander Field Office maintains staff archeologists as part of their needs to fulfill their own regulatory obligations, such as monitoring excavations, or oil and gas developments. Since the finding of human remains in any operations is also covered by state statute and notification to the coroner, and also involves NAGPRA if Native American, things otherwise could get very complicated if not laid out in a procedure. For non-native remains, other Federal laws apply, such as the [1]Antiquities Act of 1906, the [2]National Historic Preservation Act of 1966, and the [3]Archaeological Resources Protection Act of 1979. Running afoul of any of these regulations can cause time consuming headaches for a coroner just trying to do their job, so prevention is the best resolution through a good MOU. BLM lands are common in all areas of the state.

b. Tribal: Fremont County contains within its borders a majority of the Wind River Reservation (a small portion extends into Hot Springs County to the north), and thus has a unique position not common to most other counties in Wyoming. Recognize that reservations and tribal lands have a good deal of sovereign jurisdictions by Federal Law, and the coroner's office here has jurisdiction on the reservation only because the tribes have granted it. Since the services of the office are due tribal members the same as any other citizen of the county, agreements with the tribes are important to expedite and smooth the provision of those services. The other unique aspect is that we often work with the U.S. Attorney, District of Wyoming, and the FBI, on any case that a death is the result of a major crime, such as homicide. Some of the NAGPRA issues have already been noted previously, and I will not go into agreement details here, since most of that only applies to the Fremont County situation.

Also remember that certain crimes or events that result in death, are of concern to Federal agencies, such as the FBI in kidnapping or terrorist acts, or the FAA and NTSB in air crashes, regardless of where they occur.

c. Mass Fatality: Some agreements and MOUs in this area will be through the county emergency management agencies, and the State Department of Homeland Security, in which the coroner has a role to play in general organizational procedures. Fremont County does have an MOU with the State Wyoming Life Resource Center for the use of a vacant building in the case of a mass fatality event, and has an agreement with the same institution and the Department of Health for expanding available resources in such an event. We also have an agreement approved by the commission and Dept. of health to use a particular land parcel for unclaimed & indigent burials, saving the county considerable cost over private funeral homes and cemeteries.

The significance of pre-planning for an event can be put simply: what would you do if your office suddenly had to handle 10 fatalities? Or 100? Or 500? Having worked Hurricane Katrina in New Orleans in 2005, I can assure you that no plan will cover everything, nor eliminate all confusion or issues. But having a plan can keep you from being totally unprepared and overwhelmed. Another example is the Total Solar Eclipse in 2017 across Wyoming... all agencies prepared for the worst case scenario of doubling the county population for a day. Luckily everything went pretty good in consideration, and life returned to normal shortly after. It could have gone badly in an instant, however, and it is best to be prepared.

d. Donor Organizations: As previously noted, W.S. 35-5-201 through 225, the Revised Uniform Anatomical Gift Act, has direct relationship to the duties of the coroner, and by law, coroners in each county must have an agreement with the authorized recovery organizations in their area. One main difference here, is that rather than an agreement between government agencies, these are agreements with private or non-profit entities. Each time these are renewed, these organizations usually offer a template, or 'boilerplate' agreements, and it is important to look them over carefully and have them reviewed by the county civil attorney before signing. In some instances in the past, the basic agreement offered conflicted with other Wyoming statutes, and under no circumstances are you required to sign anything that mandates you violate the law.

Some donor organizations are easy to work with on developing agreements, and understand the realities of working in Wyoming, and some are not. As noted previously, time frames for procedures that are suitable for metropolitan or urban areas, are simply not practical in Wyoming. At other times we have had a problem with donor organizations contacting next of kin before we had had a chance to notify them of the death, which is obviously a terrible way to find out a loved one has died – so we insured that they must verify with our office that notification has been completed before any contact from them, as part of the written MOU. Also, the particular policies of the coroner as to when to allow donation or not on a case under jurisdiction, is up to that coroner. As long as that policy is in writing as a part of overall department policies, that serves as justification required by the Gift Act. For example, to protect chain of custody and evidence, prior to autopsy, I allow no donations from a suspected homicide case. It can be done in conjunction with, or after a forensic autopsy, but not before the forensic pathologist breaks the evidence seal on the body bag. Otherwise, I am left to explain the break in chain of custody and alteration of evidence (the body) in court. Some coroners disagree with this approach, and that is their prerogative, and their responsibility to justify and explain if needed. The Fremont County policy on donations is included in the appendix as a reference.

e. Inter-County: As noted, W.S. 16-1-104 gives counties the ability to create working agreements or MOUs either with another county as a whole, or between different agencies of different counties. This would include arranging an option for one elected service to cover more than one area in an emergency or absence, coordination of search and rescue assets and coverage, change or ceding specific jurisdiction for convenience and access, or other administrative issues. The terrain of Wyoming does not much care for man-made lines in some circumstances, and it just makes more sense either for expedience or necessity to work out some sort of plan. Sometimes these are more informal, such as where one county's search and rescue will cover an area just because they can reach it better, even though the event is across the county line. If it is a more permanent arrangement, then those things should be in the form of a written "joint powers" agreement. One example would be the agreement the various local, county, and state law enforcement agencies have with the tribes for cross-jurisdiction in some instances. Another would be where a smaller county combines coroner coverage with the coroner of another small county.

Part VI: Coroner Agency Policies

Policies and procedures for an individual agency should be a living document, subject to updates, revisions and changes periodically and when needed. Policies that were good in 1950 are not sufficient for today, and policies today will not be sufficient in 2050. In many cases, if you do not have certain policies written and in place, you can get into legal trouble. Without others, it complicates getting consistent performance from staff in the area of investigations if they do not have a framework of reference. Policies are developed through need, and often altered when a particular situation arises that was not previously covered. Parts should also be dropped or revised when no longer applicable. There are many resources available for developing policies, and those of the Coroner's Office of Fremont County are offered only as an example, not as a set requirement. The needs of each county and coroner will be different within the required framework of statutory duties. For example, the basic framework for procedures on investigations draws a lot from [1] *Death Investigation: A Guide for the Scene Investigator,* by the U.S. Department of Justice, Office of Justice Programs, National Institute of Justice. There is no need to reinvent the wheel on a lot of this when other agencies and resources have spent a lot of time and effort in developing standards.

a. Disclaimers and Provisions

Manuals are usually started with employment disclaimers and provisions that are pretty standard as a part of employment law. This sort of "legalese' is similar to all the irritating stickers you find on ATVs, power tools, or other equipment that notify you something could cause injury. In this case, the background is "injury" to the employer from unemployment or other liability claims, usually in an attempt for monetary gain. Governments are seen by the public to have big pockets, although by nature, they are immune to some types of claims that often afflict a private business or employer. Still, in this day and age, a decent disclaimer at the beginning of your manual is recommended by most government attorneys. Here is the beginning of the Fremont Coroner's manual:

THE PREFACE TO THE CORONER'S PROCEDURE MANUAL WILL CONSIST OF ALL WYOMING STATUTES RELATING TO THE CORONER'S OFFICE
Policies Will Also Conform To Those Established By the Wyoming Board of Coroner Standards
Updated August 2017

MISSION STATEMENT:
The primary task of the Coroner's Office is to fulfill the obligations under Wyoming Statutes in investigating and certification of deaths, in a professional and compassionate manner.

Important – Please Note:
This manual is meant to outline the basic policies and procedures for employees of the Fremont County Coroner's Office. Due to the nature of service and situations that may arise in the course of employment, no manual can be all-inclusive for every circumstance. It is required that each employee become familiar with the information contained herein, to enable using good judgment in a situation. If there are questions on the application of policy or procedure in a particular instance, or should any other need arise, it is expected that the employee will contact their immediate supervisor or the Coroner for assistance. The Coroner reserves the right to add to, adjust, interpret, or change any of the contained policies or procedures, at any time, without prior notice. This manual replaces all previous manuals issued, but does not necessarily negate other policies issued separately and not included herein. The effective date is immediate on issue.

Employment with the Fremont County Coroner's Office is At-Will. The employee has the right to end the work relationship with the Coroner's Office, with or without advanced notice, at any time. The Coroner's Office reserves the same right. The language, policies, and procedures outlined in this manual are not intended to constitute a contract of employment, either express or implied, nor are they a guarantee of employment for a specific time. The responsibilities of employment include but are not limited to those outlined in this manual.

An employee of the Fremont County Coroner's Office is subject to, and covered by, all applicable Federal and State of Wyoming Statutes or regulations relevant to employment. In addition, employees certified as deputies under Wyoming Statute are subject to those relevant statutes that refer to coroners or their deputies. It is highly recommended that all employees be familiar with their rights, obligations, and responsibilities under the law.

As employees of Fremont County, deputies and administrative staff are also subject to applicable policies and procedures as established by the County Commission of Fremont County.

Additional Policies Referenced Herein Are On File In The Coroner Office

Commentary: *Note that right off at the beginning, the authority of the manual is stated as being based in statutes and the rules of the Coroner*

Board of Standards. While statutes and rules leave a lot of leeway in how the individual coroner can create and adapt policies for the particular situation, it is a primary obligation of the elected official to insure the department and staff work within the structure of the law. In addition, there is a listed effective date and a note that this version replaces all previous versions, with the loophole of plainly stating that it also is not all inclusive with reference to other resources. This puts the responsibility for the most part on the employee to stay aware, current, and updated on policies and procedures... in other words, "ignorance is no excuse." The "at will" section is usually suggested by attorneys in employment law, as it is the most common status for Wyoming and much of government here. One notable exception would be Peace Officers, like the Sheriff, which have their own specified status that usually includes processes to account for due cause. Among the external references is a notice that employees are also subject to Fremont County Policies, which is a choice on my part and not required. I just think it is fair that if the county is going to pay you, then the rightful policies should apply. This also saves my office from having to come up with all the details on benefits, vacations, sick time, and the other particulars of employment. Mission statements are meant to be a brief notice of the basic reason the job exists and how it is to be performed.

b. General Duties: These sections are a mix of basic clauses defining duties, and other 'legal notices' that the employee must be aware of, many of which are defined and illustrated in more detail later in a manual. While these are principles and applicable to all, they are not considered adequate job descriptions. Those are further documented in detail elsewhere for the different positions within the agency. Most of this is self-explanatory, and in some cases after reviewing the statutes, obvious in their basis. The Fremont Coroner manual portion follows:

A. DUTIES:
In all cases of reportable deaths as defined by this document, the Coroner's Office will:
1. Receive all reports of sudden, unexpected, or unexplained deaths.
2. In the absence of a physician, pronounce death.
3. Provide accurate identification of all human remains when possible.
4. Provide for notification of next of kin of the deceased.
5. Take custody of the body and all articles on or with the body.
6. Take custody of all medication prescribed to, or in possession of the Decedent, if appropriate.
7. Maintain the chain of custody of the body and all articles obtained therefrom.
8. Conduct an investigation following established procedures leading to the determination of the cause and manner of death & issue a written report detailing the investigation.
9. Obtain toxicology samples from the body, maintain the proper chain of custody on those samples.

10. Certify the cause and manner of death; forward written certification to designated agencies upon request.
11. Maintain records of each official death investigation and provide reports to official agencies upon request per established procedures.
12. Properly see to the disposition of human remains through release to family, or designated and authorized entities.
13. Cooperate with authorized agencies having involvement with death investigation.
14. Provide professional, objective testimony in state and local courts of law.
15. Observe and be aware of all Statutes regarding Confidentiality and the Coroner's Office.
16. During all death investigations, the deceased, family members, and all others will be shown compassion and treated with respect.

B. CHAIN OF COMMAND

The Office is set up with the Coroner, Chief Deputy and other staff. The chain of command shall be followed in any matters dealing with issues related to the Coroner's Office. In the absence of the Coroner, the Chief Deputy shall assume the role of Coroner. Other specified staff or consultants may report directly to the Coroner.

C. SEXUAL HARASSMENT & DISCRIMINATION

The Fremont County Coroner's Office shall be free from all sexual harassment and discrimination due to race, color, sex, national origin, religion, disability, or sexual preference. All incidents of harassment shall be filed in writing within three days of the incident, following the chain of command. All incident reports will be forwarded to the Coroner.

D. INTERNSHIPS

The Fremont County Coroner's Office may assist educational institutions in their quest for advanced education. All applicants for Internship must be a high school graduate, a minimum of legal age (18), pass a State & Federal fingerprint background check, and be associated with a college-level field in the Forensic Sciences.

Applications for internship must be made in writing. This application shall include a letter from the institutional supervisor of the educational program, including the minimum number of hours and requirements for credit. The applicant shall complete an employment application from the Fremont County Coroner and submit to a reference check. Fingerprint clearances must be turned in with the application prior to consideration. Note: Internships do not have deputy status and are unpaid. See the application process for details and requirements.

E. WIND RIVER INDIAN RESERVATION

Whenever the Fremont County Coroner has jurisdiction for investigating the death of any Native American individual occurring within the exterior boundaries of the Wind River Reservation, the Coroner's Office shall, to the maximum extent feasible, consider and respect the traditions of any potential party having the right to control the disposition of the remains of the Native American individual, including the Eastern Shoshone Tribe of the Wind River Reservation and the Arapaho Tribe of the Wind River Reservation. Death investigation on the Wind River Reservation involves Federal, State, and local agencies, and the Coroner's Office shall integrate its investigation with all involved agencies. Also, the Office of the Coroner is governed by, as appropriate, Federal and/or tribal law while conducting the death investigation of a Native American on the Wind River Reservation. Subject to any procedural or substantive right which may otherwise be secured to any individual or Indian tribe, the disposition of the remains of the Native American individual shall be subject to the applicable provisions of the Native American Graves Protection and Repatriation Act [2] (NAGPRA; 25 U.S.C. 3001-3013 (2016)) and its implementing regulations (43 C.F.R. Part 10 (2017)). See Appendix A, Section L.: Native American Human Remains. The Fremont County Coroner's Office shall respect and honor Native American culture and tradition, and this shall include the respect of sacred objects.

F. DISCIPLINE

All violations of the procedure manual may be subject to disciplinary action up to and including termination. All disciplinary matters shall follow the chain of command and be referred to the Coroner. The determination of any disciplinary action rests with the Coroner. An investigation shall be conducted with notification made to the employee involved when completed.

The use of drugs or alcohol by the Coroner's Investigator or employee while responding to a call or in any official duty capacity is expressly prohibited, and complaints of intoxicated behavior may be grounds for dismissal. Any conviction of a DUI, even while on personal time, may be grounds for dismissal.

G. CONFIDENTIALITY

All aspects of the Office of the Fremont County Coroner are confidential and subject to specific statutes. Failure to observe confidentiality may result in disciplinary action, termination, or legal procedure, depending on the circumstances.

H. NEWS RELEASES

All news releases or information given directly to the media will be done by the Coroner. In his absence, or in conjunction with other agencies involved in incident management, the Coroner may select a designee to act as a public information officer. News releases are also subject to all applicable State Statutes and Federal Law, and legal process. The release of docket copies as required by law may be completed on request from media sources, by Coroner staff, with the approval of the Coroner. The policies of news releases and confidentiality also apply to any commentary via the various forms of on-line 'social media' available, especially in regards to cases or case information.

I. RELEASE OF INFORMATION

All request for reports and/or information shall be submitted in writing to the Coroner. The requests will conform to the policies and procedures as established by the coroner's office and W.S. 7-4-105, as noted elsewhere in this manual.

While aspects of coroner's reports or case files are legally considered public information, medical information and files are protected by Federal Law, and secondary release is severely restricted to those agencies, individuals, or firms having the specific right to receive them.

All public questions regarding Coroner policies and procedures, or County policies as they apply to this Office, are to be referred to the Coroner. The Coroner or his designee will respond as appropriate to insure a consistent representation of policies and procedures to the public.

c. Internal Policies and Procedures: The full current policy and procedure manual is available from our office on request, if interested or for reference. These are not my documents (although I created most of them), but are part of the coroner's office, and as such, are public record and also belong to Fremont County and the State of Wyoming. To be sure, some of it is applicable only here in Fremont, but the basics of what should be included in any medical-legal procedure manual pretty much are applicable to any jurisdiction. The general areas that should be covered are as follows:

Reporting deaths: Jurisdictions, and the various areas or different basic jurisdictions that will be encountered in Wyoming; assorted other agencies that require notification in certain circumstances, such as consumer or occupational safety, social services, active armed forces personnel, etc.; state and government facilities; various housing or health care facilities. This includes what we need to report, and what is to be reported to the coroner.

Investigations: Pronouncement of death; processing the scene, including basic, criminal, and non-criminal; chain of custody; notification of next of kin; special investigations, such as archaeological finds or exhumations, hazardous or infectious circumstances, documentation of the scene, and transport or disposition of remains. Disaster and mass fatality cases may need their own section depending on your procedures.

Examination: Principles of external examination; determination for autopsy; obtaining toxicology; evidence collection. The requirements, principles, and standards for proper identification should be included or have its own section.

Certification and Burials: Obligations to the State and process; presumptive deaths; indigent and unclaimed cases; release of remains; family and home burials; other special circumstances.

Property: Inventories and documentation; chain of custody; evidence processing and storage; authorized release circumstances; property and evidence disposal.

Offices, Facilities, and Personnel: Coroners will have some unique aspects to this area that are not common to any other elected official. The procedures and policies you determine for each facility should be outlined, for example, if you have a morgue. We consider all facilities to be secure and restricted, with most, other than the office where the public is allowed, only accessible to staff or specific exceptions. This is especially important in the storage of case files, due to the confidentiality of the materials. Communications, both with the public or media, as well as internal response or availability, should be addressed. The use of vehicles and equipment is covered, including response protocols such as lights and sirens. There should be a training policy, noting what the department is responsible for, and the employee obligation to maintain certifications. These days, the use of computer systems within the department is an important subject, not only for appropriate usage, but also to protect the data. The Fremont Coroner's office has a uniform policy that is not specific, but framed in terms of being appropriate for the job being done. In addition, we list what we provide, required identifying items such as badges, coats or vests, and define what the county will pay for or replace.

That point is needed if you are going to submit a bill to the commission as a necessary expense.

Detailed job descriptions are a must, as are the parameters of availability for duty. Forms, reports, and documentation standards, whether paper or digital, should be noted. While a lot of other areas are covered within the generic policies of the county, any additions, exceptions, or diversions from that policy must be specifically addressed. In terms of employment law, if it is not in writing, it does not exist, and if the employee has not signed off on receipt of the manuals or policies, you cannot verify that they applied.

Part VII: Inquest Policies and Procedures

Since the process of an inquest is part of the unique capacity of a coroner under the law, the subject deserves some special attention and mention in this text. Inquests are sometimes referred to as [1]"soft adjudication", in that they are a public fact-finding quasi-judicial process to determine manner and cause of death, and involve a jury, but are not the adversarial process encountered in the regular court system. Attorneys can be present to represent their clients if subpoenaed as a witness but cannot cross-examine or engage in the proceedings directly. The coroner, or who he selects as a presenter, gives the jury all the available information and evidence in a case regarding cause and manner for their consideration. This presentation is an inquisatory process and does not prove guilt or innocence like a regular court, but the decisions of an inquest jury can have implications for subsequent proceedings. One reference in that regard would be [2] *Maki v. State, 18 Wyo. 481, 112 P. 334, 1911 Wyo. LEXIS 30 (Wyo.1911)* where, if at a coroner's inquest, defendant before testifying was advised of his rights and duly cautioned, his testimony thereafter given voluntarily is admissible against him.

While there can be no hard and fast rules as to when an inquest is required or necessary, there are numerous areas where an inquest is highly recommended or indicated as beneficial:
    A. Generally, in any case where the public airing of evidence and information is highly beneficial to public health and safety, especially in the absence of any other public venue of inquiry, an inquest should be considered.
    B. Any officer involved shooting that results in a death should have an inquest. Recent national cases and several Wyoming incidents show the importance of a public airing of circumstances. (In Montana coroner statutes, an inquest is required in these cases.)

C. Any "in-custody" death under W.S. §7-4-104(a)(i)(G) might be considered. An exception would be any obvious anticipated natural death of a total non-suspicious nature that may occur at a facility from a long-term medical condition.
D. Any death that is questionable or difficult to differentiate between two or more Manners.
E. Any death that is tending towards 'Undetermined'.
F. Any death where the acquisition of evidence by subpoena, or testimony under oath, is necessary for the completion of the investigation and a determination of manner or cause.

While the inquest does not adjudicate or officially assign blame, it can comment on and reveal accountability in a general sense in regard to individuals, organizations, businesses, government bodies, or public policy if relevant and in the public interest concerning a death. It is a significant tool in the coroner's arsenal of independent investigation on behalf of society.

Inquests used to be the main tool for an investigation, and were more common before the advent of investigators and detectives in law enforcement. These days, proper and thorough medical-legal death investigation as a standard usually covers the need. Since each coroner's case will have its own unique and individual aspects, the convening of an inquest should always be under consideration – however, in a majority of circumstances based on the types of cases that occur in counties, most cases will not usually warrant a formal inquest to be resolved or completed.

To understand some of the framework and process for an inquest, the following example of procedures is presented:

Procedures and Checklist for an Inquest

A. Investigations and information:
1. Completion of the Coroner Investigation – while the final report will either include a summary or supplemental report describing the results of the Inquest, all aspects of scene investigation should be in written form for presentation as evidence to the Inquest jury. This would include such things as:
   a. Receipt of toxicology report
   b. Receipt of autopsy report if performed
   c. Collection of medical records if applicable

  d. Any other information that is the Coroner's responsibility to include under the Standards
 2. Other Agency Investigations – In the same manner, other agency reports such as those from involved law enforcement may not be completed until the final Inquest/Coroner investigation is completed, but their investigations should be at a stage where adequate testimony and information can be obtained.
 3. The very fact that an Inquest is needed implies that more information is needed in the case in order to determine Manner and Cause; or that the case is of the type that warrants an Inquest Jury decision, or public presentation of the evidence and facts as known. New information, evidence, or facts may be obtained during the Inquest, but investigations must be at least at a stage where the Jury will have the adequate information to reach a conclusion.

B. Associated Agencies:
 1. The Coroner does not need approval or permission from any other agency or official to hold an Inquest if he feels one is needed, however, since other agencies will be involved, it is recommended that they be notified and the process discussed, as cooperation is vital for successful completion. This would include:
  a. Local, County, or Federal law enforcement
  b. County or U.S. Attorney's Offices
  c. Any other applicable Agency, such as BLM, USFS, NTSB, etc.

C. Preliminaries:
 1. <u>Notify the next-of-kin of the deceased of the intention to hold an Inquest, as in most cases they will want to be present</u>. Discuss the process and emphasize that <u>all</u> evidence will be presented, including much that will be graphic or upsetting. Local victim-witness staff may be a good resource to acquire to assist them through the process.
 2. Select and reserve a location – the amount of time needed for a location will depend on the type and complexity of the case, and the amount of evidence and testimony to be presented. Keep in mind that once the Jury has heard the presentation, it should have the opportunity to request more information, or recall witnesses, which may require a reconvening of the inquest the next day or at a later date. The amount of time they will need to deliberate on a decision is also a variable.
 3. Select the date and time to start

4. Obtain a court reporter for the proceedings, or arrange adequate recording equipment and a transcriptionist. Local court resources may assist with this or provide direction. If a court reporter is used, make sure the agreement includes the transcription and copies.

5. Arrange security if needed, or personnel to serve as a 'bailiff' to direct witnesses and monitor the proceedings for protocol compliance from the public, and assist in "traffic control". Local law enforcement may be able to assist with this.

6. Plan for any technical equipment needed for the presentation of evidence. Keep in mind that all evidence that is normally confidential under the law becomes public in an Inquest. Ideally, for such evidence as photos, equipment that provides detailed viewing to the witness and jury without full display to the gallery is preferable.

7. Prepare a Media Release for notification of the Inquest, location, date and time. This is a public process. With the release, it would be advisable to inform the media of the protocols for the proceedings and any restrictions imposed.

D. Subpoenas:

1. Select three Jurors and give written notice for the record. It would be recommended to have a mix of gender and race if applicable, and if the case involves considerable technical information such as in the case of a work or industrial incident, perhaps at least one juror who is familiar with the field without being unduly connected to it. Prospective jurors should also be questioned to make sure they have no relation to the deceased or those involved, or undue pre-opinions in the matter. In civil or criminal procedures, the adversarial jury selection process is geared to promote an unbiased and wide demographics for juries – in an Inquest, it is the responsibility of the Coroner to do so in jury selection, a task that must be taken very seriously. While the law gives a juror no choice on service if selected, it serves to be as cooperative as possible with a person's work or personal lives in order to avoid resentment on the part of the jurors. Also, per W.S. §7-4-202, should any juror fail to appear, the Coroner can immediately select a juror or jurors from the immediate bystanders and impanel them on the spot. [NOTE: In the past, jurors were selected and sworn in over the body, required to inspect it, and in some very old cases, even assist in recovery of the remains, but this is no longer a legal requirement. However, this is also not prohibited, and in some circumstances it may be helpful for the jury to view the body, if selection is done while it's available.]

2. Prepare a list of witnesses that will be required to testify. Issue and deliver Subpoenas to all witnesses. Local law enforcement may have a process for this that can be used to assist and deliver at standard fees.

3. Note: Subpoenas for witnesses or evidence, and juror summons, for any resident of the Wind River Reservation and within that jurisdiction, must be presented to the Shoshone and Arapaho Tribal Court in Ft. Washakie for consideration, as part of a cooperative agreement between the County and Reservation. If approved for that jurisdiction, the Tribal Court will direct service of the papers through Tribal Agencies. Time frames for completion are variable, so that must be taken into consideration when scheduling the Inquest.

E. Preparations:
1. Draw up a list of questions for each of the witnesses on the list.
    a. Keep in mind that the list will be a basic template – other questions may become applicable depending on the response and testimony.
    b. Jurors are allowed to, and may ask questions of a witness in the proceedings. It is up to the presiding Coroner to decide the process, whether a juror may indicate he has a question during the testimony, or have them hold them until the end of the testimony.
    c. If a witness has an attorney present, that attorney may submit questions in writing he would like the Coroner to address to his client, but the Coroner only has to consider them, not necessarily ask them. It is up to the Coroner to decide the process, but our office notifies the witness of that right along with the subpoenas issued. The attorney is not to ask the questions himself, address any other witness or testimony, or participate in the proceedings in any other manner.
2. Prepare all evidence to be submitted in whatever form will be needed to present to the jury. Evidence should be listed and marked as "Exhibit A., Exhibit B, etc." or some other form of organization for the official record. Since the Inquest is not a legal criminal or civil proceeding, there are no standard 'rules' or limitations on what may be introduced as evidence. It is up to the Coroner to introduce anything that is applicable, and the jury to decide relevance.
3. Confirm that all needs listed in items 'C' and 'D' above have been completed.

4. Location: Be familiar with the location for the proceedings and have all presentations available and pre-tested for working order.
    a. Be sure to check recording capability and quality if not using an actual court reporter. If using a court reporter, they usually have their own equipment for that function.
    b. In the room for proceedings, a separate area should be set up for the Jury well away from any attending public, position and seating for the witness, and position for the presiding Coroner. They will also need a separate and secluded area for deliberations.
    c. While in the past record, often all Inquest witnesses were sworn at once and/or seated together in the audience as the proceedings progressed, this is <u>not</u> a recommended option. Witnesses should have a location provided to wait to be called, that is away from the proceedings and public to avoid what is known in legal circles as "reversible error". In criminal trials, a witness cannot attend the proceedings with the idea that while still telling the truth (or not), prior testimony can influence, alter, or cause adjustments in the statements made in their own testimony. Logically this is also a good idea for an Inquest in order to keep the testimony as objective as possible.

F. Proceedings – Day of the Inquest:

1. Make sure all jurors, witnesses, staff, and other participants are present and ready.
2. Make sure all equipment, evidence, and presentations are available and functioning.
3. Convene the Inquest and Call to Order.
    a. Note officially any missing persons who were Subpoenaed, and if necessary, compel attendance. (How to handle this possibility should have been pre-arranged with law enforcement, usually the Sheriff's Office as a County Agency). For the record, name and cite the person for contempt under W.S. §1-21-901 to 909.
    b. If a juror or jurors have not appeared, select and empanel the necessary number from the citizens present.
    c. Identify and swear in the jurors for the record by the Oath prescribed by statute.
4. Coroner's introductory statements for the record.
    a. "I,(name), Coroner for (name) County in the State of Wyoming, having duly summoned and sworn this jury, convene this Inquest to diligently inquire and true

presentment make, when, how and by what means, a certain person whose dead body was found on the (number) day of (month), (year), came to their death."

b. Note general instructions for those present as attendees (these options are at your discretion for procedure):

    1. All cell phones or other recording devices must remain off.

    2. No questions, comments, or disruptions are allowed from the public.

    3. Note this is not a civil or criminal litigation but an inquiry.

    4. Note that by the very nature of the subject, information and evidence will be presented that is necessarily disturbing or graphic. There is no intent to upset, embarrass, or target any member of the public or those in attendance, but the nature of an Inquest demands that all the evidence and testimony be presented to the jury in its entirety.

    5. Note that while normally confidential material will be presented in the course of an inquest, the proceedings and resulting transcript will be part of the Public Record, available from the Clerk of District Court, once filed. The media can request that transcript from the Clerk of District Court once filed, but no partial transcripts or statements will be released officially prior to that, other than the jury's final findings.

c. Note general instructions to the Jury:

    1. Their task is to listen to and observe the evidence presented and testimony given, in order to come to a decision confirming the identity of the deceased, and the manner and cause of which they died. They are not required to determine the guilt or innocence, or the involvement of any other persons in the death, but may comment in their ruling on the involvement of a person or persons if directly related to the manner and cause of the death.

    2. Jurors may take notes during the proceedings.

    3. Jurors may ask questions to the witnesses, or about the evidence presented.

    4. Inform the Jurors how to ask a question during the testimony or presentation. Whether during the

testimony they simply raise a hand, or reserve questions until the end of the particular testimony, identify them for the record and then have them address the question.

5. During any recess or break in the proceedings, jurors may discuss this case among themselves, but should refrain from any contact or conversation with witnesses, the media, or general public regarding the case.

6. While witnesses are required under Subpoena to attend this Inquest, they retain their Constitutional rights and may refuse on those grounds to answer any questions, from either this Inquisition, or the Jury.

7. At the end of the presentations and proceedings, the Jury does have the right to recall a witness, re-examine evidence, or request if more information on the case is available in any particular area.

8. Note to the jury that all evidence, report copies, etc., are not to be removed from the Inquest location, or shared outside of the jury.

9. Does the Jury have any questions on procedure? If not move to the first witness.

5. Witness procedures:
    a. Call the witnesses in the order planned if possible.
    b. Have the Witness state their name, then swear in for the record by the Oath prescribed by statute.
    NOTE: All witnesses should be advised of their rights and duly cautioned that they may refuse to testify under the U.S. and Wyoming Constitutions, and they may have an attorney present, to advise them regarding testimony.
    c. Have the witness restate name and give age, occupation, and place of residence.
    d. Have the witness give technical or professional qualifications if appropriate.
    e. Does the witness understand the Oath, obligation to tell the truth, and their rights as indicated?
    f. Establish the witness's relationship to the case or the deceased.
    g. Establish if the witness knows or can identify the deceased.

h. Proceed with questions specific to the case and witness. [NOTE: the idea of "hearsay" and other rules of evidence from a criminal or civil litigation do not apply in an Inquest. A witness can testify to another's conversation or statements, or what they were told by others.]

i. Once initial testimony is complete, if an attorney for this witness has submitted questions, the Coroner should identify the attorney for the record and rule if the questions are relevant to the case or not, and then ask those questions. In some cases such questions may have already been covered by testimony.

j. The Coroner should then address the jury for any further questions, making sure the individual Juror is identified for the record.

k. Once finished with the witness, they should be excused but be told that the Subpoena is still in effect until the end of the proceedings in case the Jury wishes to recall them later. Witnesses should not be allowed to remain to view the rest of the proceedings if subject to recall.

6. Evidence procedures:

a. In many cases, evidence and exhibits will be presented in conjunction with a witness, who will describe or explain items, photos, or other documentation to the Jury during testimony. This will be noted as to listing and submission (Item #1, Exhibit A, etc.) for the record, and the Jury may examine such evidence or ask any questions about it, in any manner they feel necessary. The Coroner should keep in mind caution, however, for any items that may be significant for later proceedings, or may involve hazards. Actual physical evidence that could be used in later criminal proceedings should be view by photograph rather than handled to protect the chain of custody – in most circumstances this will be adequate when considering manner and cause of death.

b. After witness testimony, it may be necessary for the Coroner to introduce additional available evidence if needed. This may include additional photography, reports, records, studies, or other documentation relevant to the case. Medical records, for example, may be summarized for the record, then copies of the entire record given to the Jury for consideration. It is not required that those that prepare a report, such as an autopsy, be present to testify in person. In the case of an autopsy report, a good summation would be to read the 'face' summary to the Jury, and then submit the entire report to them as evidence.

c. In the case of an autopsy, it should be noted that the pathologist comes to his conclusion based on his physical findings, and case information known <u>at the time</u>. It is the jury that makes a conclusion based on the total evidence of the investigation, and they may disagree with the conclusion of manner by the pathologist.

d. Again, the "rules of evidence" for civil or criminal litigation do not apply, and the Coroner can introduce anything he feels is appropriate that would assist the Jury in the case. The Coroner can also issue subpoenas for evidence and additional witnesses at any time if needed.

7. Summation:

a. Once all the evidence and testimony has been presented, the Coroner should inquire of the Jury if they have any questions about the evidence, need any witnesses recalled for further testimony or clarification, or need any particular information that was not presented. Note: there is no requirement that the Inquest be completed in any particular time frame. If there is more information needed, a recess for any time frame may be called until it is obtained. Prior to any recess, remind the jury of the admonitions noted in #F.4.c.5. regarding discussions with others.

b. If no further testimony is needed by the Jury, all witnesses should be released from their Subpoenas.

c. Instructions to the Jury: Comments as to wording and form on the Ruling/Official document.

d. Instructions as to the meaning of "Cause of Death" – basically the 'medical' process that led to death, as indicated on #24 of the Vital Records Certificate, Parts I. & II. Explain that the listing can be several 'due to' items with contributing factors.

e. Instructions as to "Manner of Death", as indicated on #29 of the Vital Records Certificate:

1. Natural: exclusively a medical reason for death with no other cause or factors.

2. Accident: a non-natural cause or event that precipitated death without planning, anticipation, or intent.

3. Suicide: self-inflicted, intentional act on the part of the deceased that caused or led to the death.
4. Homicide: in these circumstances, 'homicide' is a neutral term in that simply, one person killed another. The legal criminal considerations of 'degree' or 'intent', or 'premeditation', etc., do not apply. However, it can be considered in any case where another person's 'intentional act', violation of the law, or negligence resulted in a person's death, whether that act was directed towards a particular person or not.
5. Could Not Be Determined: Either there is no clear single Manner indicated by the evidence, or, the evidence could indicate more than one Manner without defining it to a single Manner within a reasonable doubt.

f. Note to the jury that time frame between a causative act and a death, does not matter in terms of Manner of Death.

g. Note to the Jury that they are only required to come to a decision on the Manner and Cause of Death. It is not required, <u>but not prohibited</u>, that they comment on other persons involved, mitigating factors, or other elements of the death that may involve public health and safety.

h. Note to the Jury that at any time during deliberations, they may request to consult with the Coroner on matters of evidence or clarification.

8. Jury recessed for deliberations. The Jury may elect a Foreman if they feel it necessary.
9. Inquest reconvenes for the Jury return of decision and Verdict, which is read aloud for the record.
10. Jury completes and signs official verdict form (W.S. §7-4-205).
11. Jury is thanked for their participation and the Inquest is adjourned.

G. Coroner completion of Obligations:

1. Transcript of proceedings produced and verified for accuracy.
2. Per W.S. §7-4-206, the Coroner files the record and transcript of the proceedings with the Clerk of District Court. This includes the signed official Verdict form, list of evidence and witnesses, transcript and other material testimony.

3. The Coroner prepares receipts, invoices, and vouchers to be submitted to the Board of County Commissioners for payment of recording and transcribing the proceedings, Juror compensation, witness fees if applicable, reimbursement for other agency assistance, any other costs (W.S. §7-4-201(c), (e); §7-4-203; §7-4-204).

4. While the Inquest transcript is public record once turned into the Clerk of District Court, it may be advisable to issue a media release on the decision once the Inquest is completed.

Supplemental Note:

In 2019, we had an officer involved shooting in Fremont County that involved the Federal Bureau of Alcohol, Tobacco, Firearms, and Explosives (commonly known as 'ATF'), within the jurisdiction of a local police department. The incident occurred in January, with the inquest held in April – this gives an idea of the time frames involved in completing an investigation to a point where enough evidence can be presented to an inquest jury. An "officer involved" will probably be one of the most complicated inquests to do, and several factors in this case made it even more complex.

It is important to remember that by several national surveys, depending on location, "officer involved shootings" can be a manner of 'officer assisted suicide' in 10 to 20% of the cases. So the manner of death can be in question, a main reason to do a public inquest. Also, despite public perceptions, in a majority of these cases the officers are justified in their actions, but to not publically demonstrate that, invokes perceptions of a cover-up and bias. So this generally benefits the officers.

First complication here, is the involvement of Federal agents. While local law enforcement supported the policy of an inquest in this case completely, the ATF was, to put it mildly, "difficult". Dealings were through the agency counsel, with the expected legal maneuvering. The Department of Justice regulations under 28 C.F.R. § 16.21 *et seq.* govern response to subpoenas, a majority of which require the agency to be a "material party" to the incident. Since the ATF agents fired the fatal shots, that point could have been argued successfully from our justification for subpoenas.

The ATF counsel, after arguing numerous legal citations in correspondence (many of which did not apply or could have been probably refuted before a judge), cited the "sovereign immunity of the United

States" in providing documentation or having its agents appear. Personally, I think any time a Federal agency comes in and applies lethal force on a citizen, they should have to account for their actions, but to force the issue would have involved a long legal battle in the courts. As it was, with local and State agency investigations, our own, and a key citizen witness that was tracked down, we proceeded in spite of the Federal lack of cooperation. The lack of Federal cooperation and their reasons were noted to the jury during the proceedings, and they decided they had enough information for a conclusion and ruling. They could have gone the other way, however.

Second, the local county attorney publically stated his opinion that the shooting was justified and no charges would be filed, shortly after the event, before an autopsy had even been completed, or the lead investigating agency (Wyoming DCI) had completed its investigation. While the authority to decide on charges is the county attorney's jurisdiction, and not the coroner's or inquest jury's, that is not the purpose for having an inquest, especially in this sort of case – and to rule before all the evidence is in, showed bias that was not necessarily unexpected. He also tried to argue that he should run the inquest, citing W.S. 9-1-804, which in part (a)(v) gives the county attorney authority to "appear at all inquests held by any coroner in his district". My response was that he can "appear" as or on the behalf of any witness, but that statute does not give him the authority to run the inquest any more than the authority to "appear" in (iv) preliminary hearings, or (vi) grand jury, or (i) act as prosecutor, in the same statute, gives him the right to the role of a judge/administrator of the proceedings. In the "plain and ordinary meaning" of the word, "appear", does not mean "run". The whole idea runs counter to the principles of an independent inquest anyway. The Wyoming Supreme Court decision, cited elsewhere in the text, quite clearly establishes the independence of an inquest from the regular judicial system, of which he is a part.

Third, we found it beneficial to have a conference after the inquest with the family of the deceased, to get their input on how they felt about the proceeding and address any further questions. In this case, the opinion was that they felt the open and public presentation resolved the questions they had, and had eliminated the feeling of a "cover-up" by authorities, regardless of the jury ruling that the shoot was justified. The advantage of that from an inquest can be seen in all the myriad complications that have followed other similar incidents elsewhere, where an inquest was not done. But from the above, you can see that the complications that pop up can be many and surprising.

Part VIII: County Attorney and other Legal Opinions

As I have noted at several points along the way, opinions by the County Attorney or the Wyoming Attorney General, are just that, opinions. While they give a certain authority to back up interpretations of the law in the performance of your duties, they can change with administrations, or be overruled by the courts and case law. The court opinions themselves stand on firmer ground, but also can change over time through the evolution of interpretation as court personnel change. And even U.S. court opinions and rulings can change, which is obvious to anyone who is familiar with the history of the United States. The law is not set in stone, but an evolving process, as the needs and priorities of the social system alter over time.

In this last section, some examples of various opinions are presented as examples of where legal counsel from the county, state, or courts has clarified specific situations. Some may seem trivial, but there is nothing trivial about not seeking a backup opinion and proceeding with an action that has repercussions on you personally or as an elected official later. It never hurts to ask. Also keep in mind that at each level, opinions may vary from county to county, or state to state, depending on the situation or person involved. As an example, I know of some county attorneys that disdain the process of an inquest as antiquated and not useful. My opinion is that just because something is old does not mean it is ineffective, and in that case they probably do not understand or appreciate the independent value of the office of the coroner in death investigations. While we may be involved in certain aspects, prosecution of a party is not our responsibility – we work for justice for society as a whole and the deceased, in that the death is accurately worked for manner and cause.

a. Review of all MOUs and agreements: One of the basic functions of the County Attorney is to legally represent the county as a whole and the individual elected officials. In this capacity, they should review any agreement you are making on behalf of the department individually, not only to verify them as to proper form, but to make sure you avoid creating legal issues for yourself or the liability for the county itself. Their opinion in this area may not eliminate or avoid contested issues, but can minimize any fallout and create familiarity with the issue should problems occur later. Remember, words and their selection are everything in these sort of documents, and the wrong word or phrase can either at best cause you great inconvenience, or at worst a legal conflict with statutes.

      b. Policy Reviews: The same would apply for policies you develop, especially in any area of employment or administration. We even run such things as termination letters through the Clerk, who functions as an HR department here, and the county civil attorney, to check wording in the text. The County Attorney's Office will be the one representing you in any employee versus employer issues. They also have the resources and knowledge to ferret out precedence for an issue within the complex volumes of case law, and how it relates to other state or Federal regulations. Just having a policy is not enough – it needs to mesh well within the laws and regulations you are subject to or it is invalid. Again, good written policies can save a lot of headaches and complications as an elected official.

      c. Confidentiality: Besides reviewing policies and procedures you devise for dealing with requests for records under coroner statute W.S. 7-4-105, the County Attorney is also your representative and "enforcer" when you encounter difficulties obtaining records as allowed by law. A good deal of kickback is eliminated by quoting the state and federal regulations on your request form as plain justification to obtain things like medical records. An example of some interesting wrinkles can be given here, however. Department of Family Services presented several issues that were resolved with the assistance of the county civil attorney.

First, in Fremont County, a previous coroner had years ago initiated a child fatality review team, that included assorted relevant agencies and interested member of the public. While a laudable effort, once the 2011 confidentiality statutes had been passed, as Chief Deputy I questioned sharing the confidential files in those meetings (especially with the public present). The coroner at that time decided on his own to continue that format, without any check on legal backing, something I totally disagreed with. Once I was elected coroner in my own right, I consulted the county attorney for an opinion, just to be sure. The result was that especially with the public present, that sharing was clearly illegal under the new statute, at least without some reconstitution of the group to exclude the public and a written/signed restricted use agreement for other agencies.

Second, an issue came up when I requested DFS records in a double homicide/suicide case. Over past history this had not been an issue, but things change with different personnel and administrations. DFS refused to turn over records in this particular case, so I consulted the county civil attorney, and she wrote a letter to DFS outlining our side of the argument. DFS in turn consulted the State Attorney General, who had the opinion that we were only entitled to medical and psychological data, not sociological or benefits data (in spite of the "Any other reasonable procedure which may be necessary..." provision of W.S. 7-4-201(b)(v)...); and we did not meet the definition of law enforcement; *and we were not specifically listed in the DFS statutes as authorized to be a receiving party.* Rather than instigate a time-consuming legal argument in a court setting, DFS and the County worked a compromise that enabled both to do our jobs without upsetting the attorneys, or violate the law.

The same issues came up in a request for records from the State child death review and prevention team on cases that did not involve abuse or neglect. This team had also been in existence from before the 2011 statute change, and had been used to getting whatever records they wanted as previously all coroner records were public documents. Due to the DFS's own statutes, there were no clear regulations on how this team was set up, and could not be considered law enforcement, county attorney, or an actual protective agency under the statutes. *Nor were they specifically listed as a group authorized to receive the confidential record under coroner statutes.* Nor were they included under the other DFS statutes regarding child deaths that involved abuse or neglect (W.S. 14-3-207) in which the coroner is required to submit records to DFS. Federal law encouraged the creation of such teams, but left the set up to the states. California had passed legislation to specifically address records access for these teams, but Wyoming never has up to this point, thus the legal limbo. So, short of some sort of legislative alteration of the law, the coroner can only provide the team with the public docket if there is no suspected abuse or neglect. DFS itself can obtain the records under the law, but technically they are not to secondary release them either, which works at cross-purposes to the intent of the team. The option remains that the team could obtain them by court order, but as of this time, that venue has not been used, and it is unknown how they currently are working the issue. Keep in mind that cases that involve death, abuse, and neglect are covered, but these teams generally are set up to review all child deaths, and most coroner child cases, fortunately, do not involve that drastic setting. At this time an unresolved conundrum for them due to the inadequacy of statutory detail, not their efforts

This area shows the confusion sometimes over the literal interpretation, and intent of the law; and that in many cases, the legislature, being human, fails to cover or consider all the various implications or inter-workings of crafting statutes. There are people specifically hired (the Legislative Services Office) who have a main job of trying to consider all those issues, but just due to statutory complexity, some things will inevitably be missed.

d. Personnel File Access: Historically, previous coroners allowed current and former employees unlimited access to their own personnel files, which by current county attorney opinion was incorrect. It is the position of the county that such files are the property of the county, and not the employee. The policy in Fremont is that all such requests are required in writing, and forwarded to the county attorney for response, treating it as a request under the Public Records Act. Notably most aspects of personnel files are *not* public records, per W.S. 16-4-203, which has a detailed and lengthy listing to go by, and specifically addressed in item (d)(iii) in that statute. The statute also notes that the grounds for refusal must be included in the response. Federal law prohibits the release of any health information on an employee under HIPAA on top of that, and both state and Federal regulations require that personnel files be only assessable to "the duly elected and appointed officials who supervise the work of the person in interest". In the case of the Fremont Coroner, that would be the coroner and chief deputy, who also functions as administrator by job description. In order to ensure compliance, such files should be in a separate locked cabinet with limited keys. This is a very appropriate area to let the county attorney handle, as the law specifies time frames and requirements for a response.

e. Film Production and Name Permissions: This is one of the more amusing instances that have occurred. A Hollywood production company wanted to use the name and logo of the Fremont County Coroner in a film being made, and sent me a "Materials Release Agreement" in that regard. I had absolutely no idea what to do in this case, so asked the county attorney's office for an opinion. The response was that as an elected official I was in charge of the logo, equipment, and property of the department, and it was up to me to decide if we were to charge a fee. The attorney did require the company delete one indemnifying clause, as we are constitutionally prohibited from indemnifying another party. She also noted we could insist on another deletion, that of releasing the company from any claims of how the material is used in reference to libel or slander, negative publicity, etc., depending on how much we trust them, since we otherwise give up any say in how it is used. It was noted that if they have an "evil coroner" then that's our logo used in that connection. As a fee, I required a copy of the script, which they dutifully sent. I read it, no evil coroner, although the forensics in the movie were a bit silly. That in and of itself was not uncommon in movies or TV these days, so I gave permission.

f. Records Release to a Private Investigator: Another interesting instance of records release was when a family, who were dissatisfied with the conclusions of a suicide investigation by our office and the Sheriff's office, hired a private medical-legal investigator to review the case. Since such an agent is not listed in the authorized person's or agencies able to receive the confidential records by statute, I consulted the county attorney. As it turns out, if such a person has the proper legal paperwork assigning them as agent, and adequate medical and investigative release forms, then they can receive copies of the case files as that agent, the same as the statutorily listed family member. Since there are penalties on the coroner for any unauthorized release, it is always good to ask in such cases, and keep such paperwork on file. For a general application, the same assignment of agent may apply in other circumstances.

g. Release of Records from before the 2011 Confidentiality Statutes: Since the coroner's office frequently receives requests for older records out of the 8,000 or so case files we have going back to 1885, we needed to know just how the 2011 law pertained to those older records. In many cases, the *ex post facto* principle refers to criminal law and not civil or administrative law. The idea that you cannot pass a criminal law that affects previous cases goes back to [1] *Calder v. Bull, Supreme Court of the United States, 1798*, in which Justice Samuel Chase specifically stated this did not refer to civil law. The [2] *Wyoming Constitution, Article 1, Section 35 "Ex post facto laws: Impairing obligations of contracts"*, only applies to contractual agreements. While not a criminal or contractual statute, some civil cases had been decided to fall under *ex post facto*, although only a small number. So where does that leave us? Time to clarify. Per the county civil attorney, such retroactive application is generally not favored [3] *(Johnson v. Safeway Stores, Inc., 568 P.2d 908, 914, (Wyo. 1977))* and if a law is to be retroactive, it must show clear legislative intent [4] *(Mestas v. Diamond Coal & Coke Co., 12 Wyo.414, 76 P. 567, 569 (1904))*. The only exception would be if to do otherwise would result in a "manifest injustice". As a procedural statute without any specified retroactive language built into the law when passed by the legislature, the coroner would not have to produce a docket for all previous files (whew!).

However, in the opinion, the courts would probably use the definition of public records at the time the request was made, not when the file was made, so it is recommended the coroner follow the set procedures established after 2011, regardless of the age of the file. Again, remember that regardless of current law, inquests are public record, so in any case, a request for an old inquest could be filled, or referred to the Clerk of District Court as custodian of record, or the Wyoming State Archives.

h. Release of the Body in a Criminal Case: In [5]*Lopez v. State, 2004 WY 28, 86 P.3d 851*, a second-degree murder conviction appeal to the Wyoming Supreme Court, the defense argued the question *"Were the defendant's rights to due process and a fair trial prejudiced by the coroner's intentional destruction of [the victim's] body?"*. The State rephrased the question as *"Did the coroner's release of the victim's body deprive appellant of his right to a fair trial?"* This was among numerous other questions on the appeal, but this is the one of direct concern to our interests. The Wyoming Supreme Court noted in their ruling on the question:

"[41] Lopez contends that by not notifying defendant or his attorney that the State intended to release the body to relatives, the State acted with bad faith. Lopez provides us with no authority that the coroner or the State had this duty. Our study suggests that Lopez was charged with the responsibility of timely requesting retention of the body for an independent examination; however, we do not decide the issue. *Michael J. Yaworsky, J.D., Annotation, Homicide: Cremation of Victim's Body as Violation of Accused's Rights, 70 A.L.R.4th 1091 (1989).* A body is a unique type of evidence because it is subject to decay and not easily preserved for evidence purposes. Families understandably wish the release of the crime victim's body for burial or, as in this case, cremation and if, as here, all of the coroner's reports, tests, photographs, and tissue slides are available to the defendant, then the defendant has obtained comparable evidence by other reasonably available means. We find no error on the part of the trial court and affirm its order denying the motion to dismiss charges."

In two California cases, [6]*People v. McNeil (1980) 112 Cal. App. 3d 330* and [7]*People v. Vick (1970) 11 Cal.App.3d 1058, 1064-1065*, the defense argued the government should have preserved the decedent's body for the defense to conduct its own tests. The Court found that quite "apart from its more ghoulish implications, defendant's criticism overlooks the fact that prosecutorial agencies have no right to custody of the remains of a deceased; therefore no duty of preservation arises. After the autopsy or investigation is completed by the coroner, the right to control disposition

133

of the remains of a deceased and the duty of interment devolve on the family of the deceased".

i. The Requirement to hold an Inquest: In [8.]*Raigosa v. State, 562 P.2d 1009 (Wyo. 1977)* a defendant actually appealed in part to the Wyoming Supreme Court that his rights were violated because an Inquest was <u>not</u> held. The Court ruled: "[9.]*Commonwealth ex rel. Czako v. Maroney, 1963, 412 Pa. 448, 194 A.2d 867*, the only case cited by defendant in support of his claim that a coroner's jury should have been called to determine cause of death and, therefore, the testimony of an expert was improper, does not support any reason to reverse. In fact, it is to the contrary. It was there held that the finding of a coroner's jury is binding on no one as a judgment, the court going on to say: "* * * [A]n inquest is for the purpose of protecting the public interest. It is not for the protection of an offender and is definitely not a necessary ingredient of due process. A defendant in a murder case has no cause to complain that an inquest was not conducted. * * *" We agree with the Pennsylvania court. There is no requirement that an inquest be held before prosecution for murder. [10.]*Walker v. People, 1952, 126 Colo. 135, 248 P.2d 287*. The verdict of a coroner's jury is merely advisory and has no probative effect. *18 Am.Jur.2d, Coroners or Medical Examiners, § 15, p. 529.* See also *Annotation 78 A.L.R. 2d 1218*, entitled "Reviewing, setting aside, or quashing of verdict at coroner's inquest." There is in Wyoming no statutory requirement for an inquest to be held as a condition precedent to prosecution. *1016 See §§ 7-81 through 7-91, as amended and superseded. The statutory provisions are clearly only an aid to assure a death was not unlawfully caused or to the contrary in aid of law enforcement."

This was further restated in [11.]*Holmes v. State, 1986 WY 59, 715 P.2d 196*: "[5.] The second claim of error is diametrically opposed to existing authority in this state. In *Raigosa v. State, Wyo., 562 P.2d 1009, 1015 (1977)*, this court held that "[t]here is no requirement that an inquest be held before prosecution for murder." The justification for that holding is the same now as it was then. The pertinent part of § 7-4-201, W.S. 1977 (1984 Cum. Supp.) is identical to § 7-81, W.S. 1957 (1975 Cum.Supp.) at issue in Raigosa. The appellant's effort to present an issue contrary to clear precedent in this case borders upon the presentation of a specious appeal. In *Raigosa v. State, supra*, we noted that the purpose of a coroner's inquest is to aid in the determination that a death was not unlawfully caused. In light of the record in this case which establishes five bullet wounds in the victim's body and Holmes' plea of guilty, the coroner's inquest would have been an exercise in futility. Holmes admitted by his plea all the essential elements of the offense including the fact that he had killed the victim unlawfully. [citations omitted]. Holmes' plea to the district court resolved any matters that could have been of concern to a coroner's jury. The inquest was not necessary to serve the public interest and Holmes had no private interest to be served."

j. Admission of Coroner Toxicology evidence Obtained without Consent: In [12]*Johnson v. State ex rel. Wyoming Workers' Compensation Div, 1996 WY 24, 911 P.2d 1054,* part of the appeal to throw out a blood alcohol level in a case over a death, was that the coroner did not obtain family permission for the toxicology draw. The Wyoming Supreme Court ruled:

"[22] In this case Johnson died a violent death which appeared to be an accident. It was by definition a "coroner's case." Under such circumstances the coroner was mandated by statute to conduct an investigation which included an examination of the body and other reasonable procedures which may be necessary to determine the cause of death.

[23] The coroner was completely within his statutory duties and authority in this case in withdrawing blood samples from the decedent's body. Permission was not required of anyone for the coroner to conduct the taking of such samples. Under the circumstances of this case, the coroner would have been remiss if he had not done so. The coroner had a routine practice of taking blood samples from all individuals who die in motor vehicle accidents. This is a commendable procedure which is helpful in determining whether or not alcohol or drugs are involved in such deaths."

k. Coroners Inquest as an Executive Matter conducted outside of the courts: In [13] *Cassidy and Hayse v. Teton County Coroner, 2019 WY, S-18-0156,* a Wyoming Supreme Court decision clearly established the lack of jurisdiction of the judicial system as far as appeals over the rulings of a coroner and jury in an inquest.

The appellants in this case, Paul Cassidy and Bruce Hayse, M.D. filed a Wyoming Rules of Civil Procedure (WRCP) Rule 60 motion to set aside the coroner's inquest verdict (Rule 60 is basically the court setting aside or allowing relief from a particular judgement or order). The district court dismissed the motion, concluding it lacked subject matter jurisdiction, the appellants appealed to the Wyoming Supreme Court, which affirmed the district court's opinion.

The case concerned the death of an individual in Teton County in January of 2017, with an inquest into the matter held about four months later. The jury ruled a verdict of "death due to aspiration secondary to alcohol and 5-

methoxy-DMT ingestion". The verdict also listed contributing factors as "failure to timely call 911 and failure to protect [the subject's] head and airway when dragging [him] down the stairs". The initiating circumstances occurred during an event at the appellant physician's home in Teton County, and while the subject was transferred to an Idaho hospital and died there, the jurisdiction was the Teton County Coroner's. The coroner entered an order denying the motion to set aside the verdict, and in district court filed a motion to dismiss the appellant's motion due to lack of subject matter jurisdiction and several other WCRP rules. The district court granted the motion to dismiss, thus the appeal to the Wyoming Supreme Court.

The oral arguments from both sides to the Supreme Court, and the final opinion, are a fascinating study in legal maneuvering and offer great citations relating to law and inquest in general across the country. One of the appellant's arguments was that since the Wyoming statutes require the coroner to file inquest documents with the clerk of district court, that confers jurisdiction to that court. The decision noted that while other states specifically give the courts the ability to review inquest decisions in statute, Wyoming statutes do not, so the comparison does not apply. The inquest verdict is not a "judgement", more in line with Washington state statutes that establish the proceeding outside the courts, where a verdict is binding on no one.

Conclusion of the court: "A coroner's inquest is an executive matter conducted outside of the courts. The Coroner's Inquest Verdict is not a final order and has no probative effect. The filing of the Coroner's Inquest Verdict and other associated documents with the district court is ministerial and does not confer jurisdiction on the district court. The district court properly dismissed Appellant's WRCP Rule 60(b) motion for lack of subject matter jurisdiction. We affirm."

This ends the consolidation and discussion of the basic statutes, laws, regulations and procedures that involve the duties of the coroner in the State of Wyoming. Remember, opinions are opinions, and the law is the law, and your main protection, and obligation, is to be knowledgeable, informed, and up to date in this area. No text can be all inclusive, and situations will always arise that are a surprise, unexpected, or not previously encountered. That has been the standard regarding the law in my twenty years as a death investigator, much in the same manner that people constantly come up with new ways to be deceased.

If variety is the spice of life, then coroners and death investigators are pretty much guaranteed to lead a 'spicy' existence in doing the job. Humanity has never let us down in that regard.

The following is a listing and summary of the references and citations of law as listed in the text:

Citations:

Part I: History
Revised Statutes of Wyoming Territory in 1887
Session Laws of Wyoming, assorted years

Part II: Current Wyoming Statutes and Law
The Constitution of the United States of America
The Constitution of the State of Wyoming
Statutes of the State of Wyoming (Current as of 2017)

Introduction: Judicial interpretation
[1] *Mendoza v.State*, 2016 WY 31, ¶ 9, 368 P.3d 886, 891 (Wyo. 2016).

[2] *L & L Enters. v. Arellano (In re Arellano)*, 2015 WY 21, ¶ 13, 344 P.3d 249, 252 (Wyo.2015).

[3] *Adekale*, ¶ 12, 344 P.3d at 765 (quoting *Rodriguez v. Casey*, 2002 WY 111, ¶ 20, 50 P.3d 323, 329 (Wyo.2002)).

[4] *Nicodemus v. Lampert*, 2014 WY 135, ¶ 13, 336 P.3d 671, 674 (Wyo.2014) (citing *Estate of Dahlke ex rel. Jubie v. Dahlke*, 2014 WY 29, ¶¶ 36–37, 319 P.3d 116, 125–26 (Wyo.2014)). *Robert L. Kroenlein Trust ex rel. Alden v. Kirchhefer*, 2015 WY 127, ¶ 22, 357 P.3d 1118, 1126 (Wyo. 2015).

[5] *Fontaine v. Bd. Of Cty. Comm'rs of Park Cty.*, 4 P.3d 890, 894 (Wyo. 2000).

Section A: Coroner Statutes
[1] *Veile v. Board of County Comm'rs*, 860 P.2d 1174, 1993 Wyo.

[2] *Williams v. Sundstrom*, 2016 WY 122, 385 P.3d 789, 2016 Wyo.

[3] The Health Insurance Portability and Accountability Act of 1996 (HIPAA). [Code of Federal Regulations] [Title 45, Volume1] [CITE: **45CFR164.512**] Subpart E--Privacy of Individually Identifiable Health Information. *Sec. 164.512 Uses and disclosures for which an authorization or opportunity to agree or object*

is not required. (g) Standard: Uses and disclosures about decedents. (1) Coroners and medical examiners. A covered entity may disclose protected health information to a coroner or medical examiner for the purpose of identifying a deceased person, determining a cause of death, or other duties as authorized by law.

Section B: Other State Statutes
Cross references for other statutes are included in the commentaries

Section C: Coroner Testimony
Wyoming Rules of Evidence (WRE), Article VII
Federal Rules of Evidence (FRE), Article VII

[1] *Taylor v. State*, 642 P.2d 1294, 1295 (Wyo. 1982) ("Foundation testimony is that testimony which identifies the evidence and connects it with the issue in question.") (citing 3 Jones, *Evidence* § 15.2, at 4 (1972)); *Thunder Hawk v. Union Pac. R.R.*, 891 P.2d 773, 780 (Wyo. 1995) ("In order to establish a proper foundation pursuant to W.R.E. 703, the proponent of the evidence must show that the evidence is information of a type customarily relied upon by experts in the field and that the evidence is sufficiently trustworthy to make the expert's reliance upon it reasonable.").

[2] Ladd, Expert Testimony, 5 Vand.L.Rev. 414, 418 (1952)
[3] *Daubert v. Merrell Dow Pharmaceuticals, Inc.*, 509 U.S. 579 (1993)
[4] *Claar v. Burlington N.R.R.*, 29 F.3d 499 (9th Cir. 1994)
[5] Rheingold, *The Basis of Medical Testimony*, 15 Vand.L.Rev. 473, 489 (1962)
[6] National Association of Medical Examiners *"Guide for Manner of Death Classification"(1st Ed., Hanzlick, Hunsaker, & Davis, 2002)*

Section D: State Agency Rules
Records Retention: Schedules for Wyoming Political Subdivisions, Wyoming State Archives
Public Records: W.S. 9-2-401 through 9-2-415; W.S. 16-4-201 through 16-4-204
Wyoming Department of Health: General Rules; Schedule of Reportable Diseases; Vital Statistics Services
Wyoming State Fire Marshal: Powers and Investigations, W.S. 35-9-107 through 35-9-110
Board of Coroner Standards: Rules, Chapter 1 through 7

Part III: Important Federal Regulations
1. The Homeland Security Act, Section 2, 6 U.S.C. 101, (6) 'emergency response provider' definition

2. The Native American Graves Protection and Repatriation Act (NAGPRA; 25 U.S.C. 3001-3013 (2016)) and its implementing regulations (43 C.F.R. Part 10 (2017)). See Appendix A, Section L.: Native American Human Remains.

3. Ref. OSHA Standards 29 CFR Subpart I, Personal Protective Equipment, 1910.132 General Requirements; 29 CFR 1910.1030 Subpart Z: Toxic and Hazardous Substances, Bloodborne Pathogens

4. The Health Insurance Portability and Accountability Act of 1996 (HIPAA). *[Code of Federal Regulations] [Title 45, Volume 1] [CITE: 45CFR164.512] Subpart E--Privacy of Individually Identifiable Health Information. Sec. 164.512 Uses and disclosures for which an authorization or opportunity to agree or object is not required. (g) Standard: Uses and disclosures about decedents. (1) Coroners and medical examiners. A covered entity may disclose protected health information to a coroner or medical examiner for the purpose of identifying a deceased person, determining a cause of death, or other duties as authorized by law.*

Part IV: County Government
Statutes of the State of Wyoming, Title 18, Chapter 3, County Officers, 18-3-101 through 18-3-814; and Clerk of Court, W.S. 5-7-101 through 5-7-107

Part V: Inter-Agency Policies and MOUs
1. Antiquities Act of 1906, 16 U.S.C. 431, 432, 433; Public Law 59-209
2. National Historic Preservation Act of 1966, Public Law 89-665' 80 STAT. 915; 16 U.S.C. 770 as amended
3. Archaeological Resources Protection Act of 1979, 16 U.S.C. 470aa-470mm; Public Law 96-95 as amended

Part VI: Coroner Agency Policies
Policy and Procedural Manual, Fremont County Coroner's Office

1. *Death Investigation: A Guide for the Scene Investigator,* by the U.S. Department of Justice, Office of Justice Programs, National Institute of Justice

[2.]NAGPRA; 25 U.S.C. 3001-3013 (2016) and its implementing regulations (43 C.F.R. Part 10 (2017)). See Appendix A, Section L.: Native American Human Remains

Part VII: Inquest Policies and Procedures
[1.]*The Inquest and the Virtues of Soft Adjudication*, by Paul MacMahon, Assistant Professor of Law, London School of Economics, published in the *Yale Law & Policy Review,* Draft of August 25, 2014.

[2.]*Maki v. State, 18 Wyo. 481, 112 P. 334, 1911 Wyo. LEXIS 30 (Wyo.1911)*

Part VIII: County Attorney and other Legal Opinions
Public Records; Right of Inspection: W.S. 16-4-203

[1.]*Calder v. Bull, Supreme Court of the United States, 1798*
[2.]*Wyoming Constitution, Article 1, Section 35 "Ex post facto laws: Impairing obligations of contracts"*
[3.]*Johnson v. Safeway Stores, Inc., 568 P.2d 908, 914, (Wyo. 1977)*
[4.]*Mestas v. Diamond Coal & Coke Co., 12 Wyo.414, 76 P. 567, 569 (1904)*
[5.]*Lopez v. State, 2004 WY 28, 86 P.3d 851*
[6.]*People v. McNeil (1980) 112 Cal. App. 3d 330*
[7.]*People v. Vick (1970) 11 Cal.App.3d 1058, 1064-1065*
[8.]*Raigosa v. State, 562 P.2d 1009 (Wyo. 1977)*
[9.]*Commonwealth ex rel. Czako v. Maroney, 1963, 412 Pa. 448, 194 A.2d 867*
[10.]*Walker v. People, 1952, 126 Colo. 135, 248 P.2d 287*
[11.]*Holmes v. State, 1986 WY 59, 715 P.2d 196*
[12.]*Johnson v. State ex rel. Wyoming Workers' Compensation Div, 1996 WY 24, 911 P.2d 1054*
[13] *Cassidy and Hayse v. Teton County Coroner, 2019 WY, S-18-0156*

Note: The examples offered in the following appendices are those as constructed specifically for Fremont County, and may not be applicable in detail to all Wyoming Counties, however, keep in mind that the statutory and regulatory requirements of State and Federal Law in most cases require that each county coroner develop such policies in some form. These are offered as an example of policies.

Rather than re-invent the wheel, all Fremont County policies and forms are available on request in digital form so that they may be adjusted and altered to suit the need of any Wyoming coroner. Just as I did with the Federal regulations for biohazard policies, it is a lot easier to take a template and adjust it to your own particular situation and need.

Appendix A: Records Retention Policy for Fremont County

Fremont County Coroner's Office Records Retention and Management Policy

Introduction

In 2014, the Coroner's Office began working with the Records Analysts at the Wyoming State Archives to develop retention schedules for the Agency. Previously there were no specific schedules for coroners, other than processing the Inquest through the Clerk of District Court per WS 7-4-206. Per W.S. 9-2-410, all records of a political subdivision of the State, which includes elected county officials, are the property of the State. By law, management and disposal is only at the approval of the State Archives, and by retention schedules as established by the State.

Additions in rules for Coroner standards by the State Board of Coroner Standards in 2009, and statutory changes by the Wyoming Legislature in 2011 have added additional requirements for record keeping and management. Retention schedules can not only define what may or may not be disposed of, and when; but also can form guidelines for organization. The following policy and procedures are established beginning January 1st, 2015 for the Fremont County Coroner's Office.

Note: For any title that states the documents need review, that review should be completed by the State Records Analyst or their designee.

Office Administration

1. **Title:** Purchase Orders, Requisitions, Vouchers (Duplicates)
   State Reference: ADM-GMT-26 Transitory Records
   Retention Schedule: Retain one year, then destroy when obsolete or superseded. Originals are filed with the County Clerk.

2. **Title:** Travel Expense Voucher and Report (Duplicates)
   State Reference: ADM-GMT-26 Transitory Records
   Retention Schedule: Retain one year, then destroy when obsolete or superseded. Originals are filed with the County Clerk.

3. **Title:** Inventory Records and Reports
   State Reference: FIN-ASM-03 Inventories
   Retention Schedule: Retain 5 years after the fiscal year end then destroy.

4. **Title:** Personnel Files
   State Reference: EMP-PER-22 (long term) & EMP-PER-14 (short term)
   Retention Schedule: Long Term: retain 10 years after completion then destroy. Short Term: retain 5 years after separation then destroy. See State schedules for what this includes.

5. **Title:** Personnel Hiring Records
   State Reference: EMP-SAR-01 Applicants-not hired
   Retention Schedule: Applicants not hired, retain 3 years after calendar year then destroy. Successful Applicants - transfer to Personnel File and subject to Title #4 above

6. **Title:** Time Sheets
   State Reference: EMP-SAR-18 Time and Attendance
   Retention Schedule: Retain 2 years after calendar year end then destroy

7. **Title:** Coroner Policy and Procedure Manual
   State Reference: GAC-PSM-02 Policies, Procedures and Manuals
   Retention Schedule: Retain 5 years after superseded then destroy. One copy retained permanently pending historical evaluation by State Records Management

8. **Title:** Coroner General Correspondence
   State Reference: ADM-GMT-05 General Correspondence

Retention Schedule: Review for legal, administrative, or historical value. Destroy 3 years after create date.

9. **Title:** Correspondence, Elected Officials
   State Reference: ADM-GMT-04 Correspondence, Elected Officials
   Retention Schedule: Permanent. This includes records related to internal and external communications to or from elected officials of policy issues, concerns and issues, and actions taken. (Considered separate from Title #8 above)

10. **Title:** Budget Worksheets and Records
    State Reference: ADM-GMT-26 Transitory Records
    Retention Schedule: Destroy when obsolete or superseded.

11. **Title:** General Office Files (as defined in WS 9-2-405(a)(ii) only), not otherwise specified
    State Reference: ADM-GMT-26 Transitory Records
    Retention Schedule: Destroy when obsolete or superseded. Be aware that there may be a need for review of some miscellaneous records for historical value.

12. **Title:** Transitory Records
    State Reference: ADM-GMT-26 Transitory Records
    Retention Schedule: Destroy when obsolete or superseded. If not otherwise specified, this relates to temporary records, of short term value, not required as evidence of transactions, duplicate copies, miscellaneous notices, preliminary drafts, reports and worksheets, and informal communications not identified by another title.

13. **Title:** Training Programs, Materials, and Printed Copies
    State Reference: ADM-EDU-14 Training Materials
    Retention Schedule: Original: Retain 2 years after superseded then destroy. Copies may be destroyed as Transitory Records

14. **Title:** Reference Material
    State Reference: ADM-GMT-20 Reference Material
    Retention Schedule: Destroy when obsolete. This refers to records and other materials which are maintained solely for ease of access and reference

15. **Title:** Complaints and Inquiries
    State Reference: LGL-LAR-49 Complaints and Inquiries

Retention Schedule: Retain 6 years then destroy. This includes general department issues or information, and not personnel or case issues, which are filed individually.

Summary on Office Administration Files: There is no regulation that says files have to be destroyed at the above minimum retention periods. Longer period may be applicable depending on space availability, possible legal or historical value, or preference of the Coroner. These titles are to serve as a guideline for organization and minimum retention periods.

Operational Files

1. **Title:** Case Files – General: May contain any or all information and documents relating to the Rules for Death Investigations as established by the Board of Coroner Standards, Chapter 6, Section 4, in addition to all correspondence and documentation relating to a specific case, not otherwise listed.
   State Reference: LGL-COU-04 Case Files and Dockets
   Retention Schedule: Permanent, with the exception of Medical Records, as listed under separate Title

2. **Title:** Case Files – Medical Records (copies)
   State Reference: ADM-GMT-26 Transitory Records (Special circumstance defined)
   Retention Schedule: <u>Homicide or Undetermined Manner</u> – Permanent; <u>Accident or Suicide Manner</u> – Retain 2 years or until all civil adjudication completed, then destroy; <u>Natural Manner</u> – Retain one year, then destroy. <u>Autopsy and toxicology reports</u> – Permanent
   NOTE: the original or supplemental reports of the investigator must include a summary of the review of relevant information from the medical records that were critical in determining the manner and cause of death, prior to the destruction of the records.

3. **Title:** Case Files – Coroner Inquest, Duplicate
   State Reference: LGL-COU-04 Case Files and Dockets
   Retention Schedule: One copy, Permanent [Originals are filed with the Clerk of District Court per WS 7-4-206 and retained to the State Archives]

4. **Title:** Case Files – Verdict and Case Docket, as described in WS 7-4-105(a)

State Reference: LGL-COU-04 Case Files and Dockets
Retention Schedule: Permanent

5. **Title:** Public Records Requests
   State Reference: GAC-RCM-07 Public Records Requests
   Retention Schedule: Permanent. Coroner policy is that all requests under W.S. 7-4-105 be placed in the applicable case file when completed.

Legal Summary

Coroners have documentation requirements and concerns unique to the Office. The only currently defined document to be retained by Statute is the Coroner Inquest, and that is statutorily through the Clerk of District Court. The only other statutorily required document is a Verdict and Case Docket, per WS 7-4-105(a), effective July 1st, 2011. Death certificates prepared by a coroner and registrar are already filed with Vital Records, however the Docket contains additional information not found on the certificate. The Rules adopted in 2009 by the Coroner Board of Standards now define the basic (but not necessarily all) documentation that should be in the individual case file on every death that is a coroner case.

Medical and Psychological records are obtained by coroners as authorized by WS 7-4-201(f); and *The Health Insurance Portability and Accountability Act of 1996 (HIPAA). [Code of Federal Regulations] [Title 45, Volume 1] [CITE: 45CFR164.512]   Subpart E--Privacy of Individually Identifiable Health Information.* Coroners by law cannot issue any secondary release of this information or documentation, and they can be considered part of the Case File. As would be expected, this can often be a large volume of information and paper, sometimes numbering cases of documents for an individual investigation. <u>Therefore this policy defines a retention schedule under special circumstances for these records, even though they are transitory copies.</u> Homicide or Undetermined cases may remain open investigations by law enforcement agencies for years, and sometimes decades. Thus, no matter the volume, all files in a homicide should be retained permanently. Accident or Suicide cases would not have criminal legal implications, but may have civil actions, thus should be retained for a reasonable time, but not indefinitely. Medical records in Natural cases would have no criminal or civil implications, and should only be retained for a reasonable time to ensure there is no change or question on the investigation. It is emphasized that this only pertains to medical records obtained by the coroner that are <u>copies</u> of originals from the originating institution, agency, or facility.

Coroner case files after July 1ˢᵗ, 2011, per WS 7-4-105, are confidential, and exempt from inspection or availability as public records, other than an Inquest, and the Case Docket. This confidentiality statute also necessitates additional responsibility for security and storage, and magnifies the need for a consistent Retention Schedule and management.

Digital Media

For the purposes of Retention Schedules, the Fremont County Coroner's Office establishes a policy whereby all originals or copies of digital media will be dealt with in the same manner as paper documentation as listed in the above Titles. While the minimum standard established will conform to State Reference ADM-ITS-01, ADM-ITS-02, and ADM-ITS-03, the Fremont County Coroner's Office will consider the Coroner Case File Database and Coroner Docket Database as items for permanent retention under the Operational Titles as listed above. This permanent retention also includes all case information, such as digital photos or other media related to an individual case. Permanent and on-going backups will also be maintained per established best practices for digital media.

Records Destruction

The policy for records destruction will conform to best practices as established by the State Records Analyst. All confidential materials, or records that contain confidential materials as specified in W.S. 7-4-105 will be shredded or destroyed irretrievably. Per State Reference GAC-RCM-03 records relating to the destruction of records will be on the approved forms and retained permanently.

Accountability to the State

It is the policy of the Fremont County Coroner's Office to cooperate and interact with the State Archives and Records Management Division to maintain and preserve records as directed and permitted. Any changes to this policy will be transmitted to the appropriate Records Analyst for review prior to implementation. As new programs and technology become available, this office will accommodate the possible transfer of historical records, digital media, and case files, or copies thereof, to the Archives for permanent storage.

Certification of Policy

Per State Reference GAC-RCM-09, the record of this policy, and any changes, will be retained permanently on file at the Fremont County Coroner's Office, and is effective as of January 1ˢᵗ, 2015.

Appendix B: Records Request Policies for Fremont County

Commentary: While the Coroner records technically belong to the State, the Coroner is assigned by W.S. 7-4-105(n) to be "custodian of record". All records made during post-mortem exams or autopsy are your responsibility and not to be distributed or shown publically, under penalty of law.

PART 1: Policies Regarding 2011 Statute Changes

Pursuant to Wyoming Statutes W.S. 7-4-105, and W.S. 16-4-203 as established or amended by the Wyoming State Legislature in the 2011 Session, the following Policy for the Fremont County Coroner's Office is hereby in effect immediately:

Policies Regarding Statutes:
1. In compliance with W.S. 7-4-105 Confidentiality of Reports, photos and recordings; exceptions; penalties:
    a. A written verdict and case docket summary of each case completed by the coroner's office will be filled out and filed as part of the official case file. This Docket will be completed by the Coroner, Chief Deputy, Operations Deputy, or office staff as directed by the coroner.
    b. This Docket will include the information as specified in W.S. 7-4-105 (a), and be completed on the official form as approved by the Coroner.
    c. Access to this form and the information contained therein will be by the procedures specified and as allowed by the above noted Statutes, and by the additional procedures and policies as established by the Coroner.
2. The Policy and Procedure Manual of the Fremont County Coroner's Office, updated as of July 2009, is amended to include the changes included herein, with additional policies, rules, and regulations as determined by the Coroner relating to recent legislative changes. Also, specifically, Section 1(H):

Confidentiality; and Section 1(J): Release of Information; remain applicable.
3. Except as provided in W.S. 7-4-105 (b), all other information, photos, reports, or contents of the individual case files are restricted and confidential, as specified by law. Failure to observe confidentiality, unauthorized or improper access or release of information, is a violation of coroner policy, and can result in action as specified in the Policy Manual, or civil penalties as specified in W.S. 7-4-105 (k) or (m).

Policies Regarding Dockets:
1. The public record Docket is filed and available only when each case is completed. Case completion is considered to be when:
    a. The Coroner has determined manner and cause of death.
    b. All investigation and adjudication connected with the case is finished. Confidentiality of all information on the case may need to be maintained if other agencies associated with a case have not completed their investigations or adjudication is in process, per W.S. 16-4-202 and W.S. 16-4-203.
    c. Coroner investigations and completion are also defined as established in the Rules by the Board of Coroner Standards, Chapter 6, Section 4
2. Limitations or exceptions to the release of case information are determined by the Coroner, in conjunction with other procedures as established in the Policy Manual, judicial limitations, or as otherwise provided by law.
3. A database has been established, starting with 2011 records, to contain and track dockets completed for cases: Coroner Docket.mdb
4. An additional Excel file is available for use if needed to complete manually: Case Docket.xlsx, however, once the public record is available as otherwise stated, all information should be transferred and completed in the above noted database.
5. Information on the public Docket will be as complete as possible, with no blank items, as all categories are defined by W.S. 7-4-105 (a). Information that is unknown will be noted as such. If, such as in the case of property, space on the form does not allow adequate detail, general categories may be used with a notation that a full listing is on file and available by request from the coroner's office.
6. All medical information and records, including medications inventories, are *not* to be included on the Docket, per Federal law

and Wyoming Statute. This includes any other detailed information from the autopsy, other than specific cause of death.
7. W.S. 7-4-105 (a) specifies that only "relevant toxicological factors" are to be included in the public record. This means those immediately and specifically related to the cause of death, and all other toxicology information is restricted and not public record. If nothing is relevant, this item should be filed as "none relevant".
8. Description of the deceased: This section should be completed in a similar manner to a law enforcement report for identification, including sex, race, height and weight, hair and eye color, identifying marks, scars, tattoos and features. Basic clothing may be included if an identifying factor, but descriptions of trauma or injury should not be noted. Descriptions and condition of the body and other details as noted in the body description of the Coroner's Report should be left to that document and not included in the public record.
9. 'Memo' section of the Docket: database text box fields are limited to 255 characters, so any additional information or descriptions that do not fit in that limit under another field can be referenced here.
10. Each Docket, when completed to fill a request for a copy, will be stamped, certified, and signed prior to release or distribution.

Requests for Information or Documents:
1. All requests from the news media or news releases, including the official Docket, will be referred to the Coroner, as specified in the Policy and Procedure Manual of the Fremont County Coroner's Office, Section 1(I).
2. All requests for documentation, files, or information, including the Docket, must be in writing, and on the approved forms. These forms are as follows, and also are available as pdf files:
    a. Records Request – Agency.docx
    b. Records Request – Docket.docx
    c. Records Request – Family.docx
    d. Records Request – Other.docx
    e. Records Request – Ancestral Death.docx
3. All pending requests will be filed in the specified location in the coroner office. Completed requests will be filed noting completion date in the appropriate case file.
4. Exceptions, agencies, individuals, and parties of interest to a particular case, are detailed in Statute, and on the forms, as well as some specific procedures for obtaining and viewing confidential portions of the case record. All staff responsible for providing such

access or information will be familiar with, and conform to the Wyoming Statues specified. Each deputy employed by the Coroner's Office is responsible for familiarizing themselves with relevant statutory changes and contacting this office if there are any questions.
5. Instructions, rules, and availability of forms are also included on the coroner web site.
6. All previous forms for records requests are no longer valid.
7. After 7/1/2011, all requests not in the proper format or form will be contacted and mailed or faxed the form and instructions, or directed to the web site to obtain the form.
8. For law enforcement agencies or prosecutors, the notation on the forms for documentation of identification may be marked "known" or "previously provided" if the investigator making the request is personally known to the coroner deputy.

PART 2: Additional Rules and Regulations

The following instructions, rules, and regulations for obtaining records and information have been issued as public record, published on the coroner web site at http://fremontcountywy.org

Records Requests: Public Dockets; Family Requests; Agencies, Legal, and Law Enforcement Requests; General Data or Summary Reports; Ancestral, Genealogy, Research and Information. Legal Notice:

WS 16-4-202(a) All public records shall be open for inspection by any person at reasonable times, except as provided in this act or as otherwise provided by law, but the official custodian of any public records may make rules and regulations with reference to the inspection of the records as is reasonably necessary for the protection of the records and the prevention of unnecessary interference with the regular discharge of the duties of the custodian or his office.
WS 16-4-204(c) After July 1, 2003, any fees or charges assessed by a custodian of a public record shall first be authorized by duly enacted or adopted statute, rule, resolution, ordinance, executive order or other like authority. [Fees for copies are as established by the Fremont County Commission on 02/02/2010 per Resolution 2010-06. This fee schedule is available on request**.]

Note: Public Information Dockets are prepared with the information as specified in W.S. 7-4-105 (a), and are produced for release after case investigation and/or adjudication is completed. Case completion is subject to the policies, procedures, rules, and regulations as established by the Fremont County Coroner's Office, Wyoming Board of Coroner Standards, and additional applicable Wyoming State Statutes.

Secondary release of Medical Records obtained by the coroner's office is prohibited by Federal Law. Also, per W.S. 7-4-105 (m) "A person who knowingly or purposely uses the information in a manner other than the specified purpose for which it was released or violates a court order issued under subsection (g) of this section is guilty of a misdemeanor punishable by imprisonment for not more than six (6) months, a fine of not more than one thousand dollars ($1,000.00), or both."

All requests for information, dockets, or case files submitted prior to completion of the case will be documented as to the date received, and will be held and processed after that completion. Completion time frames are variable depending on the nature of the case.

Dockets:

W.S. 7-4-105(a) After viewing the body and completing his investigation, the coroner shall draw up and sign his verdict on the death under consideration. The coroner shall also make a written docket giving an accurate description of the deceased person, his name if it can be determined, cause and manner of death, including relevant toxicological factors, age of decedent, date and time of death and the description of money and other property found with the body. The verdict and written docket are public records and may be viewed or obtained by request to the coroner, pursuant to W.S. 16-4-202.

Form for Docket copy request: Records Request – Docket.pdf

Rules for a Docket Request:
    a. A separate request must be submitted for each individual case docket.
    b. Request is by completion and submission of the appropriate signed form, with a photocopy of the requesting party's identification, unless the ID is verified in person by coroner staff.
    c. The docket copies provided will be certified as a 'true copy' by the coroner's office.
    d. There is no fee for an individual docket copy. Multiple docket requests may incur a copy fee and postage charges as allowed by statute and set per resolution by the Fremont County Commission.
    e. All individuals, organizations, groups, or companies not otherwise permitted by statute to confidential information, are restricted to the public information of a docket, or to general death summary information as specified below.

Files or Specific Case Information other than Dockets:

Access to confidential case information in the file, other than the official docket, is limited to:

W.S. 7-4-105(c) A surviving spouse, surviving parent, an adult child, personal representative, legal representative, or a legal guardian

Form for family records requests: Records Request – Family.pdf

Rules for family requests:
    a. Relatives of the deceased not specifically listed in Wyoming statute can only receive a copy of the docket, and must submit the form noted above.
    b. Request is by completion and submission of the appropriate signed form, with a photocopy of the requesting party's identification, unless the ID is verified in person by coroner staff. Representatives or guardians must provide copies of legal paperwork establishing the relationship.
    c. There are no fees to the family members listed for copies of the records.

W.S. 7-4-105(d) Upon making a written request, a law enforcement entity of the state of Wyoming or United States government, a district attorney, the United States attorney for the district of Wyoming, a county, state or federal public health agency, a board licensing health care professionals under title 33 of the Wyoming statutes, the division responsible for administering the Wyoming Workers' Compensation Act, the state occupational epidemiologist, the department and the division responsible for administering the Wyoming Occupational Health and Safety Act, the office of the inspector of mines, insurance companies with legitimate interest in the death, all parties in civil litigation proceedings with legitimate interest in the death or a treating physician, while in performance of his official duty

Form for agency, legal, or medical requests: Records Request – Agency.pdf

Rules for agency, legal, or medical requests:
    a. All requests for a particular case must be in writing, as specified by statute.
    b. Request is by completion and submission of the appropriate signed form.
    c. Any non-governmental requests must also include a signed request on company stationery as documentation of identification and contact information; and parties may be charged copy fees as allowed by statute and set per resolution by the Fremont County Commission.
    d. Parties in civil litigation must also provide the case identification or court docket number.

Note: Other circumstances as referenced in WS 7-4-105 may allow release of records in specific instances, such as by court order, or due to public health concerns. Please contact the coroner's office if you have questions.

General Data, Summaries, or Analysis:

The coroner's office as part of its public service provides summaries and data on deaths in general to all organizations, agencies and individuals that request it. There is usually no charge for these summary reports unless they involve a large volume of paper or time in compilation.

It is recommended that such requests be in writing on the form: Records Request – Other.pdf

This will enable better tracking and completion of requests. General information released will conform to public information as available on the official docket, or as specified in WS 7-4-105, and will usually have specific identifiers of individuals redacted.

Ancestral, Genealogy, Research and Information:

The Coroner's Office has records on cases going back to 1885, and historic files are available to those wishing information for family or independent research.

Requests of this type should be submitted on the form: Records Request – Ancestral Death.pdf

Historical records are generally available in their entirety, and fees may be applicable depending on the volume of records in the file. A search of the database for a particular name can be done easily, so it may be beneficial to call the office first. Not all Fremont County deaths were coroner cases, and not all records have survived the passing of time.
Note: Files prior to July 1st 2011 and more contemporary in nature may not be available or only partially available, and subject to limitations as established by law, policy, and other considerations.

** $.50 p/page; $2.50 p/CD; $2.50 p/photographic print; $25.00 p/map

Appendix C: Biohazard and Infectious Disease Policies and Procedures

Commentary: This example of policy is an edited version of Federal regulations which even with that culling remains bulky and inconvenient. Regardless, this stuff is required and just one of the irritating forms necessary to cover a valid need. I did not invent this one, and sometimes I think the Federal Government has a department somewhere whose main task it is to complicate matters of importance.

INFECTIOUS OR CONTAGIOUS DISEASE

[Ref. OSHA Standards 29 CFR Subpart I, Personal Protective Equipment, 1910.132 General Requirements; this section also serves as the Exposure Control Plan as required under 29 CFR 1910.1030(c)(1)(i)]

All Coroner Staff and Deputy job classifications are considered to have the occasional possibility of job exposure to bloodborne pathogens. The tasks and procedures that involve this risk are mainly associated with body recovery and transport, and the associated scene and case investigation. The work practice controls to eliminate or minimize such exposure are listed below. All employees are to be familiar with the recommendations and prohibitions as outlined in the designated biosafety manual.

    1. Hazard assessment and equipment selection:
        a. The general every day work environment of the Coroner's office space involves no hazards requiring personal protective equipment. This environment constitutes a majority of the work-hours location for staff.
        b. Casework, general: Exposure determination - Coroner and deputy response involves locations of indeterminate variety where deceased remains may be located. While each case is unique, a majority of cases require only hand protection for sanitary reasons with single-use latex or equivalent exam gloves. This would be also required as applicable under 29 CFR 1910.1030 for bloodborne pathogens. While most cases in the field do not present a danger of exposure, gloves should always be worn when entering and investigating the death scene, even if not

handling remains, as part of the principles of proper evidence technique. Gloves are required in any circumstance where there is handling of the body, biologics, or associated materials.

    1. Only in very rare occasions would staff encounter situations where respiratory protection as defined by 29 CFR 1910.134 or 1910.1030 would be advisable or required. However, staff at any time may use the provided NIOSH approved N95 particulate respirator masks if they feel the scene environment warrants the added protection.

    2. Scene environments such as vehicular collisions or fire scenes, may offer additional laceration or puncture hazards, in which case leather palm or full leather gloves should be worn over exam gloves for extra protection.

    3. Scene environments that present any large amount of blood or biologics in the area or on scene surfaces may require full PPE Tyvek suits, shoe or boot covers, or other additional equipment.

    4. In the event where a death scene involves hazardous materials or possible exposure, the Incident Commander of a scene in conjunction with the coroner investigator and trained Haz-Mat personnel will determine access and required protection, as detailed in Part N of this section.

c. Investigation: External examination, retrieval of toxicology sample, and autopsy are all part of the possible needs for investigation of a case. Specific needs are determined by the exposure risk:

    1. In all cases, single-use gloves will be worn. Any glove that has its integrity compromised should be replaced immediately.

    2. Great care should be taken when drawing blood for toxicology in order not to stick oneself. All needles, syringes, and associated materials will be handled in compliance with 29 CFR 1910.1030 and likewise disposed of in an appropriate container.

    3. PPE needs at autopsy will depend on the level of the investigator's participation in the procedure. Those who are just observers or photographers at

the procedure in most cases will require no protective equipment as long as they are not in close proximity to, or handling anything from, the body. Any task that involves such handling or close proximity requires appropriate PPE. Special circumstances of communicable disease or hazard may require different levels of protection.

4. In external examination, care should be taken to look for sharp objects when examining the body. This is particularly true with automobile accident victims where there is sharp debris on the body.

5. In most normal circumstances encountered, handling the limited property and evidence retained by the coroner's office requires only disposable gloves as hand protection. All evidence and property is to be inventoried, bagged or contained appropriately, and sealed prior to storage in the evidence room.

2. As stated in 29 CFR 1910.1030(d)(1), Universal precautions shall be observed to prevent contact with blood or other potentially infectious materials. In circumstances in which differentiation between body fluid types is difficult or impossible, all body fluids shall be considered potentially infectious materials.

3. All materials, equipment, and supplies necessary for PPE are supplied and paid for by the employer. This includes leather or puncture resistant gloves that are to be stocked in every vehicle for scene response if needed. Waterless antiseptic hand cleaner is always available for situations where handwashing facilities are not available, and should be used frequently, and is required after the removal of gloves or other PPE used in investigations or procedures.

4. The Operations Deputy is designated as the training officer for proper use of PPE.

5. All other applicable sections of 29 CFR 1910.1030 that applies to the duties and job descriptions of the coroner's office shall be followed. This Title for Bloodborne Pathogens will serve as the biosafety manual for the Coroner's Office.

6. Any incident of possible exposure by any route will be reported immediately to the Coroner or Chief Deputy. Documentation will be by the "Ryan White" form on file, and by reporting as required by the biosafety manual. All documentation of exposure incidents will be maintained in the employee's personnel file.

7. 29 CFR 1910.133, 1910.134, 1910.135, 1910.136, 1910.137, 1910.138 do not apply to the regular and common duties of the Coroner's office, except under rare and special circumstances.

8. Infectious Disease Investigation and Reporting Protocol
    a. Investigations are sometimes conducted for patients with infectious disease who die in Wyoming unattended, with no local physician, or when the physician is out-of-state.
    b. When a call is received that involves an infectious disease related death, and the case is normally one which should be investigated by the County Coroner, it may be an expected, unattended death:
        1. Conduct a routine investigation.
        2. If the physician is out-of-state, contact the physician and confirm the status of the Decedent and request medical records, etc.
        3. Release the body to the funeral home if all is in order. Use extra caution in the external exam and obtaining toxicology. Advise the funeral home of the diagnosis in advance of transporting the body.
        4. Contact the County Health Officer or the State Epidemiologist office to report the case as indicated in the Appendix.
        5. If circumstances are such that a more thorough investigation is required, such as evidence indicating the death may have been a homicide, suicide, etc., discuss the case with the Coroner for possible autopsy.
        6. Emphasize as little handling of the body as possible, using protective gear.
    c. This protocol will be considered applicable to all contagious and reportable diseases as listed by the Wyoming Department of Health (see appendix).

Biosafety Manual – Fremont County Coroner's Office

- Part Number: 1910
- Part Title: Occupational Safety and Health Standards
- Subpart: Z
- Subpart Title: Toxic and Hazardous Substances
- Standard #: 1910.1030
- Title: Bloodborne pathogens.
- Appendix: A
- GPO Source: e-CFR

1910.1030(a): Scope and Application. This section applies to all occupational exposure to blood or other potentially infectious materials as defined by paragraph (b) of this section.

1910.1030(b): **Definitions.** For purposes of this section, the following shall apply:

Assistant Secretary means the Assistant Secretary of Labor for Occupational Safety and Health, or designated representative.
Blood means human blood, human blood components, and products made from human blood.
Bloodborne Pathogens means pathogenic microorganisms that are present in human blood and can cause disease in humans. These pathogens include, but are not limited to, hepatitis B virus (HBV) and human immunodeficiency virus (HIV).
Clinical Laboratory means a workplace where diagnostic or other screening procedures are performed on blood or other potentially infectious materials.
Contaminated means the presence or the reasonably anticipated presence of blood or other potentially infectious materials on an item or surface.
Contaminated Laundry means laundry which has been soiled with blood or other potentially infectious materials or may contain sharps.
Contaminated Sharps means any contaminated object that can penetrate the skin including, but not limited to, needles, scalpels, broken glass, broken capillary tubes, and exposed ends of dental wires.
Decontamination means the use of physical or chemical means to remove, inactivate, or destroy bloodborne pathogens on a surface or item to the point where they are no longer capable of transmitting infectious particles and the surface or item is rendered safe for handling, use, or disposal.
Director means the Director of the National Institute for Occupational Safety and Health, U.S. Department of Health and Human Services, or designated representative.

Engineering Controls means controls (e.g., sharps disposal containers, self-sheathing needles, safer medical devices, such as sharps with engineered sharps injury protections and needleless systems) that isolate or remove the bloodborne pathogens hazard from the workplace.

Exposure Incident means a specific eye, mouth, other mucous membrane, non-intact skin, or parenteral contact with blood or other potentially infectious materials that results from the performance of an employee's duties.

Handwashing Facilities means a facility providing an adequate supply of running potable water, soap, and single-use towels or air-drying machines.

Licensed Healthcare Professional is a person whose legally permitted scope of practice allows him or her to independently perform the activities required by paragraph (f) Hepatitis B Vaccination and Post-exposure Evaluation and Follow-up.

HBV means hepatitis B virus.

HIV means human immunodeficiency virus.

Needleless systems means a device that does not use needles for:

(1) The collection of bodily fluids or withdrawal of body fluids after initial venous or arterial access is   established;

(2) The administration of medication or fluids; or (3) Any other procedure involving the potential for occupational exposure to bloodborne pathogens due to percutaneous injuries from contaminated sharps.

Occupational Exposure means reasonably anticipated skin, eye, mucous membrane, or parenteral contact with blood or other potentially infectious materials that may result from the performance of an employee's duties.

Other Potentially Infectious Materials means:

(1) The following human body fluids: semen, vaginal secretions, cerebrospinal fluid, synovial fluid, pleural fluid, pericardial fluid, peritoneal fluid, amniotic fluid, saliva in dental procedures, any body fluid that is visibly contaminated with blood, and all body fluids in situations where it is difficult or impossible to differentiate between body fluids;

(2) Any unfixed tissue or organ (other than intact skin) from a human (living or dead); and

(3) HIV-containing cell or tissue cultures, organ cultures, and HIV- or HBV-containing culture medium or other solutions; and blood, organs, or other tissues from experimental animals infected with HIV or HBV.

Parenteral means piercing mucous membranes or the skin barrier through such events as needle sticks, human bites, cuts, and abrasions.

Personal Protective Equipment(PPE) is specialized clothing or equipment worn by an employee for protection against a hazard. General work clothes (e.g., uniforms, pants, shirts or blouses) not intended to function as protection against a hazard are not considered to be personal protective equipment.

Production Facility means a facility engaged in industrial-scale, large-volume or high concentration production of HIV or HBV.

Regulated Waste means liquid or semi-liquid blood or other potentially infectious materials; contaminated items that would release blood or other potentially infectious materials in a liquid or semi-liquid state if compressed; items that are caked with dried blood or other potentially infectious materials and are capable of releasing these materials during handling; contaminated sharps; and pathological and microbiological wastes containing blood or other potentially infectious materials.

Research Laboratory means a laboratory producing or using research-laboratory-scale amounts of HIV or HBV. Research laboratories may produce high concentrations of HIV or HBV but not in the volume found in production facilities.

Sharps with engineered sharps injury protections means a nonneedle sharp or a needle device used for withdrawing body fluids, accessing a vein or artery, or administering medications or other fluids, with a built-in safety feature or mechanism that effectively reduces the risk of an exposure incident.

Source Individual means any individual, living or dead, whose blood or other potentially infectious materials may be a source of occupational exposure to the employee. Examples include, but are not limited to, hospital and clinic patients; clients in institutions for the developmentally disabled; trauma victims; clients of drug and alcohol treatment facilities; residents of hospices and nursing homes; human remains; and individuals who donate or sell blood or blood components.

Sterilize means the use of a physical or chemical procedure to destroy all microbial life including highly resistant bacterial endospores.

Universal Precautions is an approach to infection control. According to the concept of Universal Precautions, all human blood and certain human body fluids are treated as if known to be infectious for HIV, HBV, and other bloodborne pathogens.

Work Practice Controls means controls that reduce the likelihood of exposure by altering the manner in which a task is performed (e.g., prohibiting recapping of needles by a two-handed technique).

1910.1030(c) Exposure Control –

1910.1030(c)(1) Exposure Control Plan.

1910.1030(c)(1)(i) Each employer having an employee(s) with occupational exposure as defined by paragraph (b) of this section shall establish a written Exposure Control Plan designed to eliminate or minimize employee exposure.

1910.1030(c)(1)(ii) The Exposure Control Plan shall contain at least the following elements:

1910.1030(c)(1)(ii)(A) The exposure determination required by paragraph (c)(2),

1910.1030(c)(1)(ii)(B) The schedule and method of implementation for paragraphs (d) Methods of Compliance, (e) HIV and HBV Research Laboratories and Production Facilities, (f) Hepatitis B Vaccination and Post-Exposure Evaluation and Follow-up, (g) Communication of Hazards to Employees, and (h) Recordkeeping, of this standard, and

1910.1030(c)(1)(ii)(C) The procedure for the evaluation of circumstances surrounding exposure incidents as required by paragraph (f)(3)(i) of this standard.

1910.1030(c)(1)(iii) Each employer shall ensure that a copy of the Exposure Control Plan is accessible to employees in accordance with 29 CFR 1910.1020(e).

1910.1030(c)(1)(iv) The Exposure Control Plan shall be reviewed and updated at least annually and whenever necessary to reflect new or modified tasks and procedures which affect occupational exposure and to reflect new or revised employee positions with occupational exposure. The review and update of such plans shall also:

1910.1030(c)(1)(iv)(A) Reflect changes in technology that eliminate or reduce exposure to bloodborne pathogens; and

1910.1030(c)(1)(iv)(B) Document annually consideration and implementation of appropriate commercially available and effective safer medical devices designed to eliminate or minimize occupational exposure.

1910.1030(c)(1)(v) An employer, who is required to establish an Exposure Control Plan shall solicit input from non-managerial employees responsible for direct patient care who are potentially exposed to injuries from contaminated sharps in the identification, evaluation, and selection of effective engineering and work practice controls and shall document the solicitation in the Exposure Control Plan.

1910.1030(c)(1)(vi) The Exposure Control Plan shall be made available to the Assistant Secretary and the Director upon request for examination and copying.

1910.1030(c)(2) Exposure Determination.

1910.1030(c)(2)(i) Each employer who has an employee(s) with occupational exposure as defined by paragraph (b) of this section shall prepare an exposure determination. This exposure determination shall contain the following:

1910.1030(c)(2)(i)(A) A list of all job classifications in which all employees in those job classifications have occupational exposure;

1910.1030(c)(2)(i)(B) A list of job classifications in which some employees have occupational exposure, and

1910.1030(c)(2)(i)(C) A list of all tasks and procedures or groups of closely related task and procedures in which occupational exposure occurs and that are performed by employees in job classifications listed in accordance with the provisions of paragraph (c)(2)(i)(B) of this standard.

1910.1030(c)(2)(ii) This exposure determination shall be made without regard to the use of personal protective equipment.

1910.1030(d) Methods of Compliance --

1910.1030(d)(1) General. Universal precautions shall be observed to prevent contact with blood or other potentially infectious materials. Under circumstances in which differentiation between body fluid types is difficult or impossible, all body fluids shall be considered potentially infectious materials.

1910.1030(d)(2) Engineering and Work Practice Controls.

1910.1030(d)(2)(i) Engineering and work practice controls shall be used to eliminate or minimize employee exposure. Where occupational exposure remains after institution of these controls, personal protective equipment shall also be used.

1910.1030(d)(2)(ii) Engineering controls shall be examined and maintained or replaced on a regular schedule to ensure their effectiveness.

1910.1030(d)(2)(iii) Employers shall provide handwashing facilities which are readily accessible to employees.

1910.1030(d)(2)(iv) When provision of handwashing facilities is not feasible, the employer shall provide either an appropriate antiseptic hand cleanser in conjunction with clean cloth/paper towels or antiseptic towelettes. When antiseptic hand cleansers or towelettes are used, hands shall be washed with soap and running water as soon as feasible.

1910.1030(d)(2)(v) Employers shall ensure that employees wash their hands immediately or as soon as feasible after removal of gloves or other personal protective equipment.

1910.1030(d)(2)(vi) Employers shall ensure that employees wash hands and any other skin with soap and water, or flush mucous membranes with water immediately or as soon as feasible following contact of such body areas with blood or other potentially infectious materials.

1910.1030(d)(2)(vii) Contaminated needles and other contaminated sharps shall not be bent, recapped, or removed except as noted in paragraphs (d)(2)(vii)(A) and (d)(2)(vii)(B) below. Shearing or breaking of contaminated needles is prohibited.

1910.1030(d)(2)(vii)(A) Contaminated needles and other contaminated sharps shall not be bent, recapped or removed unless the employer can demonstrate that no alternative is feasible or that such action is required by a specific medical or dental procedure.

1910.1030(d)(2)(vii)(B) Such bending, recapping or needle removal must be accomplished through the use of a mechanical device or a one-handed technique.

1910.1030(d)(2)(viii) Immediately or as soon as possible after use, contaminated reusable sharps shall be placed in appropriate containers until properly reprocessed. These containers shall be:

1910.1030(d)(2)(viii)(A) Puncture resistant;

1910.1030(d)(2)(viii)(B) Labeled or color-coded in accordance with this standard;

1910.1030(d)(2)(viii)(C) Leakproof on the sides and bottom; and

1910.1030(d)(2)(viii)(D) In accordance with the requirements set forth in paragraph (d)(4)(ii)(E) for reusable sharps.

1910.1030(d)(2)(ix) Eating, drinking, smoking, applying cosmetics or lip balm, and handling contact lenses are prohibited in work areas where there is a reasonable likelihood of occupational exposure.

1910.1030(d)(2)(x) Food and drink shall not be kept in refrigerators, freezers, shelves, cabinets or on countertops or benchtops where blood or other potentially infectious materials are present.

1910.1030(d)(2)(xi) All procedures involving blood or other potentially infectious materials shall be performed in such a manner as to minimize splashing, spraying, spattering, and generation of droplets of these substances.

1910.1030(d)(2)(xii) Mouth pipetting/suctioning of blood or other potentially infectious materials is prohibited.

1910.1030(d)(2)(xiii) Specimens of blood or other potentially infectious materials shall be placed in a container which prevents leakage during collection, handling, processing, storage, transport, or shipping.

1910.1030(d)(2)(xiii)(A) The container for storage, transport, or shipping shall be labeled or color-coded according to paragraph (g)(1)(i) and closed prior to being stored, transported, or shipped. When a facility utilizes Universal Precautions in the handling of all specimens, the labeling/color-coding of specimens is not necessary provided containers are recognizable as containing specimens. This exemption only applies while such specimens/containers remain within the facility. Labeling or color-coding in accordance with paragraph (g)(1)(i) is required when such specimens/containers leave the facility.

1910.1030(d)(2)(xiii)(B) If outside contamination of the primary container occurs, the primary container shall be placed within a second container which prevents leakage during handling, processing, storage, transport, or shipping and is labeled or color-coded according to the requirements of this standard.

1910.1030(d)(2)(xiii)(C) If the specimen could puncture the primary container, the primary container shall be placed within a secondary container which is puncture-resistant in addition to the above characteristics.

1910.1030(d)(2)(xiv) Equipment which may become contaminated with blood or other potentially infectious materials shall be examined prior to servicing or shipping and shall be decontaminated as necessary, unless the employer can demonstrate that decontamination of such equipment or portions of such equipment is not feasible.

1910.1030(d)(2)(xiv)(A) A readily observable label in accordance with paragraph (g)(1)(i)(H) shall be attached to the equipment stating which portions remain contaminated.

1910.1030(d)(2)(xiv)(B) The employer shall ensure that this information is conveyed to all affected employees, the servicing representative, and/or the manufacturer, as appropriate, prior to handling, servicing, or shipping so that appropriate precautions will be taken.

1910.1030(d)(3) Personal Protective Equipment --

1910.1030(d)(3)(i) Provision. When there is occupational exposure, the employer shall provide, at no cost to the employee, appropriate personal protective equipment such as, but not limited to, gloves, gowns, laboratory coats, face shields or masks and eye protection, and mouthpieces, resuscitation bags, pocket masks, or other ventilation devices. Personal protective equipment will be considered "appropriate" only if it does not permit blood or other potentially infectious materials to pass through to or reach the employee's work clothes, street clothes, undergarments, skin, eyes, mouth, or other mucous membranes under normal conditions of use and for the duration of time which the protective equipment will be used.

1910.1030(d)(3)(ii) Use. The employer shall ensure that the employee uses appropriate personal protective equipment unless the employer shows that the employee temporarily and briefly declined to use personal protective equipment when, under rare and extraordinary circumstances, it was the employee's professional judgment that in the specific instance its use would have prevented the delivery of health care or public safety services or would have posed an increased hazard to the safety of the worker or co-worker. When the employee makes this judgement, the circumstances shall be investigated and documented in order to determine whether changes can be instituted to prevent such occurrences in the future.

1910.1030(d)(3)(iii) Accessibility. The employer shall ensure that appropriate personal protective equipment in the appropriate sizes is readily accessible at the worksite or is issued to employees. Hypoallergenic gloves, glove liners, powderless gloves, or other similar alternatives shall be readily accessible to those employees who are allergic to the gloves normally provided.

1910.1030(d)(3)(iv) Cleaning, Laundering, and Disposal. The employer shall clean, launder, and dispose of personal protective equipment required by paragraphs (d) and (e) of this standard, at no cost to the employee.

1910.1030(d)(3)(v) Repair and Replacement. The employer shall repair or replace personal protective equipment as needed to maintain its effectiveness, at no cost to the employee.

1910.1030(d)(3)(vi) If a garment(s) is penetrated by blood or other potentially infectious materials, the garment(s) shall be removed immediately or as soon as feasible.

1910.1030(d)(3)(vii) All personal protective equipment shall be removed prior to leaving the work area.

1910.1030(d)(3)(viii) When personal protective equipment is removed it shall be placed in an appropriately designated area or container for storage, washing, decontamination or disposal.

1910.1030(d)(3)(ix) Gloves. Gloves shall be worn when it can be reasonably anticipated that the employee may have hand contact with blood, other potentially infectious materials, mucous membranes, and non-intact skin; when performing vascular access procedures except as specified in paragraph (d)(3)(ix)(D); and when handling or touching contaminated items or surfaces.

1910.1030(d)(3)(ix)(A) Disposable (single use) gloves such as surgical or examination gloves, shall be replaced as soon as practical when contaminated or as soon as feasible if they are torn, punctured, or when their ability to function as a barrier is compromised.

1910.1030(d)(3)(ix)(B) Disposable (single use) gloves shall not be washed or decontaminated for re-use.

1910.1030(d)(3)(ix)(C) Utility gloves may be decontaminated for re-use if the integrity of the glove is not compromised. However, they must be discarded if they are cracked, peeling, torn, punctured, or exhibit other signs of deterioration or when their ability to function as a barrier is compromised.

1910.1030(d)(3)(ix)(D) If an employer in a volunteer blood donation center judges that routine gloving for all phlebotomies is not necessary then the employer shall:

1910.1030(d)(3)(ix)(D)(1) Periodically reevaluate this policy;

1910.1030(d)(3)(ix)(D)(2) through 1910.1030(d)(3)(ix)(D)(4)(iii) not applicable;

1910.1030(d)(3)(x) Masks, Eye Protection, and Face Shields. Masks in combination with eye protection devices, such as goggles or glasses with solid side shields, or chin-length face shields, shall be worn whenever splashes, spray, spatter, or droplets of blood or other potentially infectious materials may be generated and eye, nose, or mouth contamination can be reasonably anticipated.

1910.1030(d)(3)(xi) Gowns, Aprons, and Other Protective Body Clothing. Appropriate protective clothing such as, but not limited to, gowns, aprons, lab coats, clinic jackets, or similar outer garments shall be worn in occupational exposure situations. The type and characteristics will depend upon the task and degree of exposure anticipated.

1910.1030(d)(3)(xii) Surgical caps or hoods and/or shoe covers or boots shall be worn in instances when gross contamination can reasonably be anticipated (e.g., autopsies, orthopaedic surgery).

1910.1030(d)(4) Housekeeping --

1910.1030(d)(4)(i) General. Employers shall ensure that the worksite is maintained in a clean and sanitary condition. The employer shall determine and implement an appropriate written schedule for cleaning and method of decontamination based upon the location within the facility, type of surface to be cleaned, type of soil present, and tasks or procedures being performed in the area.

1910.1030(d)(4)(ii) All equipment and environmental and working surfaces shall be cleaned and decontaminated after contact with blood or other potentially infectious materials.

1910.1030(d)(4)(ii)(A) Contaminated work surfaces shall be decontaminated with an appropriate disinfectant after completion of procedures; immediately or as soon as feasible when surfaces are overtly contaminated or after any spill of blood or other potentially infectious materials; and at the end of the work shift if the surface may have become contaminated since the last cleaning.

1910.1030(d)(4)(ii)(B) Protective coverings, such as plastic wrap, aluminum foil, or imperviously-backed absorbent paper used to cover equipment and environmental surfaces, shall be removed and replaced as soon as feasible when they become overtly contaminated or at the end of the workshift if they may have become contaminated during the shift.

1910.1030(d)(4)(ii)(C) All bins, pails, cans, and similar receptacles intended for reuse which have a reasonable likelihood for becoming contaminated with blood or other potentially infectious materials shall be inspected and decontaminated on a regularly scheduled basis and cleaned and decontaminated immediately or as soon as feasible upon visible contamination.

1910.1030(d)(4)(ii)(D) Broken glassware which may be contaminated shall not be picked up directly with the hands. It shall be cleaned up using mechanical means, such as a brush and dust pan, tongs, or forceps.

1910.1030(d)(4)(ii)(E) Reusable sharps that are contaminated with blood or other potentially infectious materials shall not be stored or processed in a manner that requires employees to reach by hand into the containers where these sharps have been placed.

1910.1030(d)(4)(iii) Regulated Waste --

1910.1030(d)(4)(iii)(A) Contaminated Sharps Discarding and Containment.

1910.1030(d)(4)(iii)(A)(1) Contaminated sharps shall be discarded immediately or as soon as feasible in containers that are:

1910.1030(d)(4)(iii)(A)(1)(i) Closable;

1910.1030(d)(4)(iii)(A)(1)(ii) Puncture resistant;

1910.1030(d)(4)(iii)(A)(1)(iii) Leakproof on sides and bottom; and

1910.1030(d)(4)(iii)(A)(1)(iv) Labeled or color-coded in accordance with paragraph (g)(1)(i) of this standard.

1910.1030(d)(4)(iii)(A)(2) During use, containers for contaminated sharps shall be:

1910.1030(d)(4)(iii)(A)(2)(i) Easily accessible to personnel and located as close as is feasible to the immediate area where sharps are used or can be reasonably anticipated to be found (e.g., laundries);

1910.1030(d)(4)(iii)(A)(2)(ii) Maintained upright throughout use; and

1910.1030(d)(4)(iii)(A)(2)(iii) Replaced routinely and not be allowed to overfill.

1910.1030(d)(4)(iii)(A)(3) When moving containers of contaminated sharps from the area of use, the containers shall be:

1910.1030(d)(4)(iii)(A)(3)(i) Closed immediately prior to removal or replacement to prevent spillage or protrusion of contents during handling, storage, transport, or shipping;

1910.1030(d)(4)(iii)(A)(3)(ii) Placed in a secondary container if leakage is possible. The second container shall be:

1910.1030(d)(4)(iii)(A)(3)(ii)(A) Closable;

1910.1030(d)(4)(iii)(A)(3)(ii)(B) Constructed to contain all contents and prevent leakage during handling, storage, transport, or shipping; and

1910.1030(d)(4)(iii)(A)(3)(ii)(C) Labeled or color-coded according to paragraph (g)(1)(i) of this standard.

1910.1030(d)(4)(iii)(A)(4) Reusable containers shall not be opened, emptied, or cleaned manually or in any other manner which would expose employees to the risk of percutaneous injury.

1910.1030(d)(4)(iii)(B) Other Regulated Waste Containment --

1910.1030(d)(4)(iii)(B)(1) Regulated waste shall be placed in containers which are:

1910.1030(d)(4)(iii)(B)(1)(i) Closable;

1910.1030(d)(4)(iii)(B)(1)(ii) Constructed to contain all contents and prevent leakage of fluids during handling, storage, transport or shipping;

1910.1030(d)(4)(iii)(B)(1)(iii) Labeled or color-coded in accordance with paragraph (g)(1)(i) this standard; and

1910.1030(d)(4)(iii)(B)(1)(iv) Closed prior to removal to prevent spillage or protrusion of contents during handling, storage, transport, or shipping.

1910.1030(d)(4)(iii)(B)(2) If outside contamination of the regulated waste container occurs, it shall be placed in a second container. The second container shall be:

1910.1030(d)(4)(iii)(B)(2)(i) Closable;

1910.1030(d)(4)(iii)(B)(2)(ii) Constructed to contain all contents and prevent leakage of fluids during handling, storage, transport or shipping;

1910.1030(d)(4)(iii)(B)(2)(iii) Labeled or color-coded in accordance with paragraph (g)(1)(i) of this standard; and

1910.1030(d)(4)(iii)(B)(2)(iv) Closed prior to removal to prevent spillage or protrusion of contents during handling, storage, transport, or shipping.

1910.1030(d)(4)(iii)(C) Disposal of all regulated waste shall be in accordance with applicable regulations of the United States, States and Territories, and political subdivisions of States and Territories.

1910.1030(d)(4)(iv) Laundry.

1910.1030(d)(4)(iv)(A) Contaminated laundry shall be handled as little as possible with a minimum of agitation.

1910.1030(d)(4)(iv)(A)(1) Contaminated laundry shall be bagged or containerized at the location where it was used and shall not be sorted or rinsed in the location of use.

1910.1030(d)(4)(iv)(A)(2) Contaminated laundry shall be placed and transported in bags or containers labeled or color-coded in accordance with paragraph (g)(1)(i) of this standard. When a facility utilizes Universal Precautions in the handling of all soiled laundry, alternative labeling or color-coding is sufficient if it permits all employees to recognize the containers as requiring compliance with Universal Precautions.

1910.1030(d)(4)(iv)(A)(3) Whenever contaminated laundry is wet and presents a reasonable likelihood of soak-through of or leakage from the bag or container, the laundry shall be placed and transported in bags or containers which prevent soak-through and/or leakage of fluids to the exterior.

1910.1030(d)(4)(iv)(B) The employer shall ensure that employees who have contact with contaminated laundry wear protective gloves and other appropriate personal protective equipment.

1910.1030(d)(4)(iv)(C) When a facility ships contaminated laundry off-site to a second facility which does not utilize Universal Precautions in the handling of all laundry, the facility generating the contaminated laundry must place such laundry in bags or containers which are labeled or color-coded in accordance with paragraph (g)(1)(i).

1910.1030(e) HIV and HBV Research Laboratories and Production Facilities. Section 1910.1030(e) through 1910.1030(e)(5) are not applicable to the coroner's office.

1910.1030(f) Hepatitis B Vaccination and Post-exposure Evaluation and Follow-up --

1910.1030(f)(1) General.

1910.1030(f)(1)(i) The employer shall make available the hepatitis B vaccine and vaccination series to all employees who have occupational exposure, and post-exposure evaluation and follow-up to all employees who have had an exposure incident.

1910.1030(f)(1)(ii) The employer shall ensure that all medical evaluations and procedures including the hepatitis B vaccine and vaccination series and post-exposure evaluation and follow-up, including prophylaxis, are:

1910.1030(f)(1)(ii)(A) Made available at no cost to the employee;

1910.1030(f)(1)(ii)(B) Made available to the employee at a reasonable time and place;

1910.1030(f)(1)(ii)(C) Performed by or under the supervision of a licensed physician or by or under the supervision of another licensed healthcare professional; and

1910.1030(f)(1)(ii)(D) Provided according to recommendations of the U.S. Public Health Service current at the time these evaluations and procedures take place, except as specified by this paragraph (f).

1910.1030(f)(1)(iii) The employer shall ensure that all laboratory tests are conducted by an accredited laboratory at no cost to the employee.

1910.1030(f)(2) Hepatitis B Vaccination.

1910.1030(f)(2)(i) Hepatitis B vaccination shall be made available after the employee has received the training required in paragraph (g)(2)(vii)(I) and within 10 working days of initial assignment to all employees who have occupational exposure unless the employee has previously received the complete hepatitis B vaccination series, antibody testing has revealed that the employee is immune, or the vaccine is contraindicated for medical reasons.

1910.1030(f)(2)(ii) The employer shall not make participation in a prescreening program a prerequisite for receiving hepatitis B vaccination.

1910.1030(f)(2)(iii) If the employee initially declines hepatitis B vaccination but at a later date while still covered under the standard decides to accept the vaccination, the employer shall make available hepatitis B vaccination at that time.

1910.1030(f)(2)(iv) The employer shall assure that employees who decline to accept hepatitis B vaccination offered by the employer sign the statement in Appendix A.

1910.1030(f)(2)(v) If a routine booster dose(s) of hepatitis B vaccine is recommended by the U.S. Public Health Service at a future date, such booster dose(s) shall be made available in accordance with section (f)(1)(ii).

1910.1030(f)(3) Post-exposure Evaluation and Follow-up. Following a report of an exposure incident, the employer shall make immediately available to the exposed employee a confidential medical evaluation and follow-up, including at least the following elements:

1910.1030(f)(3)(i) Documentation of the route(s) of exposure, and the circumstances under which the exposure incident occurred;

1910.1030(f)(3)(ii) Identification and documentation of the source individual, unless the employer can establish that identification is infeasible or prohibited by state or local law;

1910.1030(f)(3)(ii)(A) The source individual's blood shall be tested as soon as feasible and after consent is obtained in order to determine HBV and HIV infectivity. If consent is not obtained, the employer shall establish that legally required consent cannot be obtained. When the source individual's consent is not required by law, the source individual's blood, if available, shall be tested and the results documented.

1910.1030(f)(3)(ii)(B) When the source individual is already known to be infected with HBV or HIV, testing for the source individual's known HBV or HIV status need not be repeated.

1910.1030(f)(3)(ii)(C) Results of the source individual's testing shall be made available to the exposed employee, and the employee shall be informed of applicable laws and regulations concerning disclosure of the identity and infectious status of the source individual.

1910.1030(f)(3)(iii) Collection and testing of blood for HBV and HIV serological status;

1910.1030(f)(3)(iii)(A) The exposed employee's blood shall be collected as soon as feasible and tested after consent is obtained.

1910.1030(f)(3)(iii)(B) If the employee consents to baseline blood collection, but does not give consent at that time for HIV serologic testing, the sample shall be preserved for at least 90 days. If, within 90 days of the exposure incident, the employee elects to have the baseline sample tested, such testing shall be done as soon as feasible.

1910.1030(f)(3)(iv) Post-exposure prophylaxis, when medically indicated, as recommended by the U.S. Public Health Service;

1910.1030(f)(3)(v) Counseling; and

1910.1030(f)(3)(vi) Evaluation of reported illnesses.

1910.1030(f)(4) Information Provided to the Healthcare Professional.

1910.1030(f)(4)(i) The employer shall ensure that the healthcare professional responsible for the employee's Hepatitis B vaccination is provided a copy of this regulation.

1910.1030(f)(4)(ii) The employer shall ensure that the healthcare professional evaluating an employee after an exposure incident is provided the following information:

1910.1030(f)(4)(ii)(A) A copy of this regulation;

1910.1030(f)(4)(ii)(B) A description of the exposed employee's duties as they relate to the exposure incident;

1910.1030(f)(4)(ii)(C) Documentation of the route(s) of exposure and circumstances under which exposure occurred;

1910.1030(f)(4)(ii)(D) Results of the source individual's blood testing, if available; and

1910.1030(f)(4)(ii)(E) All medical records relevant to the appropriate treatment of the employee including vaccination status which are the employer's responsibility to maintain.

1910.1030(f)(5) Healthcare Professional's Written Opinion. The employer shall obtain and provide the employee with a copy of the evaluating healthcare professional's written opinion within 15 days of the completion of the evaluation.

1910.1030(f)(5)(i) The healthcare professional's written opinion for Hepatitis B vaccination shall be limited to whether Hepatitis B vaccination is indicated for an employee, and if the employee has received such vaccination.

1910.1030(f)(5)(ii) The healthcare professional's written opinion for post-exposure evaluation and follow-up shall be limited to the following information:

1910.1030(f)(5)(ii)(A) That the employee has been informed of the results of the evaluation; and

1910.1030(f)(5)(ii)(B) That the employee has been told about any medical conditions resulting from exposure to blood or other potentially infectious materials which require further evaluation or treatment.

1910.1030(f)(5)(iii) All other findings or diagnoses shall remain confidential and shall not be included in the written report.

1910.1030(g) Medical Recordkeeping.

Medical records required by this standard shall be maintained in accordance with paragraph (h)(1) of this section.

1910.1030(g) Communication of Hazards to Employees --

1910.1030(g)(1) Labels and Signs --

1910.1030(g)(1)(i) Labels.

1910.1030(g)(1)(i)(A) Warning labels shall be affixed to containers of regulated waste, refrigerators and freezers containing blood or other potentially infectious material; and other containers used to store, transport or ship blood or other potentially infectious materials, except as provided in paragraph (g)(1)(i)(E), (F) and (G).

1910.1030(g)(1)(i)(B) Labels required by this section shall include the following legend:

1910.1030(g)(1)(i)(C) These labels shall be fluorescent orange or orange-red or predominantly so, with lettering and symbols in a contrasting color.

1910.1030(g)(1)(i)(D) Labels shall be affixed as close as feasible to the container by string, wire, adhesive, or other method that prevents their loss or unintentional removal.

1910.1030(g)(1)(i)(E) Red bags or red containers may be substituted for labels.

1910.1030(g)(1)(i)(F) Containers of blood, blood components, or blood products that are labeled as to their contents and have been released for transfusion or other clinical use are exempted from the labeling requirements of paragraph (g).

1910.1030(g)(1)(i)(G) Individual containers of blood or other potentially infectious materials that are placed in a labeled container during storage, transport, shipment or disposal are exempted from the labeling requirement.

1910.1030(g)(1)(i)(H) Labels required for contaminated equipment shall be in accordance with this paragraph and shall also state which portions of the equipment remain contaminated.

1910.1030(g)(1)(i)(I) Regulated waste that has been decontaminated need not be labeled or color-coded.

1910.1030(g)(1)(ii) Signs.

1910.1030(g)(1)(ii)(A) Research Laboratory and Production Facilities; through 1910.1030(g)(1)(ii)(B) not applicable to the coroner's office

1910.1030(g)(2) Information and Training.

1910.1030(g)(2)(i) The employer shall train each employee with occupational exposure in accordance with the requirements of this section. Such training must be provided at no cost to the employee and during working hours. The employer shall institute a training program and ensure employee participation in the program.

1910.1030(g)(2)(ii) Training shall be provided as follows:

1910.1030(g)(2)(ii)(A) At the time of initial assignment to tasks where occupational exposure may take place;

1910.1030(g)(2)(ii)(B) At least annually thereafter.

1910.1030(g)(2)(iii) [Reserved]

1910.1030(g)(2)(iv) Annual training for all employees shall be provided within one year of their previous training.

1910.1030(g)(2)(v) Employers shall provide additional training when changes such as modification of tasks or procedures or institution of new tasks or procedures affect the employee's occupational exposure. The additional training may be limited to addressing the new exposures created.

1910.1030(g)(2)(vi) Material appropriate in content and vocabulary to educational level, literacy, and language of employees shall be used.

1910.1030(g)(2)(vii) The training program shall contain at a minimum the following elements:

1910.1030(g)(2)(vii)(A) An accessible copy of the regulatory text of this standard and an explanation of its contents;

1910.1030(g)(2)(vii)(B) A general explanation of the epidemiology and symptoms of bloodborne diseases;

1910.1030(g)(2)(vii)(C) An explanation of the modes of transmission of bloodborne pathogens;

1910.1030(g)(2)(vii)(D) An explanation of the employer's exposure control plan and the means by which the employee can obtain a copy of the written plan;

1910.1030(g)(2)(vii)(E) An explanation of the appropriate methods for recognizing tasks and other activities that may involve exposure to blood and other potentially infectious materials;

1910.1030(g)(2)(vii)(F) An explanation of the use and limitations of methods that will prevent or reduce exposure including appropriate engineering controls, work practices, and personal protective equipment;

1910.1030(g)(2)(vii)(G) Information on the types, proper use, location, removal, handling, decontamination and disposal of personal protective equipment;

1910.1030(g)(2)(vii)(H) An explanation of the basis for selection of personal protective equipment;

1910.1030(g)(2)(vii)(I) Information on the hepatitis B vaccine, including information on its efficacy, safety, method of administration, the benefits of being vaccinated, and that the vaccine and vaccination will be offered free of charge;

1910.1030(g)(2)(vii)(J) Information on the appropriate actions to take and persons to contact in an emergency involving blood or other potentially infectious materials;

1910.1030(g)(2)(vii)(K) An explanation of the procedure to follow if an exposure incident occurs, including the method of reporting the incident and the medical follow-up that will be made available;

1910.1030(g)(2)(vii)(L) Information on the post-exposure evaluation and follow-up that the employer is required to provide for the employee following an exposure incident;

1910.1030(g)(2)(vii)(M) An explanation of the signs and labels and/or color coding required by paragraph (g)(1); and

1910.1030(g)(2)(vii)(N) An opportunity for interactive questions and answers with the person conducting the training session.

1910.1030(g)(2)(viii) The person conducting the training shall be knowledgeable in the subject matter covered by the elements contained in the training program as it relates to the workplace that the training will address.

1910.1030(g)(2)(ix) through 1910.1030(g)(2)(ix)(C) Additional Initial Training for Employees in HIV and HBV Laboratories and Production Facilities not applicable to the coroner's office.

1910.1030(h) Recordkeeping –

1910.1030(h)(1) Medical Records.

1910.1030(h)(1)(i) The employer shall establish and maintain an accurate record for each employee with occupational exposure, in accordance with 29 CFR 1910.1020.

1910.1030(h)(1)(ii) This record shall include:

1910.1030(h)(1)(ii)(A) The name and social security number of the employee;

1910.1030(h)(1)(ii)(B) A copy of the employee's hepatitis B vaccination status including the dates of all the hepatitis B vaccinations and any medical records relative to the employee's ability to receive vaccination as required by paragraph (f)(2);

1910.1030(h)(1)(ii)(C) A copy of all results of examinations, medical testing, and follow-up procedures as required by paragraph (f)(3);

1910.1030(h)(1)(ii)(D) The employer's copy of the healthcare professional's written opinion as required by paragraph (f)(5); and

1910.1030(h)(1)(ii)(E) A copy of the information provided to the healthcare professional as required by paragraphs (f)(4)(ii)(B)(C) and (D).

1910.1030(h)(1)(iii) Confidentiality. The employer shall ensure that employee medical records required by paragraph (h)(1) are:

1910.1030(h)(1)(iii)(A) Kept confidential; and

1910.1030(h)(1)(iii)(B) Not disclosed or reported without the employee's express written consent to any person within or outside the workplace except as required by this section or as may be required by law.

1910.1030(h)(1)(iv) The employer shall maintain the records required by paragraph (h) for at least the duration of employment plus 30 years in accordance with 29 CFR 1910.1020.

1910.1030(h)(2) Training Records.

1910.1030(h)(2)(i) Training records shall include the following information:

1910.1030(h)(2)(i)(A) The dates of the training sessions;

1910.1030(h)(2)(i)(B) The contents or a summary of the training sessions;

1910.1030(h)(2)(i)(C) The names and qualifications of persons conducting the training; and

1910.1030(h)(2)(i)(D) The names and job titles of all persons attending the training sessions.

1910.1030(h)(2)(ii) Training records shall be maintained for 3 years from the date on which the training occurred.

1910.1030(h)(3) Availability.

1910.1030(h)(3)(i) The employer shall ensure that all records required to be maintained by this section shall be made available upon request to the Assistant Secretary and the Director for examination and copying.

1910.1030(h)(3)(ii) Employee training records required by this paragraph shall be provided upon request for examination and copying to employees, to employee representatives, to the Director, and to the Assistant Secretary.

1910.1030(h)(3)(iii) Employee medical records required by this paragraph shall be provided upon request for examination and copying to the subject employee, to anyone having written consent of the subject employee, to the Director, and to the Assistant Secretary in accordance with 29 CFR 1910.1020.

1910.1030(h)(4) Transfer of Records. The employer shall comply with the requirements involving transfer of records set forth in 29 CFR 1910.1020(h).

1910.1030(h)(5) Sharps injury log.

1910.1030(h)(5)(i) The employer shall establish and maintain a sharps injury log for the recording of percutaneous injuries from contaminated sharps. The information in the sharps injury log shall be recorded and maintained in such manner as to protect the confidentiality of the injured employee. The sharps injury log shall contain, at a minimum:

1910.1030(h)(5)(i)(A) The type and brand of device involved in the incident,

1910.1030(h)(5)(i)(B) The department or work area where the exposure incident occurred, and

1910.1030(h)(5)(i)(C) An explanation of how the incident occurred.

1910.1030(h)(5)(ii) The requirement to establish and maintain a sharps injury log shall apply to any employer who is required to maintain a log of occupational injuries and illnesses under 29 CFR part 1904.

1910.1030(h)(5)(iii) The sharps injury log shall be maintained for the period required by 29 CFR 1904.33.

1910.1030(i) Dates — 1910.1030(i) through 1910.1030(i)(4) regard the effective dates of the original CFR. The effective date of implementation of this biosafety manual for the Fremont County Coroner's Office shall be November 1st, 2015

Applicable Sections of 29 CFR 1910.132
Personal Protective Equipment (PPE) – General Requirements

1910.132(a) Application. Protective equipment, including personal protective equipment for eyes, face, head, and extremities, protective clothing, respiratory devices, and protective shields and barriers, shall be provided, used, and maintained in a sanitary and reliable condition wherever it is necessary by reason of hazards of processes or environment, chemical hazards, radiological hazards, or mechanical irritants encountered in a manner capable of causing injury or impairment in the function of any part of the body through absorption, inhalation or physical contact.

1910.132(b) Employee-owned equipment. Where employees provide their own protective equipment, the employer shall be responsible to assure its adequacy, including proper maintenance, and sanitation of such equipment.

1910.132(c) Design. All personal protective equipment shall be of safe design and construction for the work to be performed.

1910.132(d) Hazard assessment and equipment selection.

1910.132(d)(1) The employer shall assess the workplace to determine if hazards are present, or are likely to be present, which necessitate the use of personal protective equipment (PPE). If such hazards are present, or likely to be present, the employer shall:

1910.132(d)(1)(i) Select, and have each affected employee use, the types of PPE that will protect the affected employee from the hazards identified in the hazard assessment;

1910.132(d)(1)(ii) Communicate selection decisions to each affected employee; and,

1910.132(d)(1)(iii) Select PPE that properly fits each affected employee. Note: Non-mandatory Appendix B contains an example of procedures that would comply with the requirement for a hazard assessment.

1910.132(d)(2) The employer shall verify that the required workplace hazard assessment has been performed through a written certification that identifies the workplace evaluated; the person certifying that the evaluation has been performed; the date(s) of the hazard assessment; and, which identifies the document as a certification of hazard assessment.

1910.132(e) Defective and damaged equipment. Defective or damaged personal protective equipment shall not be used.

1910.132(f) Training.

1910.132(f)(1) The employer shall provide training to each employee who is required by this section to use PPE. Each such employee shall be trained to know at least the following:

1910.132(f)(1)(i) When PPE is necessary;

1910.132(f)(1)(ii) What PPE is necessary;

1910.132(f)(1)(iii) How to properly don, doff, adjust, and wear PPE;

1910.132(f)(1)(iv) The limitations of the PPE; and,

1910.132(f)(1)(v) The proper care, maintenance, useful life and disposal of the PPE.

1910.132(f)(2) Each affected employee shall demonstrate an understanding of the training specified in paragraph (f)(1) of this section, and the ability to use PPE properly, before being allowed to perform work requiring the use of PPE.

1910.132(f)(3) When the employer has reason to believe that any affected employee who has already been trained does not have the understanding and skill required by paragraph (f)(2) of this section, the employer shall retrain each such employee. Circumstances where retraining is required include, but are not limited to, situations where:

1910.132(f)(3)(i) Changes in the workplace render previous training obsolete; or

1910.132(f)(3)(ii) Changes in the types of PPE to be used render previous training obsolete; or

1910.132(f)(3)(iii) Inadequacies in an affected employee's knowledge or use of assigned PPE indicate that the employee has not retained the requisite understanding or skill.

1910.132(g) Paragraphs (d) and (f) of this section apply only to 1910.133, 1910.135, 1910.136, and 1910.138. Paragraphs (d) and (f) of this section do not apply to 1910.134 and 1910.137.

[NOTE: 1910.133 Eye and Face Protection; 1910.135 Head Protection; 1910.136 Foot Protection; 1910.137 Electrical Protection; and 1910.138 Hand Protection are not encountered in the regular and common duties of the coroner's office (#138 discusses industrial hand

protection, not biohazard glove use). Should in a rare or special circumstance such protection be needed, the Operations Deputy is assigned to direct proper use on scene. As stated in 1910.132(g), Paragraphs (d) and (f) do not apply to 1910.134 Respiratory Protection. The need for Respiratory Protection is not required by the regular, expected, and common duties of the coroner's office, but NIOSH approved N95 face masks are available to the employee should they desire the extra level of precaution and protection]

1910.132(h) Payment for protective equipment.

1910.132(h)(1) Except as provided by paragraphs (h)(2) through (h)(6) of this section, the protective equipment, including personal protective equipment (PPE), used to comply with this part, shall be provided by the employer at no cost to employees.

1910.132(h)(2) The employer is not required to pay for non-specialty safety-toe protective footwear (including steel-toe shoes or steel-toe boots) and non-specialty prescription safety eyewear, provided that the employer permits such items to be worn off the job-site.

1910.132(h)(3) When the employer provides metatarsal guards and allows the employee, at his or her request, to use shoes or boots with built-in metatarsal protection, the employer is not required to reimburse the employee for the shoes or boots.

1910.132(h)(4) The employer is not required to pay for:

1910.132(h)(4)(i) The logging boots required by 29 CFR 1910.266(d)(1)(v);

1910.132(h)(4)(ii) Everyday clothing, such as long-sleeve shirts, long pants, street shoes, and normal work boots; or

1910.132(h)(4)(iii) Ordinary clothing, skin creams, or other items, used solely for protection from weather, such as winter coats, jackets, gloves, parkas, rubber boots, hats, raincoats, ordinary sunglasses, and sunscreen.

1910.132(h)(5) The employer must pay for replacement PPE, except when the employee has lost or intentionally damaged the PPE.

1910.132(h)(6) Where an employee provides adequate protective equipment he or she owns pursuant to paragraph (b) of this section, the employer may allow the employee to use it and is not required to reimburse the employee for that equipment. The employer shall not require an employee to provide or pay for his or her own PPE, unless the PPE is excepted by paragraphs (h)(2) through (h)(5) of this section.

1910.132(h)(7) [original CFR effective date]

Note to § 1910.132(h): When the provisions of another OSHA standard specify whether or not the employer must pay for specific equipment, the payment provisions of that standard shall prevail.

Additional Regulations

1910.1020 Toxic and Hazardous Substances: Access to employee exposure and medical records – applies only to exposure records, and in the case of biohazard substances is superseded per 1910.5(c)(1) by the more specific requirements of 1910.1030

1910.120 Hazardous Materials: Hazardous waste operations and emergency response -- not encountered in the regular, expected, and common duties of the coroner's office. Should a death scene involve hazardous waste or materials, procedures, needs and operations are deferred to the Incident Commander and those trained in Hazmat Response.

1910.134 Appendix D to Sec. 1910.134 (Mandatory) Information for Employees Using Respirators When Not Required Under the Standard

Respirators are an effective method of protection against designated hazards when properly selected and worn. Respirator use is encouraged, even when exposures are below the exposure limit, to provide an additional level of comfort and protection for workers. However, if a respirator is used improperly or not kept clean, the respirator itself can become a hazard to the worker. Sometimes, workers may wear respirators to avoid exposures to hazards, even if the amount of hazardous substance does not exceed the limits set by OSHA standards. If your employer provides respirators for your voluntary use, or if you provide your own respirator, you need to take certain precautions to be sure that the respirator itself does not present a hazard.

You should do the following:

1. Read and heed all instructions provided by the manufacturer on use, maintenance, cleaning and care, and warnings regarding the respirators limitations.

2. Choose respirators certified for use to protect against the contaminant of concern. NIOSH, the National Institute for Occupational Safety and Health of the U.S. Department of Health and Human Services, certifies respirators. A label or statement of certification should appear on the

respirator or respirator packaging. It will tell you what the respirator is designed for and how much it will protect you.

3. Do not wear your respirator into atmospheres containing contaminants for which your respirator is not designed to protect against. For example, a respirator designed to filter dust particles will not protect you against gases, vapors, or very small solid particles of fumes or smoke.

4. Keep track of your respirator so that you do not mistakenly use someone else's respirator.

Appendix D: NAGPRA Policies

Commentary: *These particular policies were developed with the Office of the Solicitor, U.S. Dept. of the Interior, NAGPRA Compliance Division of Parks and Wildlife, and the Fremont County civil attorney. As such they meet the acceptable language and presentation to both State and Federal regulations. While Fremont (and part of Hot Springs) are the only counties of Wyoming that contain lands that are part of a reservation, other counties need to be aware that the Federal NAGPRA applies to any Federal jurisdiction lands in the state, and in most cases any Native American remains recovered anywhere. This law applies nationally, so it is something every coroner needs to be familiar with. In addition, many border counties in this state are near reservations on the other side of the state line and in other jurisdictions. Developing good tribal relations is appropriate and knowing the law in this area may come into play if a death in your jurisdiction involves those from other areas, even if out of state.*

NATIVE AMERICAN HUMAN REMAINS – NAGPRA POLICIES

Subject to any procedural or substantive right which may otherwise be secured to any individual or Indian tribe, the disposition of the remains of a Native American individual shall be subject to the applicable provisions of the Native American Graves Protection and Repatriation Act (NAGPRA; 25 U.S.C. 3001-3013 (2016)) and its implementing regulations (43 C.F.R. Part 10 (2017)) where the human remains are found –

- on "Federal lands" (25 U.S.C. 3001(5); 43 C.F.R. 10.2(f)(1));

- on "tribal land" (25 U.S.C. 3001(15); 43 C.F.R. 10.2(f)(2)) (including within the exterior boundaries of the Wind River Reservation); or

- in the "possession" (43 C.F.R. 10.2(a)(3)(i)), or under the "control" (43 C.F.R. 10.2(a)(3)(ii)), of a "Federal agency" (25 U.S.C. 3001(4); 43 C.F.R. 10.2(a)(1)) or a "museum" (25 U.S.C. 3001(8); 43 C.F.R. 10.2(a)(3)).

Following the Fremont County Coroner's investigation of the human remains of a Native American individual, the Coroner's Office shall return physical custody of the human remains, as appropriate, to the Indian tribe, Federal agency, or museum on whose behalf the County Coroner's Office investigated the human
remains as follows:

- o Where the human remains are found on Federal land after November 16, 1990, physical custody of the remains shall be returned to the "Federal agency official" (43 C.F.R. 10.2(a)(2)) of the Federal agency managing the land on which the human remains are found. Except that, where the human remains are found during an intentional excavation (see 43 C.F.R. 10.3) pursuant to a permit issued under the Archaeological Resources Protection Act, physical custody of the remains shall be returned to the permittee.

- Where the human remains are found on tribal land after November 16, 1990, physical custody of the remains shall be returned to the "Indian tribe official" (43 C.F.R. 10.2(b)(4)) of the Indian tribe on whose tribal land the human remains are found. Where the human remains are found on the Wind River Reservation, physical custody of the remains shall be returned to a representative or, jointly, representatives for the Eastern Shoshone Tribe of the Wind River Reservation and the Arapaho Tribe of the Wind River Reservation. Except that, where the human remains are found during an intentional excavation pursuant to a permit issued under the Archaeological Resources Protection Act, physical custody of the remains shall be returned to the permittee.

- Where the human remains are in the possession, or under the control, of a Federal agency, physical custody of the remains shall be returned to the appropriate Federal agency official, or to a party as directed by the Federal agency official.

- Where the human remains are in the possession, or under the control, of a museum other than the Fremont County Coroner's Office, physical custody of the remains shall be returned to the appropriate "museum official" (43 C.F.R. 10.2(a)(4)), or to a party as directed by the museum official.

Where the human remains are not found on Federal lands after November 16, 1990; not found on tribal land after November 16, 1990; not in the possession, or under the control, of a Federal agency; or not in the possession, or under the control, of a museum other than the Fremont County Coroner's Office, then pursuant to State law, the Fremont County Coroner's Office has possession or control of the human remains and, as a museum, shall comply with the requirements of NAGPRA and its implementing regulations with respect to the human remains.

Appendix E: Anatomical Gifts – Procurement Agencies

(Note: This section is only the short policy statement in this area from the coroner procedure manual. This does not include the more lengthy individual agreements signed with the organ procurement agencies, but does cover the basic principles codified by those agreements.)

ANATOMICAL GIFTS - PROCUREMENT AGENCIES
1. It is the policy of the Coroner's Office to cooperate in cases of reportable deaths where organ procurement has been authorized by the family. In those cases where an investigation is required by the Coroner's Office, the circumstances of the death must be reported to the Coroner's Office prior to any tissue harvest being made.
2. Being a Coroner's case does not exclude a body from donation. Certain limitations or circumstances may apply, however, as noted below.
3. ORGAN PROCUREMENT PROCEDURES: The following will outline those procedures to be followed when organ donation is sought in Coroner cases. Prior to approaching the family for permission for procurement:
    a. A hospital must notify the Coroner's Office and request approval to initiate organ procurement.
    b. If the death is clearly due to natural causes (expected and/or attended), the physician may be allowed to proceed with organ procurement procedures; however, approval must first come from the Coroner's Office.
    c. If the death merits jurisdiction, the Investigator must obtain enough information that indicates a thorough investigation of the circumstances of the death prior to authorization.
        i. HOMICIDES: Generally, homicides are not eligible for donation of any type.
        ii. SUICIDES (NON-GUNSHOT WOUND): To the extent that all parties (law enforcement, DA, Coroner's Office) are convinced that the manner of death is suicide, and all injuries and abnormalities are documented, the Coroner's Office may give permission to proceed with organ procurement.

iii. SUICIDES (GUNSHOT WOUND): Documentation of the exit and entrance wounds must be completed prior to organ procurement if approved. If the missile is still in the body, appropriate documentation on the entrance wound, with photography, will be required prior to authorizing organ procurement. If the law enforcement agency of jurisdiction, or the County Attorney, requests removal of the missile as an item of evidence in the case, then arrangements will be made for an autopsy for the purpose of obtaining or preserving evidence of the cause of death (W.S. 7-4-209).

iv. ACCIDENTAL DEATHS: All injuries must be documented prior to giving authorization for the organ procurement team to proceed.

v. DEATHS DUE TO UNKNOWN CAUSES: Frequently, cases are reported in which the cause of death has not been determined and cannot be determined without further investigation. In most of these cases, organ procurement will not be permitted for obvious reasons, as it is indeterminate what may or may not be significant evidence.

vi. In General, cases that are determined to require a forensic autopsy are eligible for organ donation **only** with the approval of the Coroner and attending Pathologist, and if allowed, are done in conjunction with the autopsy, not before.

4. Specific Details on the policies and procedures for tissue and organ recovery are on file in the Coroner Office. Two organizations are applicable in Wyoming and have specific protocols by signed agreement: Donor Alliance Wyoming Organ and Tissue Donation Coroner Protocol, and Rocky Mountain Lion's Eye Bank Donation Protocol.

5. NOTE: In all cases, Fremont County facilities, equipment & supplies, or staff, will not be used for recovery by private procurement agencies or organizations.

Commentary: *Item #5 is included due to questions of conflict of interest if employees are used and/or paid for assisting or performing recoveries; issues with receiving payment for county required charges for use of facilities; and lack of reimbursement for county supplies and deputy time.*

Appendix F: Disaster Plan

A. **GENERAL**: The Coroner's Office Disaster Plan for field personnel provides a series of steps to be taken in the event that at least five (5) deaths occur suddenly and simultaneously, and the situation is such that standard Coroner operating procedures are not satisfactory in processing those deaths.

B. **DEFINITION:** In the term "Disaster", the situation can only officially be declared a disaster from the Coroner standpoint by the Coroner, or the Chief Deputy Coroner. Often a disaster will be declared by a variety of outside agencies, including but not limited to the Office of the Governor, the National or State Departments of Homeland Security, the Department of Corrections, Department of Health, the National Transportation Safety Board, Emergency Management, or a branch of the military. In general terms, a disaster is any situation that overwhelms the ability of local agencies to cope with an emergency.

C. **NOTIFICATION:** The first member of the Coroner's Office becoming aware of the disaster or potential disaster shall immediately contact the Coroner and specifically relay that information to the Coroner, or the Chief Deputy Coroner. It shall be the duty and responsibility of the Coroner's staff member being so notified of notifying the others in the department. There is a specific procedure in place nationally and in Wyoming for general disaster notifications.

D. **SECURITY**: If the first member of the Coroner's Office to become aware of a disaster is at the scene, it is secured to the best of their ability. In the absence of a definitive agency or jurisdiction, such as law enforcement, any means to secure the scene must be employed. Since disasters may initially conceal the true extent of damage, injury, or mayhem, all concerns must focus on survivors. Only when authorized personnel have indicated that there are no survivors can any true security be implemented at a scene of a catastrophe. Security may mean that only those individuals designated as rescuers or emergency medical personnel may enter a scene, and that all others, including Coroner personnel, are excluded from scenes of obvious multiple fatalities until life-saving efforts are completed.

E. **INFORMATION GATHERING - PRELIMINARY**: This step must be performed by an individual at the scene, or a person with whom they are in direct contact to provide preliminary information for purposes of mobilizing investigators and resources for immediate response.

F. **CORONER DISASTER PLAN**: This pre-prepared plan is on file in the main Coroner's Office for the county. It is used by the office to outline resources, facilities, manpower, and capabilities of the community in which the disaster occurs. This information will be considered by the Coroner's Office in offering direction and support for any scene activity. The Disaster Plan should be reviewed by all personnel.

G. **COMMUNICATION**: Specific means for Coroner Personnel to communicate to-and-from the scene shall be determined. This can range from having a unit with a 2-way radio to transmit a message to the investigators, to relaying from commercial telephones, to using any available telephone at the scene. Initial communication may be piecemeal, but nonetheless, must be established. Any individual communicating with the Coroner from the actual scene of a disaster shall always relay information as to how that scene can be accessed. If there is no way to communicate into the scene, this information has to be relayed to the Coroner's Office. (Telephone communications, in many disaster situations, have been demonstrated to be potentially vulnerable to damage, and extremely high usage by the public. Radio-based systems not requiring commercial power exhibit the highest degree of reliability).

H. **OPERATIONS**: The primary base of operations remains in the Coroner's Office for receipt, identification, examination, and release of human remains. No area of the county can be overlooked in determining means of providing a death investigation capability in the event of mass disaster with multiple fatalities. In addition, a forward base of operations and Command Center can be provided through the Coroner Mass-Fatality trailer.

Mass Fatality / Pandemic / Emergency Operations Plan

The duties and responsibilities of the Coroner's Office will conform to State and Federal regulations and statutes, as well as the policies and standards for death investigation as established by the Fremont County Coroner's Office.

A. **Planning Responsibilities**
1. Coordinate and determine needs with Incident Command
    a. Scene and Personnel Safety
    b. Scope and anticipated numbers and duration
    c. Participating Agencies
2. Assure adequate supply materials for recovery and identification.
    a. Body Bags or envelopes
    b. Biohazard Bags
    c. Property containers/bags
    d. Identification bands or tags
    e. Scene Documentation materials, equipment, and markers
3. Transportation and Vehicles
    a. Vehicles: 3 response/transport vehicles
    b. Transport
        1. Mass Fatality Trailer & mobile IC
        2. Gurneys & flexible stretchers
4. Remains Storage
    a. Cooler, County Morgue, Lander
    b. Cooler, EMA garage, Riverton
    c. Wyoming Life Resource Center – Barn facility storage/processing and interment area
    d. Arrange temporary facilities as needed
        1. Funeral Home facilities and coolers
        2. Refrigerated trucks and associated fuel/power needs
        3. Temporary processing facility, building, or structure
5. Remains Examination
    a. County Morgue, Lander
    b. Temporary processing area near scene if applicable
    c. WLRC Field station and set-up
6. Security for Facilities
    a. Law Enforcement
    b. Contractual Staff
7. Transportation, Scene to Morgue/Storage
    a. Coroner vehicles and trailer
    b. Funeral Home assistance if available
8. Personal Protective Equipment
    a. Gloves and masks

    b. Protective suits
    c. Disinfecting materials
    d. Other misc. biohazard and protective gear
  9. Remains Disposition and other Disposal
    a. Remains to Funeral Home custody
    b. Possible temporary or permanent interment at WLRC
    c. Biohazard materials and used PPEs
    d. Property release or Secured Storage
  10. Organized Documentation and Administration
    a. Data entry and documentation of scene and remains
    b. Chain of Custody for remains, property and evidence
    c. Identification of remains and detailed interment location information
    d. Victim information, family contact and documentation
    e. Critical Incident Stress needs and referrals
    f. Safety issues, incidents, and violations
    g. Personnel, Logistics, Planning, Materials and Supplies, Operations

B. Procedures

1. The responsibilities of the coroner begin with the notification that the incident involves multiple fatalities. All deputies will be called and requested to respond to the incident command center. The notification will be accomplished by the Coroner, Chief Deputy, or designated representative. Mutual aid is available.
2. **CONSIDERATION WILL BE GIVEN TO ALL DISASTER DECLARATIONS MADE BY THE GOVERNOR OF THE STATE OF WYOMING.**
3. **Fremont County is in the emergency response region with Teton County and Sublette County.**
4. The coroner will proceed to the command center for briefing with the incident command. An approach to the incident will be determined. The emergency response trailer will respond to the command center. The incident will work under a unified command with an incident commander.
5. No body or body part will be touched or moved without the consent of the coroner, except for the preservation of life.
  A. **LOCATION:** The coroner's office will gather all incident information. The scene will be searched for bodies and body parts with locator flags being placed. They will be identified by number and mapped into location, as well as photographed.
  B. **RECOVERY**: The remains will be recovered and transported to an area designated for a temporary morgue. Then they will be transported to the Fremont County Morgue or other selected site for

examination. Recovery and transport of bodies will be conducted as hazardous materials, if the incident warrants.
- C. **IDENTIFICATION**: The bodies will be identified through forensic processes and standards. Fragmentary remains or those not identifiable by immediate methods may have to be stored or temporarily interred pending long time frame methods of identification. All available methods of identification will be utilized.
- D. **CAUSE OF DEATH**: Remains will be examined to determine the cause of death, and all suspicious deaths will be autopsied, if possible.
- E. **MANNER OF DEATH**: A complete incident investigation will be completed to determine the manner of death. All deaths determined to be homicide will be autopsied, if possible.
- F. **DISPOSITION OF REMAINS**: At the completion of the described procedures, the remains of the deceased will be released to the family for disposition per standard policies. All unclaimed bodies will be interred in accordance with Wyoming Statutes and Fremont County Policy.
- G. **NEXT OF KIN**: The next of kin will be located and notified of the death. All local families will be notified in person if possible. Families living in areas other than Fremont County will be notified through the assistance of an agency in that area. No telephone notification will be made, if it can be avoided.

The Fremont County Coroner and staff are subject to call and response when requested by the Wyoming Office of Homeland Security. Additional resources and assistance, State and Federal, may be available, depending on the scope of the incident, and declarations made through the Governmental Chain of Command, such as in Disasters or States of Emergency.

Public Health Emergency

A public health emergency as defined in W.S. 35-4-115(a)(i) is declared by the governor and involves the risk of a significant number of fatalities. During such time the coroner will cooperate with the state health officer and county health officer to mitigate the consequences of such an event, as mandated by W.S. 35-1-223. W.S. 35-4-114 provides immunity from liability for those acting under such as declared event.

W.S. 35-1-241 defines the safe disposal of corpses in emergency circumstances during the period of such an emergency. The statute includes the following:
(a) The state health officer in consultation with the appropriate county coroner, during the period that a public health emergency exists, may:
    (i) Adopt and enforce measures to provide for the safe disposal of corpses as may be reasonable and necessary for emergency response. These measures may include the embalming, burial, cremation, interment, disinterment, transportation and disposal of corpses;

(ii) Take possession or control of any corpse;

(iii) Order the disposal of any corpse of a person who has died of an infectious disease through burial or cremation within twenty-four (24) hours after death;

(iv) Compel any person authorized to embalm, bury, cremate, inter, disinter, transport or dispose of corpses to accept any corpse or provide the use of his business or facility if the actions are reasonable and necessary for emergency response. The use of a business or facility may include transferring the management and supervision of the business or facility to the state health officer and granting the right for the state health officer to take immediate possession for a limited or unlimited period of time, but shall not exceed beyond the termination of the public health emergency.

(b) Every corpse prior to disposal pursuant to subsection (a) of this section shall be clearly labeled with all available information to identify the decedent and the circumstances of death. Any corpse of a deceased person with an infectious disease shall have an external, clearly visible tag indicating that the corpse is infected and, if known, the infectious disease.

(c) Every person in charge of disposing of any corpse pursuant to subsection (a) of this section shall maintain a written record of each corpse and all available information to identify the decedent and the circumstances of death and disposal. If a corpse cannot be identified, prior to disposal a qualified person shall, to the extent possible, take fingerprints and one (1) or more photographs of the corpse, and collect a DNA specimen. All information collected under this subsection shall be promptly forwarded to the state health official.

(d) As used in this section "public health emergency" means as defined by W.S. 35-4-115(a)(i).

As of 2018, there were no specific administrative rules on file with the WY Secretary of State, under the Department of Health that add any other procedures to the above.

In the case of a mass fatality, declared disaster, or other public health emergency, the coroner's office will facilitate and document all large number or mass burials, as required by law, in an appropriate area for either permanent or temporary interment. Large numbers may require the use of the facility and land set aside at the WY Life Resource Center, per MOU agreement with the Dept. of Health for indigent and unclaimed burials.

If interment is considered temporary, or relatives of the deceased wish to claim, disinter, and rebury elsewhere at a later date, those persons must obtain all required permits prior to removal, and are responsible for all costs and arrangements of that removal, unless specific exception is approved by the County Commission. A representative of the coroner's office will be present for any such removal to insure accurate documentation and identification of the location of the individual being removed.

Appendix G: Indigent and Unclaimed Policies

Fremont County
Unclaimed & Indigent Burial and Cremation Policy

This policy is established and amended to comply with W.S. § 42-2-103(c), W.S. § 18-3-504(c), and W.S. § 19-14-101, and shall be effective as of May 5, 2014. (Amended by County Commission 2019)

1. Authority: Pursuant to W.S. § 19-14-101, the County Commissioners are responsible for the costs of burial or cremation of indigent veterans who have not been dishonorably discharged, and who served on behalf of the United States during any conflict or war. The County Commissioners are also responsible, as per W.S. § 18-3-504(c), for burial or cremation of other indigent persons who were not receiving certain public benefits. As per W.S. § 42-2-103(c) the State of Wyoming Department of Family Services is responsible for burial or cremation of those indigent persons receiving aid under POWER (Person Opportunities With Employment Responsibilities) program, SSI (Supplemental Security Income) or Medicaid. Pursuant to W.S. § 7-4-104(a)(i)(K), a case involving an unanticipated death where the identity of the victim is unknown or the body is unclaimed, is a coroner's case, and under W.S. § 7-4-207(a), when the coroner investigates the death of a person whose body is not claimed by a friend or relative within five days of the date of discovery and whose death does not require further investigation, he shall cause the body to be decently buried. The expense of the burial shall be paid from any property found with the body. If no property is found, the expense of the burial shall be paid by the county in which the investigation occurs.

2. Initial Determination of Eligibility: The family or friends, as claimant for the deceased, or the funeral home as their representative, shall be responsible for discovering whether the decedent was indigent at the time of death, or a recipient of the public benefits named above. Failure to diligently pursue information regarding indigency will result in refusal of payment by the County.

3. Veterans:

A. Any veteran who was not dishonorably discharged and who served during a war or conflict (as defined in Title 38, United States Code, section 101) on behalf of the United States, and who dies leaving insufficient funds to defray the necessary funeral expenses, is eligible for preparation of the body and transmittal to and interment in the Oregon Trail State Veterans' Cemetery in Evansville, Natrona County, Wyoming at 89 Cemetery Road, Evansville, WY 82636.

B. The amount expended for preparation of the body shall not exceed one thousand eight hundred dollars ($1,800.00). The amount expended for the transportation of the body shall not exceed five hundred dollars ($500.00)

C. Pursuant to W.S. § 19-14-101(c)(i), the claimant for the deceased, or funeral home as their representative, shall assemble and provide a complete record of all the facts relating to any veteran of the armed forces of the United States who is buried or cremated as per this policy, and shall submit the record to the County Coroner, who shall keep a complete record of all such facts. The County Coroner on behalf of the County Commission, will be responsible for verifying the veteran status by established procedure.

D. If a veteran was also in receipt of the public benefits named in paragraph 1 above at the time of death, the County shall assume responsibility for costs for interment in the Veterans' Cemetery.

4. Non-Veteran Indigents:
A. After the responsible party named in Section 2 above determines that a decedent was not receiving POWER assistance, SSI income, or Medicaid under the Wyoming Public Assistance and Social Services Act at the time of death, and that the decedent was without sufficient means in his own estate or other resources to provide burial or cremation, arrangements may be made for burial or cremation at the County's expense.

B. The total cost to the County of such burial or cremation shall not exceed one thousand eight hundred dollars ($1,800.00).

C. If the body is claimed by a friend, relative, or other person, and the decedent is not determined indigent, that person shall be responsible for burial or cremation at the rates charged by the funeral home in non-indigent cases.

D. If no property is found with the body, and no other estate or resources as listed on the application exist against which the responsible party or funeral home may make a claim, the responsible party or funeral home may then file an application for payment by the County, by submitting an itemized invoice or accounting and a sworn affidavit stating that diligent inquiry was made regarding potential property, assets, or funding.

E. If the Board of County Commissioners finds that no other means of payment are available, they may authorize payment to the funeral home, not to exceed $1,800.00. Any available funding resources as listed on the application will be deducted from the payment amount, and the funeral home may seek reimbursement in that amount from the estate.

F. Fremont County has arranged district or public locations for interment of both indigent or unclaimed remains, and is not responsible for interment or costs thereof, for non-veterans at any other location.

5. Non-veteran Unclaimed: If no one claims a body, or if the body remains unidentified, the expense of burial or cremation shall be paid from any property found with the body, as per W.S. § 7-4-207(a), and by the County in which the jurisdiction of the death occurs. The manner of disposition of the body and any itinerant funeral services are at the discretion of the Coroner and Fremont County, and may not be dictated by friends, family, or other interested persons, absent payment therefor.

6. Non-veteran Recipients of Certain Public Benefits: If the decedent was indigent and a recipient of POWER assistance, SSI income, or Medicaid under the Wyoming Public Assistance and Social Services Act at the time of death, the Wyoming Department of Family Services shall be responsible for payment for burial or cremation, as per W.S. § 42-2-103(c). Also per W.S. § 42-2-103(c), no Board of County Commissioners shall be responsible for any burial or cremation expenses in excess of the amount paid under this subsection.

7. Claim of Remains After Burial or Cremation: If a relative or friend of an unclaimed decedent wishes to claim the remains of the decedent after burial or cremation, that person must first reimburse the

County up to and including all burial or cremation fees, and any transportation fee paid for a decedent who was a veteran under Section 3 above, and shall pay the funeral home the costs over and above the amount paid by the county, as per their normal and customary rates, as well as any or all fees charged by the mortuary or cemetery for the cost of disinterment.

8. Coroner's Policy: The Fremont County Coroner's Disposition Policy and Resources for Unclaimed or Indigent Veteran's Remains, and assistance information handout of Resources for Funding Funerals and Burials, are attached hereto for reference. Policies and procedures for the disposition of property found on or with the body are public documents and are available from the Coroner's Office.

Additional section(s) to approved policy:

9. Determination and Usage of the Cemetery Area at the Wyoming Life Resource Center (WLRC)

    A. A Memorandum of Understanding (MOU), as approved by the County Commission, is in place between Fremont County and the Department of Health, Wyoming Life Resource Center at 8204 Wyoming Highway 789, Lander, WY 82501. Procedures and terms of use of this cemetery area for indigent and unclaimed burials are referenced in that MOU.

    B. The established area will be the primary burial site for unclaimed remains cases under W.S. § 7-4-207(a), with interment and procedures as established by the policies of the Fremont County Commission and Coroner's Office. This area will also be an optional burial site for indigent remains cases under applicable statutes, with interment and procedures as established by the policies of the Fremont County Commission and Coroner's Office.

    C. Should an indigent applicant prefer burial at a location other than as the County provides, an equivalent amount of interment cost may be deducted from the County's indigent compensation at the sole discretion and decision of the County Commission. [See Section 4.F]

    D. All access by the public to the burial site at WLRC is subject to the rules and regulations of that institution and the responsibility of compliance rests with the public.

E. If relatives of the deceased, or other parties, wish to claim, disinter, and rebury the remains elsewhere at a later date after interment at WLRC, those parties must obtain all required permits prior to removal, and are responsible for all costs and arrangements of that removal, unless specific exception is approved by the County Commission. A representative of the coroner's office will be present for any such removal to insure accurate documentation and identification of the location of the individual being removed [See Section 7].

F. All parties wishing to disinter and remove remains from the WLRC facility may be required to reimburse Fremont County for all costs incurred in the original interment prior to permission for removal, at the discretion of the County Commission.

10. Public Health Emergency and Mass Fatality

A. A public health emergency as defined in W.S. § 35-4-115(a)(i) is declared by the governor and involves the risk of a significant number of fatalities. During such time the coroner will cooperate with the state health officer and county health officer to mitigate the consequences of such an event, as mandated by W.S. § 35-1-223. W.S. § 35-4-114 provides immunity from liability for those acting under such as declared event, if following the instruction of the State Health Officer.

B. W.S. § 35-1-241 defines the safe disposal of human remains in emergency circumstances during the period of such an emergency. As of 2019, there were no specific administrative rules on file with the WY Secretary of State, under the Department of Health that add any other procedures to this statute. Should any such rules be promulgated by the Department of Health and certified by the Secretary of State, they will be added to this section as an Appendix.

C. In the case of a mass fatality, declared disaster, or other public health emergency, the coroner's office will facilitate and document all large number or mass burials, as required by law, in an appropriate area for either permanent or temporary interment. Large numbers may require the use of the facility and land set aside at the WY Life Resource Center, per MOU agreement with the Dept. of Health for indigent and unclaimed burials.

D. If interment under this section is considered temporary, or relatives of the deceased wish to claim, disinter, and rebury the remains elsewhere at a later date, those persons must obtain all required permits prior to removal, and are responsible for all costs and arrangements of that removal, unless specific exception is approved by the County Commission. A representative of the coroner's office will be present for any such removal to insure accurate documentation and identification of the location of the individual being removed. Other restrictions and procedures as noted in county policy may apply.

Approved and adopted by the Fremont County Board of Commissioners this 16th day of April, 2019.

Afterword

While attempting to make this text as comprehensive as possible, keep in mind that a set of Wyoming statutes in print form looks like an encyclopedia set on your shelf – twelve or more large volumes. Each agency, official, department, and political subdivision has their own statutory obligations, and in addition, may have comprehensive and detailed rules on file with the state. These rules, if authorized by statute, have the effect of statute. A great effort is made by the legislative services office and the attorney general's office to make the laws and rules consistent within themselves, but conflicts will arise, usually after the fact when it goes to implementation over time.

While interpretation can only be codified and set by judicial case law, or by other legal opinions, those too can change over time. Fighting in the judicial process can be time-consuming and expensive, even if your view is correct. When a conflict arises, the best approach is to have an objective discussion with an adversarial opinion and try to come up with a work-around that allows both parties to fulfill their obligations, without resorting to legal measures.

For example, W.S. 3-1-418 concerns death registration under the Dept. of Health, Vital Records, and states "The nonmedical coroner shall not diagnose the cause of death without the assistance and advice of a competent physician, advanced practice registered nurse or physician's assistant" in certifying the medical portion of a death certificate. Basically, unless a licensed physician, coroners obviously do not diagnose the cause of death, rather, we investigate and then conclude on the basis of that entire investigation, and all factors in it. Having an autopsy, consulting with the pathologist, talking to the attending ER doctor or personal physician, obtaining and reviewing medical records, is all "assistance and advice". The final conclusion is yours for manner and cause, based on the entirety of the investigation, and not a physician's. Just make sure your reporting and documentation justifies your conclusions thoroughly, and vital records will usually not question a conclusion.

Coroners are independent medical-legal death investigators for good reason under the law and society. Know what is expected under the law. Do your job. The dead deserve our best effort.

Subject Index

Anatomical Gifts
    General, *52, 80-82, 106*
    Policies, *185-186*

Authority
    Acting Coroner, *15, 18, 41*
    Archaeology sites, *31-34*
    Arrest, *14*
    Burial or Cremation, *49-51*
    Certification, *24, 58, 199*
    Child Abuse, *25, 59*
    Contempt, *13, 37, 47*
    Court Testimony, *86-88*
    Custodian of Record, *30, 142-147*
    Election & Term, *23, 69*
    Inquest, *31-35, 115-127*
    Joint Powers, *60, 106*
    Jurisdiction, *25, 34, 35*
    Medical records, *35, 100*
    Oath, *23*
    Office Space, *62-63*
    Position Defined, *25, 69*
    Subpoenas, *14, 37, 126-127*
    Term, *23, 69*
    Toxicology, *135*

Autopsy & Physicians
    Board of Standards, *43*
    Fees, *47*
    Historic, *15*
    Consultation Records, *28*
    Liability, *41, 51*
    Physician Appointment, *35*
    Post-mortem Exam, *41, 199*

Board of Coroner Standards
    Education, Training, *24, 58*
    General, *43-45*
    History, *18*
    Rules, *93-96*

Clerk of District Court, *15, 39, 40, 102, 125*

Confidentiality
    Coroner, *27-31, 129-131*
    Court Order, *29*
    Deceased Identity, *28-29*
    History, *19*
    Public Records, *27-28*
    Research & Training, *28*

Coroner case, Definition
    Child abuse, *59*
    Current, *25*
    Historic, *13*
    Presumed death, *49*

County Attorney
    Access to Records, *28*
    Autopsy Order, *41*
    Board of Standards, *43, 45*
    Child Abuse, *59*
    Complaints, *45*
    Duties, *102*
    Opinions, *128-133*
    Removal of Official, *65-68*

County Commission
    Autopsy Fees, *47*
    Bonds, *23*
    Board of Standards, *45*
    Complaints, *45*
    Coroner Office Space, *62*
    Coroner Salary, *42*
    County Policies, *101-103*
    Deputy Wages, *23, 42*
    Duties, *102*
    Education payment, *24*
    Fees & Mileage, *42*

Indigents/Costs, 64, 68
Investigation Costs, 35, 38
Inquest Costs, 37, 38, 126
Records Location, 62-63
Unclaimed, 15, 39-40, 84

Definitions
Archaeological burial, 33
Attended & anticipated
Death, 18, 25, 26
Coroner as Official, 25
Coroner Case, 25
Dead Body, 73
Determination of Death, 84
Dockets, 27, 62
Final Disposition, 74
Human Remains, 70
"In turn", 36
Live Birth, 73
Person in Charge of
Disposition, 74
Public Emergency, 77
Still Birth, 73
Viability, 82

Department of Health
Access Records, 28, 30, 75
Cause of Death, 71, 199
General, 92
Health Officer Coroner, 37
Public Health Emergency,
30, 72-73, 77
Reportable Diseases, 75-76
Transport, 71

Deputy Coroners
Appointment, 23
Certification, 24, 58
Duties, 110-111
Office, 25
Personnel Files, 131
Salaries, 42
Standards, 44, 93-96
Training, 58

Disposition of the Body
Archaeological Sites, 32
Burial Authorization, 49-51
Crim. Case Release, 133
DFS Responsibility, 84-85
Emergency Disposal, 72-73
Funeral Director, 71
Historic, 15
Indigent, 64, 68
Policies, 193-198
Possession, 77-79
Unclaimed, 40, 51, 77-79
Veterans, 68, 78, 193

Federal Regulations
BLM, 104
First Responder, 97
HIPPA, 37, 100
Incident Mngmt, 99, 105,
189-192
NAGPRA, 34, 98, 182-184
OSHA, 98, 155-181
Tribal, 105

Inquests
Authority, 34-39
Contempt, 37, 47-48
Deceased Testimony, 46
Jurors, 37, 39
Juror Costs, 37
Juror Fees, 37, 46
Juror Impaneling, 13, 37
Juror Instructions, 124-125
Juror Number, 13, 35
Juror Oath, 13, 37
Policies, Proced., 115-127
Post Mortem Exam, 41
Records, 15, 39
Required to hold, 134
Subpoenas, 14, 37, 126-127
Witness Oath, 14, 38
Witness Rights, 122
Verdict, 14, 39

Investigations
Autopsy, 35, 41
Costs, 35

General Policies, 108-114
Genetic Testing, 59
Inclusions, 34-35
Inquest Preparation, 116
Reasonable, 35
Standards, 93-95

Law Enforcement
Access to Records, 28
Archaeological sites, 32
Background Checks, 57
Child Abuse, 59
Coroner notification, 31, 34, 36
Fire Marshall, 93
POST Authorization, 58
Reporting Death, 31, 34
Sheriff Duties, 41, 104
Standards (POST), 44
State Agencies, 93
Training Standards, 58

Law, General
Board of Standards, 43-45
Conflict of Interest, 53-56
Interpretation, 20-22
Joint Powers, 41, 59, 106
Liability, 41
Remove from Office, 65-67

Native American & Tribal
Affiliated tribes, 32, 34, 105
Archaeological sites, 32
BIA, 97
Ethnic respect, 33
Identification, 32
Inquests, 119
Joint powers, 60, 107
NAGPRA, 34, 98, 182-184
Policies, 111
Protocols, 32-33

Penalties
Acting before oath, 55
Archaeological remains, 33
Body Trafficking, 78

Concealing a body, 53
Confidential Violation, 29
Conflict of interest, 53
Contempt, 37, 47-48
Desecration, 51
Duty failure, 55
Failure to Certify, 24
Failure to Dispose or Deliver Body, 78
False certification, 53
Kickbacks, 56
Mutilation, 52
Public Health Violation, 71
Public records, 63
Reportable Disease, 76
Removal from office, 55, 65
Body trafficking, 78
Unauth. Transport, 71
Unreported Death, 34
Wrongful appropriation, 54

Property and Disposition
Estate, 39
General, 39
Historic, 15
Release Value, 40

Records and Documentation
Board of Standards, 93-95
Court Release, 29
Inquest Filing, 39, 125
Inquest Reporting, 39
Inspection, 62
Next of Kin Access, 28
Location, 62
Management, 58, 132
Medical Records, 35
Permitted Agencies, 28
Policies, 90
Private Investigators, 132
Property of the State, 58
Public Docket, 27, 62
Reporting Child Abuse, 59
Reporting Diseases, 75
Reporting Death, 31, 34
Requests, 148-154
Retention, 142-147

Verdicts, 62

2019 Additions
Archaeology sites, 31-34
Co. Attorney opinion, 126
Desecration, 51
Human remains defined, 70
Inquests, officer involved shooting, 126
Inquests, Wyoming Supreme Court, 135
Mass fatality, 197
Presumed deaths, 49
Public records (revised), 60-62
Subpoenas, 38, 126-127
Vital records, 199

www.ingramcontent.com/pod-product-compliance
Lightning Source LLC
Chambersburg PA
CBHW050210230526
45470CB00001B/326